A DICTIONARY OF OMENS AND SUPERSTITIONS

Did you know that:

If a woman's apron suddenly falls off for no apparent reason it is an omen that she will have a baby within a year?

A man with a hairy chest makes a better lover than one without?

The appearance of bubbles on the surface of a cup of tea can mean you are in for some money?

If you get out of bed on the left-hand side, you should put your right sock and shoe on first to counter the bad luck?

If you find a button it is a sign that you are going to make a new friend?

Pipe smokers who light their pipes from lamps will have troublesome, even unfaithful, wives?

If you move into a new house, you can ensure good luck for yourself and your family by walking into every room carrying a loaf of bread and a plate of salt?

INTRODUCTION

'No natural exhalation in the sky,
   No scape of nature, no distemper'd day,
No common wind, no customed event,
   But they will pluck away his natural cause,
And call them meteors, prodigies, and signs,
   Abortives, presages, and tongues of heaven,
Plainly denouncing vengeance.'
                William Shakespeare
                King John

Dr Johnson, that most inquisitive and urbane of men, tells us in an entry in one of his journals that he was quite sure that something unlucky would happen to him unless he touched every wooden post as he walked along a particular road. He could offer no reason why this was so – just that it was, and he had no intention of going against it.

Superstition, for such it was, plays a part in all our lives, and although many people would argue that reason should always triumph over instinct, the question is – does it? Let me quote you an example which will certainly put you in the kind of quandary that faces anyone who takes a firm line in such discussions. Suppose, for arguments sake, you stand behind a reinforced glass partition, and ask someone on the other side to take a swing at you with their fist. What will happen when they do? You'll flinch, and even step back even though you know the glass will prevent the fist touching you. Instinct has triumphed over reason, has it not?

We may apply exactly the same argument to omens and superstitions. They form the mental instincts that for thousands of years have swayed our reason and no matter how far we advance in science and technology, they still lurk in the corners of our consciousness, often affecting our social behaviour and attitudes to life. Perhaps, the very speed of our progress has played a part in the persistence of these beliefs. With man in space, 'miracles' being worked in medicine, and fresh discoveries constantly stretching the boundaries of our knowledge, it is hardly surprising that we are anxious and doubtful about the future as were our forbears in their unsettled times, so many of whose superstitions are now in our canon.

The historian T. S. Knowlson, in his fascinating work, *The Origins of Popular Superstitions and Customs* published over half a century ago expresses the matter succinctly. 'The true origin of superstition,' he wrote, 'is to be found in early man's effort to explain Nature and his own existence; in the desire to propitiate Fate and invite Fortune; in the wish to avoid evils he could not understand; and in the unavoidable attempt to pry into the future. From these sources alone must have sprung the system of crude notions and practices still obtaining.'

By and large, superstitions take three forms which can be defined thus:

1. The idea that if a certain action is taken bad luck will result.
2. The performing of a specified ritual which will bring about desired results.
3. The reading of omens by which a definite event, good or bad, will occur.

The first two are, I think, self-explanatory, but the third relating to omens ought perhaps to be expanded a little further. According to my understanding, an omen is an event

8

which is supposed to indicate destiny, the chief feature being the gratuitous nature of the happening. In a nutshell, it is a message about the future which we do not seek, yet find difficult to ignore. Let Knowlson again explain:

'There is no origin for omens; they are as old as man himself. From time immemorial the changing aspects of nature have told him about the changes which might happen in his own life; the flight of birds, a rabbit crossing his path, and an infinity of other matters have been taken as "signs" of something that forbodes good or ill – generally ill – a testimony to the almost universal fear with which man has regarded the forces surrounding his life.'

But being able to define and to a degree explain both omens and superstitions, has done nothing to diminish their influence, and an old cynic like Francis Bacon can with some justification point out that 'men mark when they hit, and never when they miss.' Nor is he done at that. 'It is also worthy of notice', he writes, 'that a genuine and solemn citation may tend to work to its own fulfilment in the minds of superstitious men who, by permitting the thing to prey upon their own spirit, enfeeble the powers of life, and perhaps at the critical date arouse thus some latent or dormant disease into deadly action.'

So we cannot win either way, and that famous English clergyman and naturalist, Gilbert White in his classic work, *Natural History and Antiquities of Selborne* only underlines this state of affairs when he adds:

'It is the hardest thing in the world to shake off superstitious prejudices; they are sucked in as it were with our mother's milk; and, growing up with us at a time when they take the fastest hold and make the most lasting impressions, become so interwoven with our very constitutions, that the strongest sense is required to disengage ourselves from them.'

It must also be said that a number of superstitions persist because they, in some respects, concern matters of which we are still largely ignorant, and this is a good reason why those who profess to be only a little superstitious should not be too quick to criticize others who have real apprehension about

9

such matters. It is probably one of the great myths of this scientific age that superstitions can and will be disproved of by science when the facts show (as will be seen in pages of this book) that they are either adapted or dished up again in a kind of pseudo-scientific guise.

Having said that, let me explain that what I have tried to present in this book is a wide-ranging selection of the omens and superstitions which still exist in the Western World at this moment in time. Many of them are of considerable antiquity, while others are quite recent and have evolved out of new developments in either human or scientific progress. I have collected the entries from many sources, both oral and recorded, with the major emphasis being on those found in Britain, Europe and America where I have had the chance to travel most extensively in recent years. This is not to say, however, that I have excluded examples from other distant places, just that they are less fulsome and representative than the rest.

Of course I have found that certain superstitions have different versions in different places, and in these instances I have selected that variation which seems to have most general acceptance. Just as I have gone for those beliefs which are still repeated, at the expense of those archaic traditions which might make delightful reading but are hardly relevant to a modern audience. As far as the origins are concerned – where it is possible to establish *any* kind of origin – again I have gone for the version most widely accredited. It should perhaps also be pointed out that people in Europe and America share many omens and superstitions in common, a great number having been carried unchanged to the new world by the early immigrants, and while a single location for the belief may be given, they can equally apply in many others: I have merely listed those countries which have come to light during my research. (I should also add that I have not delved deeply into the many folk cures and remedies which could well be cited as having their origins in superstition as this is a considerable topic and requiring a book of its own: nevertheless, I have quoted certain

10

such cures where they seemed appropriate and help an understanding of the superstition in general.)

Collecting this material has been a fascinating and rewarding task affording some revealing insights into the fabric of societies on both sides of the Atlantic. I particularly enjoyed, and was grateful for, the openness of folk in many places talking about their fears, and while noting the efforts of people like the members of the American 'National Society of Thirteen Against Superstition, Prejudice and Fear' (meeting on Friday the 13th) to deliberately defy superstition, found them still surrounded by countrymen with as many beliefs as a rural English backwater!

There are, in total, over 550 entries in this volume, which makes it as far as I can tell the most wide-ranging work of its kind – but this said it would be quite wrong to say it does more than very fairly represent the major omens and superstitions. There must still be many more to be collected, just as there are new ones emerging all the time, for this is very much a living folk tradition underlining and emphasizing those lines in the tale of *Oedipus*:

> 'For when we think fate hovers o'er our heads,
> Our apprehensions shoot beyond all bounds.'

PHILIPPA WARING
Somerset Island,
Bermuda.
1977.

ACCIDENT

In Japan there is a superstition that if a cup or glass containing medicine for a sick person is accidentally upset, then it is an omen of that person's speedy recovery.

ACORN

To carry an acorn on your person prevents you growing old, says an ancient British superstition. The origin of this belief probably arises from the fact that the acorn comes from the oak tree which was considered by the ancient Druids to be a sacred tree with special powers. The charm is said to work best for women, especially if they carry the acorn in their pockets or handbag.

ACTORS and ACTRESSES

There are probably few groups of people more prone to omens and superstitions than actors and actresses, and this no doubt is due to their artistic temperament. Very much at the mercy of the public's fickle taste, they look for any signs that may encourage them in their art and try to avoid those which may indicate pitfalls. It would be quite impossible to list all their superstitions – particularly as many adhere to a single company or a particular individual, and change over the years – but here is a selection of some of the most widely observed and generally held. Things can go wrong for actors and actresses right from the moment they enter the dressing room – and naturally there has never yet been one numbered 13! It is said to be unlucky to have pictures hanging in the room, and no performer ever likes to be 'overlooked' by another member of the company as he or she is making up in front of the mirror. The lucky rabbit's foot charm is used to bring good fortune, and of course serves the dual purpose of applying rouge. It is invariably kept in the make-up box and to lose it would presage disaster. Make-up boxes should always be kept untidy, and to knock one over is a bad omen. (An interesting variation of this is held by chorus girls who believe if they spill any powder on the floor they should quickly dance on it as this will bring them good luck!) Wigs are said to be harbingers of good luck, and many actors will wear them when there is really no need. There is an omen to be read in the simple process of kicking off a pair of shoes: if they both fall on their soles and remain upright then it is a sign of good luck, but if they fall over, misfortune will follow. And, incidentally, no actor would court disaster by putting his shoes on a chair in the dressing room. The profession believe they should always leave their dressing rooms with their left foot going out first, and should their shoes squeak as they make their first entrance on the stage, this is a sign that all will go well with the production. Apart from the embarrassment, to stumble on entering will result in missing a cue sometime during the evening, while to catch any part of a costume on a piece of scenery will also herald lines being 'fluffed' – unless the actor retraces his steps and makes a new entrance. In contrast, though, if a player spontaneously falls during a performance, he can be sure of another engagement at the same theatre. As far as costumes are concerned, peacock's feathers should never be worn as they will bring disaster – indeed if these feathers appear anywhere in the theatre, even if worn by a member of the audience, it is an ill omen. (In America, even a picture of an ostrich on the stage is unlucky.)

Only artificial flowers should be used as props, and the colour yellow should be avoided at all costs. (Yellow is adversely affected by the footlights.) Indeed superstition decrees that no real food, drink or jewellery should be used, only imitations, or the production will fail. On opening night, an actor should never be wished good luck so that the gods of chance are not affronted, and a typical wish is 'May you break your leg!' No play should ever open on a Friday unless the company wants a flop, and it is widely held that Shakespeare's *Macbeth* is the unluckiest play to perform mainly because it is believed the famous 'Witches' Song' has the power to raise evil and strike the cast. (And certainly, only the most foolish actor would think of humming any of the music used with the play while in rehearsal.) Interestingly enough, stage people believe *Robin Hood* and *The Babes in the Wood* are both ill-omened panto-mimes, while *Cinderella* promises nothing but good. American vaudeville performers believe it is unlucky to change the style of costume in which they first achieved success – some even think that they should not change the original suit itself. If an actor or actress should happen to try the handle of the wrong door when they are seeking the manager of the theatre or an agent then this is a sure omen of failure. And just a final note for members of the acting profession in particular: an old tradition in Germany and Scandinavia says that if you wish to commit any difficult lines to memory, put the book or script in question under your pillow before you go to sleep. You'll wake up with them firmly committed to memory – so the super-stition says!

ADDER

The adder is said to be an omen of good luck, and if you kill the first one you see in the spring this will ensure your triumph over your enemies. To allow this same reptile to escape alive is, however, to court disaster and bad luck. An adder seen by the front door is an omen of death, according to an old English belief. In many forest areas of the world it is believed that if you hang the dried skin of an adder by the chimney it will bring you good luck, while to place another skin in the rafters or the hearth will ensure that the house never catches on fire. Most of the omens associated with the adder, which is the only veno- mous snake in the British Isles, are said to have originated with the gypsies who maintain that the most effective cure for its bite is to kill the creature and rub its dead body over the wound.

AEROPLANES

The crews of modern aeroplanes have a strong fear of using the words 'crash' or 'prang' before a flight, and in many airlines there persists the belief that any accident or crash will be followed by two more. Many pilots and their crew carry small charms, and there is a universal dislike among all these people against taking flowers on board – particularly red and white ones. Air Force crews believe that when 'touching wood' for luck, the wood should be a living tree, as wood used for tables, chairs, etc is 'dead' and therefore not a good omen. A pilot is also said to be able to preserve his luck by emptying the contents of his pockets on the ground after landing as a kind of sacrificial offering. American airmen always cross unused seat- belts before taking off so as not to offend the spirits of the unknown.

AGE

Although women are not aware of the fact, the widespread practice of concealing one's real age (usually for reasons of vanity) may well have its origins in superstition. In many country districts of Britain in particular, it is said to be unlucky to disclose your age, an idea that apparently arose from the ancient prejudice against numbering things lest by doing so they became identifiable to evil spirits. There is, though, according to an English superstition, an infallible way of getting at the truth. First, you must obtain a hair from the lady's head and tie it to a small gold ring. Then hang this inside a glass tum- bler and wait for it to begin oscillating. According to the belief, the ring will strike the sides as many times as the woman's age.

ALBATROSS

From the earliest days of sail, an albatross flying around a ship heralded stormy weather. The birds were also particularly revered because each was said to contain the soul of a dead seaman, and for any sailor to kill one was to bring bad luck upon himself for the rest of his life – as Samuel Taylor Coleridge immortalized in his great poem, *The Ancient Mariner*.

ANGLING

Anglers share quite a number of the superstitions attributed to fishermen and mentioned in detail later in the book. However, angling has several peculiar to itself which deserve to be mentioned. For instance, it is believed to be unlucky to change rods during fishing; that a float which has been successful in the past should not be exchanged for a new and supposedly more efficient kind; and that because of the special powers of spit, bait should never be cast without first being spat upon. It is said to be an ill omen to place the keep net in the water before a catch has been made and it is bad luck to ask a fisherman how many bites he has had, for this will doom the rest of his fishing. Finally no angler who sits on an upturned bucket will ever have the slightest luck!

ANIMALS

Many British farmers still believe it is very unlucky to allow anyone to express admiration or expectation for an animal entered in a show, or it will certainly fail. And only by expressing some terrible fate for the creature such as breaking its neck can he hope to lift his ill luck.

ANTS

There is a common belief in many countries that 'stepping on ants brings rain' and indeed ants are said to be an omen of bad weather whenever they are seen to be particularly active in carrying their eggs to new places of safety. There is also a widespread superstition that it is unlucky to destroy a colony of ants, for should they build a nest near your door you can expect security and riches in the future. Two curious beliefs which are still occasionally mentioned about ants is that they never sleep, and that if their eggs are eaten with honey it is a most effective antidote to love!

APPLE

The apple, according to tradition, was the fruit with which the Devil tempted Eve in the Garden of Eden, and superstition says that to eat one now without first rubbing it clean is a challenge to the Evil One. Despite this association, the apple is universally regarded as a holy tree, and since the very earliest times it has been considered very unlucky to destroy apple trees or orchards. There are a number of love omens associated with the apple, the most popular of which enables a girl to find out who her future husband might be by peeling the skin off one in a continuous piece and flinging this over her left shoulder. If the peel stays in one strip it should fall in such a way that it makes the shape of a letter – which will indicate the initial of the man in question. If it breaks, she will not marry at all. In Austria it is believed that a girl can learn her future by cutting open an apple on St Thomas's night and counting the number of seeds. If there is an even number then she will marry shortly, but if she has carelessly cut one or more of the seeds then she will have a troubled future and end up a widow. Should a girl have several lovers, says another European super-stition, and she is unable to choose between them, then an apple pip will do the job. She should take one of these and, reciting one of the men's names, drop it on the fire. If it goes off with a popping sound, then the man is 'bursting' with love for her; if it makes no noise then he is not in love. A German tradition says that if the first apple on a young tree is picked and eaten by a woman who has had many children then it too will have many fruitful seasons. Another interesting belief is that in Britain an apple tree which blossoms out of season while there is still fruit on it is an omen of death in the family, but in Europe the same thing means the owner can look forward to some good fortune. It is also said to be lucky to leave an apple or two on the ground after they have fallen to keep any wandering spirits happy. Finally, the saying 'An apple a day keeps the doctor away' is actually rooted in superstition, for the fruit was once said to be the food of the gods, but such are its health-giving qualities that science now recognizes there is more than a little truth in the saying.

APRIL FOOL'S DAY

The origin of this practice of fooling people on the first day of April is probably lost in the mists of time, but in its modern form it seems to have come to Britain from France in the sixteenth century. In 1564 the French instigated the creation of January 1 as the first day of the year, bringing it forward from its previous date of March 25 (now known as Lady Day). It appears that prior to this people had been in the habit of giving presents to one another to celebrate the first day of the new year, but as the old date of March 25 usually fell in Holy Week, the Church insisted that this rite be postponed until the first of April. When, therefore, the New Year was moved back to January, a custom grew up among the French of paying visits to their friends on April 1 in the hope of 'fooling' them that it was still the first day of the new year. From this modest beginning, the custom travelled throughout Europe and indeed now embraces the world.

APRON

The apron has earned itself quite a significant place in superstition primarily, of course, because it was once virtually part of every woman's attire day in and day out. In England, for instance, it is lucky to inadvertently put on an apron inside out, and should you be having a day beset by small accidents this can be changed by reversing the apron. Throughout much of the British Isles it is said to be a sign of bad luck if an apron suddenly falls off, while in some places it is an omen that the wearer can expect a baby within a year! In both Britain and Europe this belief among young single girls is a sign their lover is thinking of them at that moment. The apron also features in two German traditions still very much alive today. The first is that if a man wipes his hands on a girl's apron he will fall passionately in love with her. Once a girl is engaged, though, she is best advised not to let her fiancé use her apron for this purpose for it is said this will lead to a quarrel. The explanation of this superstition is said to be that it is the smell of a person's perspiration which plays a major part in the attraction of the sexes, and naturally a man would smell a woman on her apron.

ASCENSION DAY

In certain parts of Britain, notably Wales, it is still considered very unlucky to do any kind of work on Ascension Day, as those who do lay themselves open to accidents. It was once claimed that the figure of a lamb was always seen among the clouds on this day, but nowadays it is only the weather omens that are noted. If it rains on this day, says superstition, it is a sign of a poor crop and sickness among cattle; if it is fine then there will be a long, hot summer.

ASHES

Ashes are believed throughout the world to be a fertility charm, and in many places the ashes from special ritual fires like those at Midsummer have been spread over crops to ensure good harvests. In many European countries the remains from Easter bonfires have actually been mixed with seeds being prepared for the next sowing. Similarly ashes were put into the feed of cattle and other animals such as pigs and chickens to ensure that they grew strong and healthy. In some places, too, ashes were regarded as good luck charms: in France they would prevent damage by thunder and lightning if scattered over houses, while in England and America they were utilized as a protection against witches and evil spirits. Among more primitive peoples, the ashes of a human being were thought to help crops when scattered to the winds as they turned to rain and thus fertilized the land as well as protecting it. There is also a superstition still prevalent in England and Wales that if the ashes of the fire are spread smoothly over the hearth on New

Year's Eve and footprints leading in the direction of the door are found in the morning, someone in the family will die during the year. If, however, the footmarks go in the opposite direction, there will be a birth.

ASTHMA

A sixteenth century superstition still on record in rural areas of Europe claims that asthma can be cured by eating raw cat's meat or with foam from a mule's mouth. If those seem just a little too unpleasant, a fortnight's diet of boiled carrots will apparently be just as effective!

ASTROLOGY

Astrology and fortune telling overlap the fields of superstition, but are such huge and diverse subjects that they need no more than passing mention here – the reader is doubtless familiar with the columns about 'The Stars' which appear in most daily papers, and there is a veritable library of books available on both topics. What began with a natural veneration for the heavenly bodies primitive man saw above him, today has become a flourishing science – but the basic belief that their movements can affect people's lives remains unchanged. The twelve star signs are, of course, instantly familiar, and although much fortune telling tries to give the impression that 'reading' these signs is easy, in fact to deduce accurate and meaningful information requires exact details and careful analysis.

ASTRONAUTS

Superstition has even found its way into the realms of man's very latest technological achievement – spaceflight. The traditional ill-omened colours are carefully avoided by astronauts, and a good number of those who have taken part in space missions firmly believed it was important for there to be some small error or hitch in the rehearsal stage for a successful mission – which is surely an extension of the same belief found among actors. Many of the recent changes in weather have been put down by the superstitious to rocket launchings (or alternatively the exploding of nuclear weapons) and numerous other phenomena have been credited to man's intruding across the frontiers of space into the unknown heavens. All the superstitions in this area have, needless to say, been somehow underlined in many people's minds by the disaster of the ill-numbered Apollo 13 mission.

AXE

In all the European nations which have been troubled by witchcraft at some period in their history, there is a belief that if cattle are made to step over an axe when they are taken out to pasture for the first time in spring they will be invulnerable to evil magic and spells. To carry an axe (in some places a hoe) into the house will bring about death in the family, according to a widespread American superstition. This belief seems to have its roots in the old Scottish tradition that to take a spade indoors is very unlucky; the tool symbolizes the profession of the gravedigger, and thereby death.

B

BABY

There are a great many superstitions associated with babies and it is only possible here to mention those which are most widely noted. It is believed that to rock a cradle without the baby in it is to doom it to an early death, and to protect a child at birth a knife should be placed on the doorstep as no witch or evil spirit can cross iron or steel to do the new infant harm. In Ireland, it is said that to spit on a new-born baby is to ensure it luck, while the Welsh to achieve the same end have the more pleasant alternative of rubbing the offspring's head with honey. Concerning the actual birth an easy delivery for the mother can be effected by opening all the locks in the house at the time of the mother's labour. If the child is born feet first, says another British superstition, it will be lamed in an accident while still young unless bay leaves are immediately rubbed on its legs. However, this child is believed to have the power to cure muscular pains, and as adults such 'footlings', as they are called, are much in demand in country areas. A child whose mother dies in giving birth to him or her is also credited with special healing powers and will be called upon to administer the 'kiss of life' to respiratory ailments in particular. Throughout many nations it is considered unlucky to let a child see itself in a mirror before it is six months old or it will die before the year is out. In many places to cut a baby's finger or toe nails before it is twelve months old will cause it to grow up a thief and the mother will chew the tiny nail ends off rather than use scissors. In Wales to ensure a baby grows well the water in which the child is washed should be thrown under a tree in leaf, and a child that has been weaned should never be put to the breast again – for if it is it will grow up to become a terrible swearer! Mothers should always pull clothes on a new born baby over its feet first unless they want it to grow up unhealthy, because superstition says the feet are inferior to the head and should always be covered first. Although it is a natural enough thing to want to kiss a new-born baby, it is also lucky – for infants are said to be harbingers of good luck. Some country people say that a child born with teeth will be selfish, while if the baby has its right hand open at birth it will be generous. However, if a child first clasps anything with the left hand it will prove unlucky in life – another example of the misfortune associated with the left. In several European countries it is also held to be unlucky to weigh a new born baby – because it is a gift from God and such checking of God's bounty is an insult. And another piece of advice from Central Europe tells all mothers – never give away *all* your baby's clothes after he or she has finished with them, for superstition warns that if you do you will be needing them again before long, whether you want another child or not! Jewish superstition says that the evil eye is threatened whenever anyone comments on how beautiful a baby is, but this can be offset by saying three times in Yiddish, 'Whoever gave you the evil eye may it fall on them'. The Jews also believe a child should never be watched when it is asleep as this action is like watching the dead and may result in the same end. American mothers are warned by superstition from putting an old nappy, or diaper, on their baby or else he will grow up to be a thief. And when first nursed, a child should be carried on the left side or he will become left-handed. Also a child that is weaned in early Spring is said to be most likely to become prematurely grey haired. Never throw a baby into the air, says another American superstition, for this will cause it to grow up a dimwit. But take comfort if your child is bald – he or she will grow up to be a brilliant scholar. A Louisiana belief says you can predict you baby's future if you place a Bible, a pack of cards and a silver coin within its reach. If the child picks the Bible, then he will have a good future; if he grabs the cards then he will be a gambler; but if it is the money he takes then he will be successful in all financial dealings. An old English superstition says that if a new born baby is allowed to urinate in the fireplace he or she will quickly become clean and grow up to be well-behaved. It is very unlucky to dress a baby in black as this is an omen that it will not live beyond childhood. Finally, it is still held in many parts of Britain that it is unlucky for a woman who has given birth to go anywhere but to church the first time she leaves her home. If she ignores this, says superstition, she will bring misfortune on herself, and more than likely on any friend or person whom she meets. In some rural areas it is further claimed that if such an 'unchurched' woman visits another woman then this other person will have a child herself within a year.

BACON
Bacon is believed to be a powerful curative for fever and constipation according to a European superstition – but only, apparently, if it has been stolen!

BADGER
The badger was an animal much favoured by old-time gamblers because according to a European tradition one of its teeth kept on your person made you unbeatable whenever you made a wager!

BAKING
The thrifty habit of most housewives to use up any scraps of pastry left over from their baking to make small items for their children has an element of superstition about it, although the ladies concerned may be unaware of the fact. For centuries ago

it was believed that if any flour or meal was left over after the last loaf or cake had been prepared, then the entire baking would be spoiled unless the remnants were made into a small additional cake and given to a child. To throw such scraps away was said to court disaster. It is also unlucky to count the number of loaves or cakes again when they are taken from the oven for this will make them go stale quickly. If a loaf emerges from the oven broken open, then this is a sign that a stranger is coming to share it with you.

BALDNESS

Baldness, the curse of many a man, has according to an old British superstition, a cure though not a very pleasant one; it requires liberal amounts of goose dung to be rubbed into the bald patches! perhaps men would prefer a preventive measure supplied by another superstition – never cut your hair when the moon is waning for it will thin and fall out.

BAPTISM

There are almost as many superstitions about the baptism of a child as there are about babies in general. It used to be widely believed that a child should be baptised as soon after birth as possible or it ran the risk of being carried off by the fairies or evil spirits. It could, though, be protected in the interim by covering it with an item of its father's clothing whenever danger seems imminent. In many European countries this is augmented by hanging herbs, bread, salt and a piece of steel over the cradle. In the North of England there is a superstition that if a child does not cry at its baptism then it will grow up naughty and disobedient because the inherent evil spirit has not been driven out by the holy water. It is important, too, that the font water is not wiped from the face, but is allowed to dry naturally, and if the baby wore a christening cap this should be kept on for at least the following twelve weeks. A baby girl should never be baptised in the same water that has been used for a boy, says a German superstition, or else she will grow up to have a beard! And in America it is claimed that if a child's baptismal water is saved and given to him or her later then it will become an excellent singer. In many places it is said to be unlucky to call a child by its name before it is christened. The Scots believe that children who die unchristened take the form of ghosts and can often be seen wandering in woods and lonely places bewailing their fate. There is an extraordinary superstition recorded in Cheshire that an unbaptised child cannot die. In the North of England it is regarded as an evil omen for a child to be the first one christened in a new church as he or she will be claimed by the devil. (This tradition seems to have its origin in the ancient custom of burying alive a child or a man under the foundations of a new church to ensure its sound construction!) The Welsh believe that a baptism following immediately after a funeral is an omen of death and that to ensure a full and happy life for a child its christening should follow a wedding. In most superstitions the baptism is of paramount importance in ensuring the child's future, and many a story is told of children who were weak and sickly until the ceremony had been performed. To finally seal the child's future a feast should be held immediately afterwards, the more lavish the better, and plenty of drink is essential. Indeed, the orgies which accompanied many christenings in the past were the origin of that popular saying about 'wetting the baby's head'!

BARNACLES

There is a curious superstition still repeated among some old fishermen that the barnacles on a ship's bottom will turn into geese. This appears to have originated from a much older belief that the well-known Barnacle Geese once hatched from timbers rotting in the sea.

BASEBALL

American baseball players have been described by a famous member of their ranks, Christy Mathewson of the New York Giants, as 'children of superstition' and indeed they are certainly very prone to strange beliefs. For instance it is said to be very unlucky for a player to see a cross-eyed woman in the stands, for if he does he will not get a hit during the entire game. On the other hand, if he sees a red-headed woman then it is his lucky day—particularly if he can get her to give him a hairpin. These items are said to be especially valuable to the baseball player because each one found represents a base hit driven home. Gloves can also influence luck, and it is said to be essential for a player to make sure that the fingers of his glove are left on the ground pointing to his own team's dugout when he goes out to bat. Naturally, there are superstitions about the baseball bat, and it is said that as each bat contains a given number of strikes, it is unlucky to lend it to a team-mate and thereby give away some of your luck. It is also considered that a split bat is unlucky and no team will prosper that allows a bat to lie crosswise in front of a dugout. Finally a dog that walks across the playing field will bring bad luck to the team at bat, and throughout baseball the belief still persists that no season should ever begin on a Friday.

BATHING

There is an old superstition about swimming in the sea or rivers for the first time, exemplified in this verse recorded all over the British Isles:

> 'He who bathes in May will soon be laid in clay
> He who bathes in June will sing a merry tune
> But he who bathes in July will dance like a fly.'

The origin of these verses would seem to be the ancient idea that the act of washing cleansed a man not only of the dirt from his body but also the sins from his heart. In many countries it has been held that to wash the body all over washes away a man's luck, and in Wales, miners would often deliberately leave their backs dirty for fear that if they cleaned them they ran the risk of the mine roof falling in on them. It is said to be very lucky to see a naked person bathing – although it is vital that you come across the person unexpectedly. It is obviously not so lucky if you happen to be the person so rudely discovered!

Bathers should also note that the old superstition that it is unlucky to bathe feet first 'because the feet are below the head and thus inferior' is actually medically sound for to moisten the head first will alleviate the risk of a headache due to blood pressure which can of course lead to cramp.

BATS

The uneasiness which these creatures arouse in many people, has led them to be considered important omens in several respects. Should one fly near you, says a widespread belief, then beware, for someone is trying to betray or bewitch you. Should one fly around your house three times, or actually fly into a room this is an indication of a death or very bad luck to someone you know. A bat hitting any building is a sign of rain, while bats flying around at twilight before their normal time of emergence means good weather is on the way. Some superstitions maintain that the bat is the luckiest of all animals and to ensure luck for himself a person should keep a bat's bone in his clothes. Another belief of European origin claims that the right eye of a bat kept in the waistcoat pocket will make a man invisible! In Africa and Australia, among other places, there is a belief that the life of a bat represents that of a man and to kill one will shorten the life of a man. The most extraordinary, and persistent, belief about bats is that if one flies into a woman's hair it will become entangled and can only be released by cutting the hair. Despite actual experiments to establish whether there was any truth in this belief – and the emphatic result that there is not – the creature is still universally loathed by women.

BEANS

The flowers of all beans have been widely associated with death and the spirits of the dead, and in many countries – notably in the Far East – they are scattered about the house to placate the demons. In England it is said that if one bean in a row should come up white instead of green a death will occur in the coming year. Throughout the South West of England it is

28

also believed that kidney beans will not grow unless they are planted on the third day of May and you are asking for trouble putting them in at any other time.

BEAR
Among the backwoodsmen of America there was a superstition that bears breed only once every seven years, and when they did this caused such a disturbance in the atmosphere that any cattle in the district which were about to calve would lose their young. Curiously, these same people also held that a child could be cured of whooping cough if he was able to ride on a bear – though the peril of his life would seem to outweigh the advantage of such a cure.

BEAUTY
One of the simplest ways of acquiring beauty according to a superstition found in rural Britain and throughout much of Europe is to bathe the body in dew collected fresh on the first day of May. For an all-the-year-round course of treatment, the Germans simply recommend cups of cold coffee, while the Hungarians have the horrible idea that taking a bath in human blood will do the trick!

BED
There can be few more famous superstitions than the one about 'getting out of bed the wrong side' leading to a bad day. The 'wrong side' has traditionally been the left because it is associated with the Devil who, of course, sat on the left hand side of God before he was banished from heaven. Apparently the only way you can avoid the ill luck is to make sure you put your right sock and shoe on first when dressing. Many people also believe that bad luck follows if you get out of bed from the opposite side to which you got in. It is said too, that no more than two people should ever make-up a bed or a death will surely result in the family. Perhaps of some practical use, is the claim of folk in Northern England that bed sores may be avoided by placing two buckets of fresh spring water under the

bed daily. Under no circumstances though, use cold boiled water for this is said to anger the Devil, and should he by some chance pass in the night it will certainly catch his eye and he may well do you some harm. According to the superstition of several European nations, it is not advisable to clean out the room where a guest has slept until at least an hour after he has left or bad luck will follow. Perhaps the bad luck might be an unwelcome guest returning! Looking under the bed before retiring is often referred to jokingly, but the idea has its roots in superstition. Many country people used to believe it was essential to do this to ward off the Devil who liked skulking in such places. The Americans believe it is an ill omen to lay a hat on the bed at any time, and it is unlucky to turn a mattress on Friday and Sunday – the latter particularly for this would result in a week of bad dreams! Many European housewives believe a bed should always be pointed in an east-west direction (the path of the sun), and should it face north to south by any chance then the sleeper is in for restless nights.

BEES

Bees have long played an important role in rural superstition where they are considered wise creatures with a special knowledge of the future. Tradition says they originated in Paradise and are known as 'The Little Servants of God' so it is very unlucky to kill one. Country people believe it is particularly important to tell them when any member of the bee keeper's family dies or gets married. After a death a relative must go to the hive and repeat three times the phrase, 'Little brownies, little brownies, your master (mistress or whoever) is dead.' If this is not done, says the superstition, then the bees will either die themselves or fly away. Similarly a bride must inform them of her marriage or they will certainly leave the hive and not return. After both these rituals, a few moments must be allowed and if the bees begin to buzz once more then they are content and will remain as they are. A piece of bridal or funeral cake, whichever is appropriate, should also be left by the hive for the bees to feed on. Bees which swarm on a dead tree or hedge are an omen of a death in the family, and it is also bad luck if a stray swarm lands on your house or land. Bees should never be sold, but bartered, and to actually give a hive to someone not only provides them with honey but good luck also. Never move bees without telling them, says a Cornish superstition, or they will sting their owner, and if they are moved on Good Friday they will die. Bees which become idle or lazy presage disaster of some kind, and if they are all seen to enter the hive and none to come out again within a short time, then rain is in the air. A bee flying into your house is an omen that a visitor will shortly arrive, while in Wales it is claimed that a bee flying around a sleeping child indicates that he or she will have a happy life. The bee sting is, of course, well known as a cure for rheumatism, but there is probably not another belief quite as extraordinary as the one, held on both sides of the Atlantic, that any girl who is a virgin can always pass safely through a swarm! The clever little creatures are apparently able to tell the difference!

BEETLES

The most widely held superstition about the beetle is that it is an omen of death if one walks over your shoe. Bad luck, says a Scottish superstition, is in store if one enters a room of your home while the family are seated, and the misfortune will certainly be increased if you kill it. In many parts of Europe it is said a beetle will bring on a terrible storm. All in all, it is an ill-omened insect and should one emerge from a shoe you have left standing by the door, bad luck will follow.

BELLS

Throughout much of Europe church bells are said to drive away evil spirits, and at one time it was believed that if they were rung during a storm they might distract the spirit of the storm from his work and cause the bad weather to abate. In England especially it is said that if two bells ring in a house at the same time somebody is shortly going to leave, and it is also an ill omen if a bell rings for no apparent reason.

BIBLE

The Bible has been a source of omens for centuries, and apart from the belief that if left open it will keep evil spirits at bay, it is most commonly used in divination. In both Britain and America to open the Bible at random on New Year's Day and place a finger on a passage without looking, will foretell events in the reader's coming year. There is also a quaint belief in America that the Book of Proverbs can be utilized by a young man to determine the character of his girl-friend and consequently whether or not he should marry her. He has to first find out her age and then apply it to the appropriate verse of the first chapter of Proverbs. Whichever verse it leads him to will be a clue to her nature and temperament – always assuming, of course, that she has given him her real age! A girl can get the answer to the same question by placing her door key in the Song of Solomon section of the Bible, leaving the key ring protruding. The Bible must next be tightly bound with her garter or stocking and two other people asked to hold it by placing a finger under the key ring. The girl should then repeat this verse from the Song of Solomon: 'Many waters cannot quench love, neither can the floods drown it. Love is as strong as death, but jealousy is as cruel as the grave, and burneth with a most vehement flame. If a man should give all the substance of his house for love, it would be utterly consumed.' Should the Bible when these words are spoken turn under the fingers or fall to the ground then the girl will marry, if nothing occurs she is unhappily going to be a spinster.

BIRDS

There are numerous omens and superstitions concerning birds primarily because they are often believed to be the returned souls of dead people. The more general ones are recorded here and those associated with specific birds are to be found under their individual names. Ever since earliest times birds have been treated by man as symbols of good and evil, and indeed the Greeks made a science of this called Ornithomancy. By far the most widespread bird omen says that if a bird flies in and out of a room through an open window it signals the death of someone living in the house. A variation of this says that if birds hover or fly constantly around a house, or when resting on a window sill tap against the glass, then this too portends a death. The Irish, Brazilians and Australians all believe that black and grey birds seen flying around trees at night and never settling contain the souls of evil-doers who are doing penance. In France it is said that unbaptised children who die become birds and remain so until they are baptised by John the Baptist. The Scots also have the unhappy superstition about caged birds that if one should die on the wedding morning of a member of the family, the marriage will be unhappy and the couple will eventually separate. On a happier note it is claimed that if you see a flight of birds just before you are about to undertake a journey, their direction will indicate the success or otherwise of your trip. If they are flying to the right of you, all will be well; but if to the left, it would be as well to stay at home! Finally – and perhaps not surprisingly – a British superstition says that if bird droppings fall on you it is a sign of misfortune!

BIRTH

The enormous progress in obstetrics has made the birth of children a much safer process than in the past, and this has naturally obliterated many of the old superstitions which were observed in the home to ensure a successful delivery. Although most of the charms have gone, in many rural areas of Europe it is still the custom to open doors and locks – even knots on any items of clothing the mother may be wearing – to ease the birth. Many people living in coastal fishing areas say a child cannot be born until the tide comes in, and should one be born at the ebb this is an ill-omen. In England it is said that a child born as a result of a Caesarian operation will develop great strength and possess the power to see spirits and find hidden treasure. It is also believed that if a boy is born during the time the moon is waning, the next child born will be a girl, and vice versa. Similarly when a birth takes place during the waxing of

33

the moon the next child will be of the same sex. Sunday is still widely regarded as the best day on which to be born, although any child born on Christmas Day is doubly favoured. According to a Yorkshire superstition, an infant born during the hour of midnight is given the special power of being able to see ghosts; and to bring luck to the newborn, say the people of this same country, it should first be placed in the arms of a maiden, which perhaps accounts for the great popularity of young nurses at the confinement. A more general superstition instructs that the infant should be carried up to the top of the house to ensure that it will 'rise in the world'; if this is not possible, a pair of steps will do just as well. To ensure that the baby is successful with the opposite sex later in life, Kent people put a boy's night shirt on a girl and vice-versa so that they would later be 'surrounded' by love. In Yorkshire the same result could be obtained by laying some of father's clothes over a daughter, and mother's over a boy. It is an ill-omen if a child is born with teeth – even one – for in several superstitions this is said to be a sign that he or she will die a violent death. At the time of the child's birth, if you have time to think of such a thing, take a look up at the clouds; a German superstition says, that if they have the shape of droves of sheep or lambs then this is a sign that the baby will enjoy much good fortune during its life. In the American states of Maine and Massachusetts there is a popular superstition about the birth of children summed up in these lines:

'First a daughter, then a son,
The world is well begun.
First a son, then a daughter,
Trouble follows after.'

No section on birth would be complete without repeating that famous verse describing a child's character based on the day it is born, and which is clearly rooted in superstition:

'Monday's child is fair of face,
Tuesday's child is full of grace,
Wednesday's child is full of woe,

Thursday's child has far to go,
Friday's child is loving and giving,
Saturday's child works hard for a living,
But the child that is born on the Sabbath Day
Is blithe and bonny, good and gay.'

BIRTHMARK

The birthmark has a place in superstition, though only the most primitive peoples still believe it is the result of the mother having seen something unpleasant or been touched by some demon or evil spirit during her pregnancy. In the Mid-West of America it is still believed that a baby born with a double crown marking on its head (actually the shape of the parietal and coronal suture bones) will travel a great deal and live on at least two continents during its lifetime. Any child born with a caul (a thin membrane which sometimes covers the head) will become a gifted speaker, and there are still seafaring folk who believe that a caul will protect them from shipwreck or drowning. For this reason there was for many years a profitable trade in the buying and selling of these items. The belief that birthmarks can be removed if the mother licks the mark for several days after the child's birth is still very widespread, and because of the known curative powers of spittle is said to be effective in certain cases.

BLACKBERRIES

Although the blackberry is such a delicious fruit and found in such abundance in rural districts, it has become associated with the Devil in two old superstitions. In France, there are still people who will not eat the fruit because they believe its colour resulted from it being spat upon by the Devil. And in England there is a widely held rural belief that blackberries should never be gathered after October 11 because on this day (the old Michaelmas Day) the Evil One fell into a blackberry thicket and left his curse on the thorns which had injured him. Conversely, though, these brambles are said to be a cure for several illnesses including rheumatism, whooping cough and boils!

BLACKBIRD

If two blackbirds are seen sitting together it is said to be a good omen almost everywhere, except in Wales where the sight is believed to indicate that someone in the household will shortly die. This is a particularly remarkable superstition because the blackbird is well known for 'staking out' its territory and fiercely driving off any other of its kind which appears in the vicinity!

BLACK CAT

Perhaps the most famous of all superstitions is the belief that a black cat crossing your path will ensure good luck. Indeed so widespread and firmly held is this tradition that there are many instances in history where people have pampered black cats to an amazing degree so that misfortune should never attend them. Apart from crossing in front of you, it is also held that a black cat walking into your house will bring good luck and naturally, to kill one is extremely unlucky. The animal is said to have curative powers, too, and some blood from its tail will cure many minor illnesses if rubbed on the affected part. In many primitive areas of the world the black cat has been used in special rituals to appease the gods, though it is never killed. Not surprisingly we find that it became much sought after and changed hands for large sums of money. It is always stressed by those with most implicit faith in the black cat's powers that it must be *totally* black, that even a fleck or hair of white disqualifies it. The origin of this superstition dates back to the ancient Egyptians who greatly revered cats in general, one of their most important Goddesses being Bast, a black female cat. There are many other superstitions associated with the feline and these are listed under the heading Cat.

BLACKHEADS

Superstition has a cure for these annoying and troublesome disfigurements when modern medication and all else has failed: locate a bramble bush which forms an arch and on a sunny day crawl backwards and forwards under it three times going as nearly east to west as possible. This, if the thorns have not torn you to ribbons, should cause the blackheads to fade and disappear!

BLACK SHEEP

It is interesting to find that despite the popular expression that someone referred to as 'the black sheep of the family' is troublesome, the black sheep itself is mostly considered a harbinger of fortune. Throughout much of the British Isles one of these animals brings good luck to a flock, although in certain counties, and in Shropshire in particular, it is believed that bad luck will strike a shepherd into whose flock a black lamb is born, and disaster will result from an ewe having black twins.

BLOOD

Among British country folk there is an old superstition that a drop of blood taken from the little finger of a man's left hand and secretly put in a woman's drink will make her fall passionately in love with him. A less savoury belief is that anyone who bleeds on the day of Halloween, October 31, will not live long thereafter.

BLOSSOM

Trees and shrubs that bloom out of season are considered to be omens of misfortune in many places. In Wales, for instance, the flowering of Christmas roses late in spring is said to be ominous, while fruit trees which bud and flower out of their normal time presage sickness or death. Another superstition maintains that if plants of any kind flower out of season in large numbers in any one district, then there will be a hard winter followed by much sickness and death.

BLOWING OUT CANDLES

An essential part of any birthday party is the blowing out of the candles and should the person whose birthday it is blow them out with a single breath then he or she can be sure of good luck during the following year. This world-wide superstition appears to have originated with the Greeks who held that candles symbolized life and that the number displayed should represent the number of years that had already past in a person's life. You may also make a wish while blowing out the candles, and if you succeed in blowing them all out at one go – and do not tell a soul what you have wished – then the wish will come true.

BORROWING

'Never a lender or a borrower be,' goes an old phrase still recited today by thrifty parents to their offspring, and certainly superstition holds that the first three days in February and the last three in March are particularly unlucky for anyone who tries to borrow. Indeed in Scotland it will not only bring you bad luck to ask for a loan on these days but it is also unlucky to plant any seeds at this time for they will not flourish. If you have to borrow, says a Yorkshire superstition, always return what you have borrowed 'laughing', in other words with good grace and thanks, or bad luck will attend you.

BOXERS

Boxers are another group of sportsmen prone to omens and superstitions, and many great champions have carried or worn their own personal good luck charms ranging from a rabbit's foot to a ten dollar bill! It is said to be unlucky for a fighter if he sees a hat lying on a couch or bed before a fight, and no fighter likes to be first in the ring – believing this to be unlucky – so any challenger for a title must duck under the ropes before the champion. New shoes are believed to be unlucky in any important bout, and the boxer who does not spit on the palms of his gloves before confronting his opponent dares the gods of fortune.

BRAMBLE BUSH

This bush is believed to be particularly effective in the cure of numerous ailments including blackheads, boils, rheumatism and whooping cough. The sufferer has to be passed under a natural arch formed by the brambles for the cure to be effected.

BREAD

Because bread has always been considered one of the staple foods of life it is naturally considered unlucky to waste it or throw any away – for you will surely go hungry later, says superstition. With an ever increasing number of women making their own bread, it is as well for them to remember the old belief that anyone who pricks the loaf with a fork or a knife will never be 'a happy maid or wife'. Pricking the loaf to see whether it is sufficiently baked should, of course, be done with a skewer, and the belief is really a commentary on the fact that anyone who cannot bake something as basic as bread correctly can hardly be experienced enough for the harder tasks of housekeeping. If the loaf should split at the top while baking this is said to be an omen of a funeral. The old expression about 'a baker's dozen' is thought to have its origins in superstition, especially in view of the couplet, 'Twelve for the Baker and one for the Devil'. The truth is much more mundane. Bread was originally sold by the pound weight and since a loaf shrinks after a while, the baker selling his wares either in a shop or on a round did not want complaints about 'short weight'. He would therefore add an extra loaf to every dozen to make up each of the twelve to the required weight, and there are thirteen loaves in a baker's dozen. There is another superstition primarily held by the American Indians that a loaf of bread weighted with quicksilver and dropped into a river will float along and stop over the place where the body of a dead person is lying. This is known and has been tried with a certain amount of success in the British Isles as well. In the North of England it is unlucky to turn a loaf upside down after cutting a slice since the breadwinner of the family may fall ill. Similarly if the loaf crumbles in your hand while you try to cut it, there is going to be argument and dissension in the family. Should you find a hole in the centre of the loaf this is said to represent a grave and the death of a member of the family is imminent.

European superstition says that bread baked on Christmas Eve will never grow mouldy, and while to put scraps of bread out for the birds is an act of kindness, it is claimed that to burn a loaf is unlucky. Should you drop a slice of bread and it falls with the buttered side up then you can expect a visitor shortly. Particular good fortune is in store for the girl who eats the last piece of bread and butter at tea time for superstition says she will then be in line for 'a handsome husband or ten thousand pounds a year'.

BREASTS

There is a quaint old superstition to be heard in Devon that a woman whose breasts are sore may cure this by going to church at midnight and removing some lead from one of the ornamental windows and shaping it into a heart which she then wears on a chain around her neck.

BREEZE

Sailors would be well advised to take note of the widely recorded European superstition that a breeze – as distinct from a wind – can be raised by scratching a nail on the foremast.

BRIDE

There has always been a great deal of superstition attached to weddings and the bride in particular. There is hardly a country in the world where rites of some kind are not carefully observed so that the marriage may go off happily. Superstition is, of course, at the back of the old verse dealing with the bride's ensemble:

> 'Something old, something new,
> Something borrowed, something blue.'

According to tradition, the 'something old' should be her shoes or handkerchief; while the 'new' and 'borrowed' speak for themselves. (In some countries this latter word varies as something 'golden' or even 'stolen'!) The 'something blue' is, of course, the only exception to the rule that the bride should wear nothing coloured – but it has to be stressed that for the good luck to be ensured the blue should be sky-blue, the colour of the heavens. Tradition decrees that the bride should be dressed in white the symbol of innocence and purity, and any bride who is given a dress which her mother wore is said to be lucky. Coloured dresses are usually given to the bridesmaids and the luckiest shades are believed to be blue, pink and gold. Red is said to be very unlucky, and if a bride spills even the tiniest drop of blood on her gown this is an omen that she will not live long. Green is also an unhappy colour because it represents jealousy, although the Irish take quite the opposite view! Silk is the most widely accepted material for the wedding dress, while satin is said to be unlucky, and velvet – of all things – is said to presage poverty! There should be no designs on the dress, particularly not incorporating birds which are an ill-omen, or any vine-like pattern as this signifies death. Superstition also brought about the bridal veil for in years gone by it was felt evil spirits might try to snatch a woman whose charms appealed to them, and consequently the veil was used to hide her features until she was in the church and safely under the protection of her new husband. (In many countries when the bridegroom raises the veil to kiss his new bride it is said to be important that she has a little cry or else all her married life will be full of tears.) Any bride will certainly court unhappiness if she makes her own wedding dress or tries it on before the wedding day, especially if she sees herself in a full-length mirror. Unable to resist this temptation, though, most girls leave off a shoe or a glove out of respect for this old tradition. It is also said that to make sure everything goes without a hitch, a last stitch should be added to the bride's dress just as she leaves for the church. Because flowers symbolized sex and fertility among the ancients, the bride carries a bouquet to ensure her own marital happiness. The ribbons knotted around the flowers are said to be good luck bringers, symbolizing the wishes for health and happiness proferred by the bride's friends. On the way to Church it is an ill-omen for the bridal party to meet either a policeman, a doctor, a lawyer, a priest or a blind man, and the party should also enter by the door which it is planned to leave from or the signs are not good. When leaving after the ceremony it is an evil omen for a bride to meet a pig or a funeral party, while it is a good sign if her path is crossed by a black cat, a chimney sweep or an elephant. Although few brides go to their receptions in a horse-drawn carriage, grey mares are said to be the best animals to pull it, but should they prove troublesome or difficult to start when the couple are on board then bad luck is in store for the newly weds. The throwing of confetti over the happy couple – it used to be rice – is another time-honoured superstition to bestow fertility on the couple. In some countries a slipper is also sometimes thrown at them – symbolizing the womb and a charm to ensure they have children. Although guests at a marriage take great trouble to make sure they hit the happy couple with their confetti, superstition originally decreed that it should fall around them, and they would be unlucky if actually hit by it! Wedding gifts are also a continuation of the old idea of presenting the new couple with fruit to ensure fertility – in Germany, for instance, it is still quite common for a bride to be given nuts and the phrase 'to go a nutting' is a euphemism for love-making. So to the final stage – the bride must, of course, always be carried across the threshold of her new home to avoid bad luck. This tradition is said to come from the days when men carried off their brides and the girl might well still be struggling to escape when they reached their new home! Another superstition, found through much of Europe and Asia, says if the bride goes to sleep first on her wedding night she will certainly die first.

BRIDESMAIDS

The bridesmaids at a wedding, along with the best man, are actually relics from the days when marriage ceremonies were not infrequently attacked by enemies wishing to carry off the bride, and their presence was to prevent such an outrage. Bridesmaids, of course, always hope to catch the bride's bouquet when she throws it among them and thus ensure a wedding for themselves. There are other omens for them, too

It is, for example, very unlucky for a bridesmaid to stumble on her way to the altar for this is said to be a sign that she is destined to become an old maid. Strangely, it is unlucky to be a bridesmaid three times – for unless a girl undertakes the job four more times she will never marry (the lucky number seven again!). A bride who has a matron of honour in her retinue is said to attract particular luck to herself for this married woman represents the happy state of matrimony.

BRIDGE
In several European countries it is considered an ill-omen to take leave of a friend on a bridge, for to do so means that you will never meet again. And it is unlucky to go under a railway bridge either on foot or in a car when a train is passing overhead.

BROAD BEANS
Superstition maintains that the broad bean contains the soul of the dead and when these plants are in flower accidents are most likely to happen. The shape of the broad bean is also associated with death and it is said that ghosts may be warded off by scattering some of the beans around the house on December 31 each year and reciting the words, 'With these beans I redeem me and mine.' The spirit is said to pick these up and not trouble the household for the following twelve months. The bean has also been widely used in foretelling the future. On Midsummer Eve three beans should be prepared – one left as it is, the second half-peeled and the third with its skin totally removed. These must be hidden and the person wishing to know his future sent to find them. Whichever he finds first will indicate what life holds in store – the unpeeled bean indicating wealth, the second a comfortable life and the poor little stripped bean, poverty. Perhaps the most curious of all beliefs about the broad bean is that it grows upside-down in Leap Years!

BROOM
The most widespread superstition attached to the broom was that it was used by witches to fly on – a belief that has been proved to be false as the only 'trips' the witches actually took

were provided by drugs. In its everyday use, people in a great many countries believe that a new broom should be used to sweep something *into* the house before sweeping dust out, or else your luck will go out of the door with it. In parts of England it is believed to be unlucky to buy a broom in the month of May or you will 'sweep your friends away', while Yorkshire folk maintain that if a girl walks over a broomstick she will become a mother before she is married. Never take an old broom with you to a new house or else you will carry all your bad luck with you – and indeed a new broom, some bread and a little salt are prerequisites when moving to a fresh home to ensure a happy future there. It is unlucky to sweep after dark and it will certainly prevent you making your fortune, while if a child picks up a broom and begins sweeping then unexpected guests are on the way. Never step over a fallen broom; it means bad luck, as does a broom which falls over as you pass by. The omens are also said to be bad if you borrow a broom, lend one or – worse still – burn one. In African superstition one of the worst things you can do is to strike a man with a broom, for unless he grabs the broom and retaliates with seven blows he will become impotent. If it happens to a woman, though, it is an omen that she is going to lose her man, and unfortunately there is no prescribed remedy.

BUBBLES
In both Britain and America the sight of bubbles floating on the surface of a cup of tea or coffee is an omen that the drinker is going to come into some money.

BUCKET
If you pass a bucket full of liquid of any kind when you first leave your house in the morning it is a good omen for the day; but if it is empty watch out for misfortune.

BUILDING
One of the worst omens that can befall a new building is if someone engaged in its construction is accidentally killed. A

superstition found on both sides of the Atlantic says this is a sign that the building is going to be an unhappy one and many deaths will subsequently occur there. The consequences are thought to be even worse if the luckless worker should be burnt to death.

BURIAL

In Ireland and parts of Britain it is believed that the last corpse to be buried in the churchyard or cemetery on any given day has to 'watch over' all the graves until the next coffin arrives. This superstition has, apparently, led to some unfortunate and even hilarious scenes when two funeral parties have approached the burial ground at the same time and a race has developed between the groups to ensure that their charge is not the last to be buried! The French also have a superstition that the last person to be buried each year becomes a symbol of death and will be seen again in the locality where he lived by those who are to die within the next twelve months. There is a widespread belief that a coffin should always be carried to the grave 'with the sun' – in the direction the sun travels from its rising in the east to setting in the west – otherwise both the living and the dead are ill-omened.

BUTTERCUP

For generations children have delighted in holding buttercups under the chins of their friends to see if they like butter by the appearance of a yellow glow – which there always is when the sun is out!

BUTTERFLIES

Perhaps the most widespread belief about butterflies is that they are the souls of the dead, and from earliest times there are references to these creatures being looked upon with favour and treated kindly lest they should be the soul of a departed loved one. However, in many parts of England it is claimed that unless you kill the first butterfly you see each year, you will have twelve months bad luck. Similarly if the first butterfly you see is a yellow one then sickness is in store, although most folk claim the sight of a white butterfly bodes nothing but good. In Scotland great faith is placed in the old tradition that if a golden butterfly is seen fluttering near a dying person it is a good omen; in Ireland, too, the sight of a butterfly hovering near a corpse presages eternal happiness. To see three butterflies together on a leaf at any one time, though, is unlucky, and to spot one of the creatures flying at night is an omen of death.

BUTTERMAKING

Superstition decrees that you should throw a pinch of salt into the fire before you begin to make butter or the milk will not churn. In some coastal areas of Britain it is maintained that the milk will not curdle until the tide is coming in, and across the channel in France, the best time for butter making is at high tide just as the water begins to flow. The Scots believe that witches delight in preventing milk from turning into butter and consequently make their churn staffs of rowan wood which is well known to be feared and hated by those in league with the Devil.

BUTTON

It is a very common superstition that if you button up a shirt, coat or any garment incorrectly than you are in for some bad luck that day unless you take the item of clothing off and start all over again. However, if you find a button it is a sign that you are going to make a new friend. Many an American mother will teach this verse to her small daughter so she may learn the profession of her future husband by counting the buttons on her skirt:

'A doctor, a lawyer, a merchant, a chief,
A rich man, a poor man, a beggar-man, thief.'

In Britain, a very similar verse is recited by young boys to determine their future while counting the stones left from eating a plate of fruit.

CABBAGE

That old vegetable garden favourite, the cabbage, can be an omen of good luck if one should be found growing 'double' – that is with two shoots from a single root.

CALF

The calf is an object of considerable superstition in the British Isles, and several authorities have recorded that in the past farmers whose herds were struck by illness or infertility would often burn a calf alive, believing the very ancient tradition 'burn one (a calf) to save the herd'. The origin of this lies in witchcraft, for the illness of cattle was often put down to the work of witches and it was believed that whatever was done to one of the animals which had been spelled would happen to the originator of the curse. A less drastic and horrifying superstition to cure illness among calves is found in the Midlands where the leg or thigh of a beast who had died was hung by a rope in the vicinity of the herd. This probably originated from the practice of early man of hanging an animal from a tree in sacrifice to the old gods. The creature is seemingly considered unlucky in life but lucky in death, for to put your hand on a calf's back is to court misfortune for yourself and presage illness or an accident for the beast; while to carry a tip of its tongue in your pocket will protect you from danger *and* see you are never short of money. This superstition is the origin of Northumberland folk referring to the tip of a calf's tongue as 'the lucky bit'. Many farmers believe that to give a piece of mistletoe to the first cow to calve after New Year will bring good luck to your entire herd. In parts of Southern England, it is thought to be unlucky for a farmer if any of his cows have twins, and a double misfortune if one or both of them should have a white streak on its back. On many farms it is unlucky to step over a calf when it is lying on the ground for this is an ill-omen for man and beast.

'CALLING THE DEAD'

Many American and African negroes still hold to a super- stition of very great antiquity that if a sick person either knowingly or unknowingly calls out for anyone who is dead, then his own death is not far away. There would seem to be sound psychological reasoning behind this, for often when the mind is in a feeble or decaying state it recalls people and scenes from earlier times in the person's life. An extension of this superstition is that the last person whose name a dying person speaks will be the next to die. In Germany there is a belief that if you call a dead person by their name three times then they must appear – although this only works on Christmas Eve. In India to imagine you hear someone calling your name after dark is an omen of death.

CANCER

A quite useless superstition still to be found in parts of Europe is that toads have the power of sucking cancer from the system, and there are on record several instances of people who have swallowed small toads or frogs in the hope that they would eat away the disease. Any cures attributed to this practice can no doubt be ascribed to the fact that the patient did not really have cancer in the first place! In the West of England the claim is still occasionally made that a poultice made of earth from a churchyard will cure cancer.

CANDLE

Superstitions and omens associated with candles are widespread around the world. In one of the oldest it is used to predict the future: if a candle will not light there is a storm on the way, while if the flame gutters and waves in a room where there is no wind or draught then bad weather of some kind is imminent. If the flame burns blue this indicates frost or a death in the offing. Should one gutter and cause grease to form in what is called a 'winding sheet' then this is a death omen for whoever is sitting nearest to it. Superstition holds that it is important to light candles at moments of birth, marriage and death to ensure that evil spirits are kept at bay at these crucial times. It used to be said that a candle showing a bright spark indicated that the person sitting opposite would receive a letter – but nowadays it is more likely to mean the arrival of strangers! The French and Germans believe that the candle is a test of virginity, for only a girl who is pure can blow back into life one that is spluttering and dying. In the North of England the candle is used as a love charm and it is believed that if two pins are stuck through a lighted candle, by the time it burns down to the pins the sought-after lover will have arrived. It apparently helps to recite the following verse while inserting the pins, 'It's not the candle alone I stick, but (name of the man or woman)'s heart I mean to prick; whether he (she) be asleep or awake, I'll have him (her) come to me and speak.' Mind you it is difficult to understand how raising someone in the middle of the night would put them in the most loving frame of mind! To light a candle from the fire will prevent you ever growing rich, while to leave a candle to burn itself out is to court misfortune. Accidentally knocking a candle out is a sign of a wedding. The delightful custom of lighting candles in the window at Christmas time – even on the Christmas tree – originates in the idea that they lit the way for the Holy Family on their way to Bethlehem. Today, they can still ensure a year of light, warmth and plenty for the family.

CANE

Faced with corporal punishment, schoolboys in many parts of Britain still believe that a strand of horse hair – particularly one plucked from a living horse – stretched across the palm of their hand would cause the cane of a master punishing them to split.

CARROTS

The idea has persisted for many years that eating carrots improves the eyesight, and during the Second World War the story was widely propagated that British RAF Pilots were fed a special diet of these vegetables to make them superior night fighters to the Germans. The story was mainly a screen to cover the development of Radar, but there is a certain truth in it for they contain medicinal salts which will help some eye troubles. Carrots have also featured in love-philtres and aphrodisiacs, and eating quantities of the vegetable boiled is said to help asthma sufferers for they contain certain constituents that relieve constriction of the bronchial tubes.

CATERPILLAR

A favourite superstition of Yorkshire people to bring good luck on themselves is to throw a hairy caterpillar over their left shoulder whenever they find one!

CATS

The cat has a special place in superstition as a good luck token, primarily because it was held in the highest esteem by early man: the Egyptians, in particular, looked upon cats as gods, the male cat representing the sun, and the female the moon. The claim that the creature has nine lives originated from this veneration as well as its well-known tenacity for life. The most famous cat superstition relates to the black cat which almost everywhere is said to be lucky, especially if one crosses your path (always make a wish if one does) and should a stray arrive at your home then this is an omen of money to come. In America, though, the black cat is thought to be unlucky, while black and white and grey cats are said to be lucky. In both America and Europe the white cat is looked upon with some suspicion, and a stray tortoiseshell coming into your home is an omen of misfortune. For a time all cats were believed to be the familiars of witches, and witches to have the power to turn themselves into felines to carry out their evil intentions. Of the less sinister beliefs about the cat, the following are among the most common. If a cat sneezes, it is said to be a lucky sign for the household; but if it sneezes three times the family where it lives will all develop colds. (Some country folk also maintain a sneezing cat indicates rain.) A cat sitting with its back to the fire is an omen of a storm to come, while if it scratches the leg of a table there will also be a change in the weather. Many country people believe that when one of these animals washes its face over its ears then a long period of wet weather is on the way and if it licks its tail then a shower may be expected. Sailors say that a cat heard meowing on a ship presages trouble, while one seen leaping about in a playful manner or clawing at objects is an omen of a gale. In Wisconsin, America, a cat that washes itself seated in the doorway is an omen that a clergyman is due to visit the house. Finally, it is thought to be unlucky to hear a cat crying before setting off on a journey – if it does, return and find out what it wants. And remember that no cat which has been bought will ever be any good for catching mice!

CATTLE

Cattle for centuries have been believed to be one of the main targets of witches and consequently a number of charms have been developed. To protect them in the stalls the Irish scatter primroses on the ground and hang a piece of Rowan or Mountain Ash at the door, and the Scots maintain cows should be tarred behind the ears and at the root of the tail or the witches will steal their milk. Cattle are also seen as omens, and should an ox or a cow break into your garden there will shortly be a death in the family. An Irish superstition says that to see a woman before a man while driving cattle to market will lead to bad luck in your dealing. If a herd of cattle all feed close together, or lie down near each other, or low excessively, then rain is on the way; while if they rest on high ground fine weather can be expected. A tradition is also widespread that cattle turn to the east as midnight strikes on Christmas Eve and kneel to worship the baby Christ as their forebears did centuries ago. In some European countries it is even held that they acquire human speech for this one night. Perhaps not surprisingly, it is said to be unlucky for humans to witness this spectacle!

CHAIN LETTERS

There has been much controversy over the years about chain letters and the effect they can have on even the most apparently sophisticated people. Although originally used as a means of passing useful cures from one person to the next, the letters have subsequently become vehicles for extravagant claims about acquiring a fortune by passing them on – and equally sinister threats as to what might happen if the recipient does not do so. The very earliest chain letters date from the Middle Ages and carried details of simple cures and prayers to be recited with them. They were sold by travellers or fortune tellers and widely believed to be most effective. In the last hundred years, however, they have degenerated into what are little more than begging letters in which people are instructed to send money to names given on the accompanying list and then copy out the letter themselves and send it on to a dozen or more people who will, in turn, send the writer money. In this way, the missives claim, each writer will receive a considerable amount of money in the weeks that follow. But woe betide he or she who breaks the chain! There is no doubt that the chain letter has a place in the annals of superstition, but it cannot be stressed too strongly that there is no reason to believe they carry any likelihood of a fortune – or even misfortune – for the recipient, and can be destroyed without hesitation.

CHAIR

On leaving someone's house never put the chair on which you have been sitting back against a wall, for this is not only unlucky but means that you will never visit that house again. There is also a superstition of indeterminate origin in Ohio, America, that if three chairs are accidentally placed in a row, then a death will occur either in the house or in the family.

CHEEKS

Throughout much of the world it is said that if your cheeks feel as if they are burning, someone is talking about you. There is, though, usually a simple explanation of emotional stress or other psychological influence behind the blush.

CHESTNUT

The horsechestnut has for centuries been credited with the power to draw out pain such as backache, rheumatism and arthritis, and for this purpose country people throughout Britain and Europe still carry a conker or two in their pockets. The same belief also holds good in America where the chestnut is known as the 'buckeye', which may be the origin of the superstition, for anything resembling an eye has always been credited with magical powers.

CHEWING GUM

There is a superstition which has developed in America that if a young man presents his girl-friend with a stick of chewing gum over which he has secretly and earnestly requested that she fall in love with him, then if she takes it and chews it thoroughly, she will be unable to resist his charms.

CHICKENS

Many country people in Europe believe that it is unlucky if a hen lays an even number of eggs, and should this occur one should be removed or no chicks will hatch. On the other hand if all the eggs of one laying turn out to be cockerels this will bring luck to the owner and his family. Any egg laid on Good Friday, it is said, will ensure the strength and fertility of all the hens if preserved intact. As to the birds themselves, a widespread superstition says that a crowing hen presages evil, while if a cock crows outside the back door the housewife may expect a stranger to call. In the Midlands of England there is also a belief that immediately before the death of a farmer his chickens will roost at midday rather than at their usual time.

CHICORY
Superstition has credited the chicory plant with the power of making a person invisible, but on a more practical level it is said to be a harbinger of good luck and especially equipped to aid those on exploring trips. For this reason many of the early American settlers – and later the prospectors – carried a root of the plant in their pockets for luck. To this day it is still credited with the power of being able to open locks or remove obstacles.

CHILBLAINS
In the Channel Islands and much of France there is an ancient superstition that if a partly burned Yule Log is placed under the bed it will protect the family from chilblains – and thunder and fire into the bargain! There is also a very peculiar cure for this complaint that involves pricking the chilblains with holly leaves while sitting with your feet crossed. Absurd and even painful though it may seem, there is no disputing that the action would stimulate blood circulation in the feet, lack of which is the primary cause of the complaint.

CHILDREN
In many areas of the world it is thought to be a good omen for a child's future to present it with certain specified gifts as soon as it is old enough to understand what they represent. The items are bread, salt, an egg, money and some matches – which symbolize food, intelligence, friendship, wealth and light to lead it to heaven. It is a bad omen for anyone to step

over a child crawling on the floor as this may stunt its growth, while the same thing will happen to an infant who carries a basket on its head. The Japanese also believe that a child who carries a gun on his head or even under his arm will be stunted in his growth. Whether there is any truth in the superstition or not, the advice to keep guns away from children is certainly sound!

CHIMNEY SWEEP

Any bride coming from church who meets a chimney sweep is believed to secure for herself and her husband good luck and happiness for the rest of her life says a very old superstition, and may account for the popularity of these gentlemen at 'smart' weddings. The bride is, of course, required to kiss his grimy face to ensure her fortune. Why sweeps are believed to be lucky – a belief strongly held in Britain and also noted in Europe and America, too – is not easy to explain, but it has been suggested that a sweep once saved the life of an English king, and to show his gratitude, the monarch doffed his hat and bowed low to his saviour. However, as there was no way the king or his courtiers could again recognize the man because of his grimy countenance, and no one wished to give offence to a man who had performed such a noble act, it became common practise to show respect to all sweeps – and from this grew the idea that they were lucky. Consequently it is said to be lucky to meet a chimney sweep on his rounds, and any horse racing enthusiast who comes across one while on his way to place a bet is sure to enjoy success. To absolutely ensure the luck you should touch the man, or better still, shake his hand. (Interestingly, before his marriage in 1947 to Princess Elizabeth – now Queen Elizabeth – Prince Philip left his apartment in Buckingham Palace to shake hands with a sweep who just happened to be loitering nearby!) That commodity in which the sweep deals, soot, is also recorded as another marriage omen. If some of it should fall down the chimney while the wedding feast is in progress this unfortunately means the couple will not enjoy the best of luck in their life together.

CHINA ORNAMENTS

China ornaments, particularly those of animals, should always face into a room and never towards the door, or else they will allow the luck of the place to 'run out of the door'. The origin of this superstition seems to lie in the power of association. When a man's wealth was measured by the animals he owned, to face them in such a way that they might escape and thereby impoverish him was obviously something to be avoided. Hence the china animals, now standing in their stead, carry the same association.

CHOLERA

In several districts of Britain, including a number of the major cities, there is a tradition that cholera can be detected by throwing a piece of raw meat up into the air and if the disease is about it will immediately turn black. In Australia, a superstition decrees that to cure cholera the sufferers should go and sleep in a churchyard.

CHOPSTICKS

Wherever chopsticks are used there is a belief that to break one is a very bad omen. In Japan specifically it is said that a child who strikes anything other than their plate when they are eating with chopsticks will be struck dumb – although this sounds more like a directive to encourage good manners rather than a superstition!

CHRISTMAS

The majority of superstitions and omens associated with Christmas are of a happy nature – not a few dealing with love and affection as seems only right and proper. On Christmas Eve, for instance, if a girl walks backwards to a pear tree and then walks around it nine times she will see an image of her husband (or perhaps be dizzy!). If there are no pear trees available, the girl should try the hen house and tap sharply on the outside: if a hen cackles she will not be wed that year, but if the cock replies her luck is in. As a last resort there are always sage leaves, and the girl seeking news of her lover-to-be should go into the garden, pick twelve sage leaves and scatter them to the winds. As she does so a shadowy figure of a man will present itself to her. A test for true love is said to be a rose which has been picked on Midsummer Day and put away until Christmas. It is then examined and if found to be still fresh, the love of the girl who plucked it and her intended will run true and flourish. Despite widespread belief to the contrary, superstition maintains that ghosts do not appear on Christmas Day, although it is as well to open all your doors at midnight to let out evil spirits. For the gardeners among you, if you have time to bind straw around your fruit trees on Christmas evening then you can be sure of a rich crop later in the year. Apart from their attraction, Christmas decorations of holly and mistletoe are also guardians against evil, although it is bad luck to keep them up after Twelfth Night – January 6 which coincides with the date of the Old Christmas Day. Evergreens should not just be thrown out of doors but carefully burnt or a death will occur in the family. That lovely superstition maintained for children that Father Christmas fills stockings left for him has its origins in a legend told about St Nicholas, the patron saint of Christmas Day. He is said to have gone to the home of three sisters living in the most dire poverty and thrown some coins down the chimney. Instead of landing in the hearth, however, they fell into some stockings which the girls had left hanging to dry and were discovered there in the morning. Hence the legend of gifts appearing in stockings on Christmas morning and the idea of Father Christmas coming down the chimney! If the sun is shining on Christmas morning it is said in many places to presage a fine harvest during the coming year, but in Huntingdonshire there is a verse which runs, 'Light Christmas, light wheatsheaf; dark Christmas, heavy wheatsheaf' – so take your choice! In the North of England the custom of 'First Footing' is still held, although in most other areas the tradition belongs to New Year's Day. A dark man must be the first to enter the house on Christmas morning to ensure luck – but a woman coming at this time will bring disaster. A man with red hair is said to be no better, either! It is believed to be unlucky to carry anything out of the house on a Christmas morning before something has been brought in. The delight in a white Christmas should not overlook the fact that it is an omen of fewer deaths in the coming year while lack of snow signifies quite the opposite. Finally, when you are all settled around the roaring fire take a careful look at the shadows flickering on the walls. Any that appear without heads belong to people who will die during the coming twelve months.

CHRISTMAS PUDDING
Stirring the Christmas Pudding while it is being made is lucky for all those who take part – but it is absolutely essential to stir the pudding 'sun-wise' (that is, east to west) as the custom is a throwback to one of the earliest ways of honouring the Sun God. Each person as they stir the mixture can make one wish, and as long as they do not repeat it to a soul it should come true.

CHURCH
One of the most sinister omens associated with churches is that a bird seen perched on the weather vane signifies a death in the parish in the following week. On a happier note, if a bird flies into a church while a service is taking place it will bring good luck to all those present. In many districts it is said that you will have twenty unlucky Sundays if you turn over a hassock in your pew; you should use it whatever way up it is to avoid this misfortune. The sound of a church door rattling when there is no discernible cause is said to be a signal that it will be opening before long to admit a coffin. Anyone brave enough, and perhaps one might think ghoulish enough, who wants to see those from his parish who are going to die during the next twelve months has merely to sit in the church porch at midnight on Hallowe'en, and the forms of those who are to pass on will be seen entering the building as the clock chimes twelve. In Scotland it is believed that the names of the doomed are actually called out and the person situated in the porch can save

them from their immediate fate by throwing off an item of clothing at each call. One hopes that the night would not prove too cold for such a noble strip-tease!

CIGARETTES

The superstition that it is bad luck to light three cigarettes from one match appears to have originated during the Boer War. It was said that a sniper could spot where men might be as the first cigarette was being lit, take aim as the second was ignited and fire with deadly effect at the third. Two lights was enough for any group of men who valued their lives.

CIGARS

The girls of that famous American 'witch town' of Salem in Massachusetts have a superstition that if you accidentally step on a cigar end then you will marry the first man you meet thereafter!

CLOCK

In America it is still widely believed in rural areas that a person's favourite clock will stop at the time of their death. This belief has been immortalized in the song, 'Grandfather's Clock', and the explanation may be that until this century many favourite clocks were of such a temperamental nature that only their owners really knew how to operate them. If this person was confined to bed during his final illness it was highly likely that they would wind down and then stop as the man himself expired. Americans also believe that the clocks in a house should be stopped when a person dies to indicate to Death that his job is done and he should leave and let life go on again. The clocks themselves should not be re-started until after the funeral. There is an eerie omen in Britain that a clock which suddenly strikes or chimes after not going for some time signifies a death is imminent in the household. In the West of England there is a superstition that if a clock strikes during the reading of the text or the last hymn a death will shortly occur in the parish. However in Wales it is said that if the local town clock strikes while the parish church bells are ringing watch out for a fire in the vicinity! It is an ill-omen if a clock chimes during a wedding ceremony, similarly during a funeral, for another will then follow soon afterwards. If there is a sudden change in the rhythm of a clock – particularly if it goes faster – this is widely believed to be an omen of death, as is the ominous striking of thirteen.

CLOTHES

Superstition has always claimed it is lucky to put on any item of clothing inside out, while it is unlucky to button anything up wrongly. When you buy a new coat or dress it is advisable as soon as you wear it to put some money in the right hand pocket, for if you do not, says a superstition widespread throughout much of Europe, you will always be hard up as long as you wear it. In many parts of Britain it is said that a person whose clothes are stitched and mended while he or she is still wearing them will also always be needy, and apart from looking odd, it is unlucky to mend any item of light coloured clothing with dark thread. A good many nations consider the relationship between a person and his clothes important, and in Russia for instance it is said that if someone has robbed you or your house but left some small item of his dress behind at the scene of the crime, you should beat it with a stick and the man will thereafter fall ill and be more easily detected by the law. In an American superstition it is said that if a woman wants to have a happy and successful spring she must wear *three* new things on Easter Day – though some husbands may well find that a high price to pay for luck! Americans also believe that if you burn a hole in a dress this is an omen that someone, somewhere is telling lies about you.

CLOVER

To find a piece of clover with four leaves is regarded far and wide as a bringer of good fortune, and many people will spend an idle half an hour or so wandering across summer fields hoping to spot one – and they are actually not as rare as generally supposed. In some parts of Britain it is said that if a young man or woman finds such a clover they can expect to meet their future love the same day. The fact that cattle particularly enjoy grazing in fields of clover is the origin of the phrase often applied to a person doing well in life, 'He's in clover.' (Incidentally, you can enhance your chances of good luck after finding a four-leafed clover by handing it to someone else.) The reputation of the four-leafed clover springs from the tradition that Eve took one with her when she was expelled from paradise. There is an old saying associated with the leaf that goes:

> 'One leaf for fame, one leaf for wealth,
> One leaf for a faithful lover,
> And one leaf to bring glorious health –
> All are in the four-leaf clover.'

There is also a tradition that should you find one of the extremely rare five-leaf clovers then you will become very wealthy. (Irish readers might like to note that the same traditions apply to their national flower, the Shamrock.) Finally, during the war years there was a superstition that if a man wore a four-leafed clover in his button hole he would avoid military service!

COAL

Coal, being symbolic of fire, is considered lucky, and country people have for generations carried small pieces of it in their pockets to ward off misfortune. Its use in 'First Footing' on New Year's Day is well-known, although in some parts of Europe a piece is sometimes given as a Christmas present and if it is placed on the fire and a wish made, this is sure to be granted. It is lucky to find a piece on the road (and more so if there are a lot, with coal being the price it is!), although in some parts of Britain it is said that you can only obtain luck by throwing the lump over your left shoulder and then walking on without looking back. In coastal districts, a piece of coal found washed up on the shore should be given to a sailor as a protection from drowning. A piece of coal kept in the pocket or handbag is claimed to bring good luck according to a British tradition, and in the days when there were many more coal fires than there are now it was thought to be very unlucky to give a neighbour a live coal to kindle his fire with on a Christmas morning.

COBWEBS

As it is believed that it was a cobweb which hid the baby Jesus from Herod's soldiers, a certain mystique has grown up around them and to destroy one is said to bring bad luck. The web is also claimed to have the power to quickly stop bleeding when laid over a wound, and as long as it is not too deep it does work! In America, cobwebs are associated with two courting customs. If a girl finds a cobweb on her door then it indicates that her boyfriend is also making calls on another girl elsewhere. A cobweb found in the kitchen, say the people of Boston, is an omen that no love making goes on there.

COCK

The cock is held in high esteem as the enemy of ghosts and evil spirits, and because it is said to have heralded Christ's birth there is a superstition that on the Day of Judgement all cocks – even the iron ones on church spires – will set up a cacophany of noise that will awaken both the living and the dead. White cocks are universally regarded as being lucky, but the black variety in some parts of Europe are held to be consorts of the Devil. A cock crowing as you go off to work signals a good day. However, if the bird crows in the early evening bad weather will follow the next day, while a cry late at night means there is to be a death in the family. If the cock crows facing the door of the house then a stranger will arrive that day, and a cock that stays on its perch indicates rain is imminent – a sensible bird indeed! The cock is said to cure illness when rubbed on the body of a sufferer and then either cast out to sea or removed from the district 'taking' the illness with it. In many places you will find for any medicine to be effective that it must be given at cock crow.

COFFEE

Coffee drinkers in America believe they can see omens of the future on the surface of their cups. If there are bubbles which float towards you then money is on its way, while if they float in the opposite direction times are going to be hard.

COFFIN

Throughout Germany it is said that anyone who lies in a coffin, even for fun, is inviting death, and that no item of clothing belonging to a living person should ever be placed on a corpse when it is put in a coffin, for as the clothing rots in the grave so will the rightful owner decline towards death. (This superstition is one of the major reasons why some people are still afraid of giving away old clothes to the aged and infirm.)

COINS

Superstition has credited certain coins with special powers – particularly those given at Holy Communion. If two or three of these coins are immediately handed over to a person suffering from rheumatism and they rub the affected part of the body a cure will soon be effected. For many years special coins, known as 'touch pieces' and usually showing the Devil defeated, were minted in Britain and distributed amongst poor people in the belief that they would keep down disease and sickness. Many of the famous individual coins which are claimed to have special powers and have remained in the possession of certain families over the years were originally 'touch pieces'. In many countries it is believed that to be given a coin with a hole in it – either as a gift or in change – will bring good luck. In Europe there is also a rather amusing superstition that if two of the coins which are sometimes placed on the eyes of the dead are removed and dropped briefly in a glass of wine which is afterwards given to a husband or a wife, it will 'blind' them to any affairs or infidelities the other partner may be conducting! Carrying a coin bearing the date of your birth is lucky, while there is potentially no luckier way of settling a question than by tossing a coin – as long as you win, of course! In Austria it is believed that any coins found during a rainstorm are particularly lucky because they are said to have been dropped from heaven and therefore make very good charms.

COLOURS

Colours have always featured strongly in superstition and they are referred to in numerous entries to be found in this book. Many people, of course, have particular likes and dislikes and believe that certain shades are lucky for them. Superstition, though, has very clear ideas about the qualities of certain colours. For instance, blue has always been regarded as a particularly fortunate colour because it represents the skies, as has white – if it may be classified as a colour – because of its sacred connections. Apart from its popularity for wedding dresses, white has for generations been especially favoured for night dresses to protect the sleeper from the attentions of evil spirits who naturally fear the holy colour. Black, too, features in many superstitions and more often than not for the good (think of black cats, sheep and birds, for instance) although many people fear it. It is interesting to note that the tradition of wearing black at funerals is not strictly speaking a mark of respect for the dead, but continuing a Roman custom of acknowledging that, in the presence of Death, we are inferior creatures. Certain colours have always had a connection with astrology, and the planets also each have a specific colour. In this context it is perhaps not such a bad idea to utilize the colour associated with your star, for modern science has been able to prove what superstition has maintained for centuries, that colours can and do affect the human psyche. Red has always been associated with passion because it is the colour of blood and superstition credits it with strong powers to work against witchcraft and evil in general. For this reason it is a very popular colour in special ceremonies and as the dress for important people. Orange is healthy and emotional, while yellow is considered stimulating and symbolic of the sun. Green, too, is a favoured colour which has always meant satisfaction and symbolized both nature and the feeling of peace. Finally, in old English country lore, the qualities of the colours are summarized succinctly: blue being lucky, green healthy, red meaning wealth and pink pleasant anticipation.

COMB
A comb which has been used by a dead person should never be used by anyone else or it will invite death, according to Hungarian tradition. In Britain a mother is advised never to comb a baby's hair until it has finished teething, or else for every tooth of the comb that falls out so will one of the child's teeth be lost before its due time.

COMETS
Comets have for centuries been seen as omens of misfortune, and have proved uncannily correct on occasions. Similarly thunderstorms and unusual displays of static electricity have heralded trouble as did the freak electrical storm which broke over Michigan and Ohio in America only minutes before the terrible Japanese attack on Pearl Harbour.

CONSUMPTION
A bizarre superstition still persists in parts of England that consumption may be cured by swallowing baby frogs first thing in the morning before breakfast!

COOKING
Many housewives in rural districts still believe that food which is mixed in an anti-clockwise direction will never taste good, and thereby unconsciously honouring the practise of the ancient sun worshippers who believed all important functions must be conducted in an east to west direction. In Cornwall, there is a belief that one should never attempt to remove fruit stains from any item when the fruit is out of season, again paying deference to the old idea that there is an interconnection between an object and its parts however separated they may be.

CORK

A piece of cork is said to be a cure for the cramp, and old people in country districts throughout Europe still go to bed wearing garters made from bits of the material to prevent their leg muscles from seizing up during the night.

CORN DOLLIES

These delightful pieces of country handicraft made from plaited corn sheaves have become much in evidence again recently and are widely believed to be harbingers of good luck. Originally, the dollies were supposed to be made from the last sheaves taken from the harvest field as they contained the spirit of the corn, but as harvesting has now become a mechanised industry such traditions are not often observed.

CORPSE

There was once a great variety of superstitions about dead bodies, some of a most extraordinary nature, but with the advances in medical science most have been disproved and discarded. It is, though, still widely believed that if a corpse remains warm for some hours after it should have grown cold then this presages another death before long in the same family. Among the oldest superstitions about the moving of dead bodies is one that any land over which a corpse is carried becomes a public right of way. Despite numerous legal rulings that this is just not true, the belief still persists in several places. Many country folk also claim that if a dead body is carried across a field it will thereafter fail to grow good crops. Sailors as a whole think it is unlucky to have a corpse on board ship, and when a dead man is buried at sea they will not look as it disappears into the waves, because if they do superstition says they will soon be following it. In the Northern Counties of England it is an omen of disaster if an animal jumps over a coffin, and this can only be avoided by seeking out and killing the creature immediately. Throughout Britain and Europe the superstition still exists that to touch a dead body while it lies in the coffin before burial is to ensure good fortune for the living and allow the departed to go to his or her rest in peace. In America it is the custom to touch the forehead of the deceased so as not to dream of him or her or see them as a ghost.

COTTON

If you find a piece of cotton sticking to your dress or suit then you can expect an important letter. This universal superstition goes on to add that the cotton will probably lie in such a shape that it has the appearance of a single letter which will indicate the initial of the person from whom the correspondence is coming.

COUGH

A superstitious cure for a cough said to be still practised in parts of the British Isles is to boil three snails in barley water and give the liquid to the sufferer to drink. It is essential, says the recipe, that the patient is unaware of the constituents of his drink – which is perhaps not to be wondered at!

COW

The cow is, of course, regarded as a sacred animal in the Far East and religious beliefs as well as superstition give it a special place in the community. In Scotland, though, the milk from a white cow is believed to be inferior to that of any other type, while many rural Americans say the meat of a red cow is the best to eat. Should a cow low in your face three times this is believed to be an omen of death, while a cow breaking into your garden also signifies that someone in the family will die shortly. If a cow carries her tail upright it is an omen of rain, and if she slaps it against a tree or fence bad weather is also on the way. Two other superstitions surrounding the cow which once held great sway but now seem to have virtually disappeared are that cows eat buttercups to help them make better butter (in fact they dislike the plant intensely) and a herd's milk yield will dry up if the milkmaid does not wash her hands after each milking.

CRADLE

Two totally different superstitions pertaining to the cradle have been recorded: in much of England and most of Europe it is believed that to rock an empty cradle will lead to it being occupied again within a year, while in the north of England and Holland to carry out this same action will result in the death of the child who last laid in it.

CRICKET

Cricket is as beset with personal superstitions as any other sport. Players at all levels believe a certain bat is lucky for them, that a ball should or should not be rubbed on certain parts of their clothing to achieve success, and that particular caps or sweaters can mean the difference between winning and losing. The more general superstitions claim that it is lucky to see a black cat immediately before a game begins, but unlucky when leaving the pavilion; and any bowler who has to restart his run is certainly ill-omened. No cricketer would go happily out to bat if he had made the mistake of first putting his pads on the wrong legs for he will score no runs. Similarly, a batsman who takes guard twice at the same end will be bowled soon afterwards. It is also advisable that no two members of the same team wash their hands at the same time before going out to bat because, says another superstition, if they do they will both score ducks! Finally, there is, of course, no score more disliked than 13.

CRICKETS

Crickets are said to be harbingers of good luck and to kill one will bring misfortune. As it often seeks the warmth of the house, if one of these insects is seen leaving a building it is a sign that sickness or death will occur there shortly. Any white cricket seen indoors is an omen of death. The American Indians do not share this appreciation of the cricket, though, for they believe it possible to obtain a fine singing voice by drinking a liquid made of a quantity of these insects crushed and boiled!

CROCODILE

The Indians believe that crocodiles make a moaning and sighing noise like a human being in distress to attract their victims. They also have a curious superstition that the creatures shed their famous 'tears' over a victim's head after they have devoured the body – and then polish off the head to complete the meal!

CROPS

Farmers in many countries believe that the best crops are those which are sown from north to south across their land, and indeed there is a sound reason for this as all the plants will get more sun than if they were sown from east to west. It is also said that crops sown during the time of the full moon will be ready a month earlier than those sown with the waning moon.

CROSSED OBJECTS

The origin of the superstition that crossed knives and shoes are unlucky dates from the Middle Ages when such signs were said to be an affront to the Christian cross. To remove the bad luck, though, you merely need to have someone else uncross the items for you. Many people also believe it is unlucky to meet a cross-eyed woman, but lucky to meet a cross-eyed man. A partial explanation for this is that cross eyes were once thought to be a sign of the Evil Eye, and many an unfortunate soul suffering the affliction was made an outcast by society.

'CROSSING THE LINE'

Although those who take part in the hilarious sea ceremony of 'crossing the line' are probably unaware of it, the ritual actually developed from the tradition in ancient times of sacrificing a member of the crew to the sea gods to ensure a safe voyage for the ship and good luck for all those on board.

CROWS

Throughout the world and from the earliest times the crow has been looked upon as an omen of misfortune and death. The bird is widely associated with witchcraft and is said to have the gift of prophecy, hence it has proved a major ingredient in many potions of fortune telling. A crow flying about a house and cawing signifies a death to come, while to see one of the birds perched alone is an omen of bad luck. A flock of crows flying from a wood is a sign of hard times ahead, while their activities at dawn and evening are weather portents. If they are seen flying towards the sun in the morning the weather will be fine and dry, but to be spotted stalking around water at nightfall is the sign of a storm in the offing. The number of them in any one place also indicates the future of the eyewitness according to this verse from Maryland in America:

'One crow – sorrow,
Two crows – mirth,
Three crows – wedding,
Four crows – birth.'

CRYING

It may be a comfort to mothers of children who seem to cry a great deal that there is a superstition still prevalent in many rural areas of Europe that a child who 'cries long will live long'. Though whether this is much consolation after a disturbed night is doubtful!

CUCKOO

The first call of the cuckoo heralding spring, that topic so beloved of letter writers to *The Times*, is the subject of several interesting omens and superstitions. In Wales for example, it is believed to be unlucky to hear the cuckoo before April 6, but a whole year's prosperity is in store if you hear his tone for the first time on April 28. In England it is unlucky to hear it in bed, but lucky to be dressed and outdoors. In some places to hear the bird after August is an evil omen – especially in September or October when it should have left for warmer climes – and the hearer will not live another year round. It is good luck, though, to have money in your pocket when the cuckoo first calls for if you turn it over you will not go short again. If the bird's sound comes from the right of where you are standing then you are in for good luck during the year (the reverse being true if it comes from the left) and you may also get a wish granted if it is made immediately afterwards. To be looking down at the ground when you first hear the cuckoo is an omen that you will be dead within a year, while the Scots say that the number of calls you hear the bird making will indicate the number of years you have left to live. In general, it is thought that whatever a person is doing at the time he hears the calls – and whatever his state of health – so will he continue for the next twelve months. Should you remove your shoe at this time and find a hair inside, this will be the same colour as that of your future mate, says another superstition for young men. The bird's song can also tell an unmarried girl about her future; the number of notes she first hears it sing will indicate the number of years she must wait to be wed. The bird will similarly provide an old person with the answer to how many years he or she has to live, replying with a 'Cuckoo' for each year. There is a delightful suggestion still to be heard that it is because the cuckoos are kept so busy providing answers to these questions that they have no time to build a nest and consequently dump their young on other unsuspecting birds! The cuckoo has, of course, given its name to plants and natural formations with which it has nothing to do (i.e. 'Cuckoo Buds' for buttercups and Cuckoo-Spit, the white frothy substance that certain insects cover themselves with as a form of cocoon), but surely the cruellest cut of all is the use of his original Latin name as the description of a deceived husband – the cuckold!

CURLEW

The curlew is a bird of ill-omen to sailors who say that when one is seen flying overhead making its distinctive call, then a storm is brewing and it is ill-advisable to take to sea. It is also a particularly sinister omen for anyone who hears it calling at night.

CUTLERY

There is an old superstition couched in rhyme which is known in many rural areas of England which goes 'Knife falls, gentleman calls; fork falls, lady calls; spoon falls, baby squalls.'

DAFFODIL

The Welsh believe it is lucky to find the first daffodil of Spring and that to do so will bring the finder more gold than silver in the coming twelve months. Also never take a single daffodil into the house, always a bunch, or misfortune will occur.

DAISY

Little girls have always loved plucking the petals from a daisy and repeating the words, 'He loves me, He loves me not' to find if their boy friend is true. Although gardeners regard the plant as something of a nuisance when it appears on lawns, it is actually a good weather omen for when the petals are seen to be closing then bad weather is on the way. (The same is also true of the dandelion.)

DANDELIONS

Dandelion heads can serve as love omens according to English country lore. If an unmarried girl plucks one fresh from the ground and blows the head of fluff, the number of puffs it takes to remove all the 'flying seeds' will indicate the number of years she will have to wait before her wedding.

DARTS

Darts players in Britain have many individual superstitions, but there seems to be a general agreement that playing against women is unlucky. Perhaps the action most regularly seen to promote a lucky throw is a player putting his left foot forward to the line and moving it from left to right as if to remove an invisible object of bad luck between himself and the board.

DAY

The frame of mind in which you get up often has a lot to do with what kind of day you will have, and there is a British superstition summed up in verse, about the effect of waking up and mistaking which day of the week it is:

> 'Lose a day, you lose a friend,
> Gain a day, you gain a friend.'

DEATH OMENS

A great many death omens will be found throughout the book under specific headings, but here are a few general superstitions of this kind which are almost universally accepted. The sound of three knocks in the room where a person is lying ill is believed to be Death announcing his intention of carrying off another soul. The appearance of a white-breasted bird near a sick room has the same import. In Wales the discovery of a mole that has burrowed under the wash house or the dairy is said to signify that the woman of the house will die during the next year. Among other animal activities believed to portend death are dogs howling at an open door for no apparent reason, hens laying eggs with double yolks and fish making a strange noise when pulled from the water. It is interesting to note that the Death Watch Beetle got it's name from the superstition that its tapping sound in the house meant a death in the family. The insect actually bores silently through the wood, and the tapping sound is the noise the beetle makes when it calls to another of its kind.

DEATH PREDICTION

There is an old Jewish tradition that it is possible for a husband and wife to learn who will die first by calculating the numerical value of the letters in each of their names. (The formula being A=1, B=2, etc). If the result turns out to be even, the man will die first; if odd, the woman.

DEATH TIDE

Among many folk who live by the sea there is a common superstition that a person will not die until the tide begins to ebb, and this is explained by the fact that they see their lives as being ruled by the mighty ocean. Similarly it is believed that a child cannot be born until the tide is nearly in.

DEW

In rural areas throughout Europe there is a superstitious belief that dew can be used by women as a cosmetic and if we accept some of the stories told of its qualities, it can be far more effective than the most expensive toilet preparations now available on the market! Dew collected early on the morning of May 1 and rubbed on the face is said to ensure a beautiful complexion for the following year, while the skin as a whole will benefit from dew taken from plants on St Bride's Day, February 1, and rubbed gently over the body. There is also a delightful verse concerning American superstitions about the dew which reads:

> 'When the dew is on the grass,
> Rain will never come to pass.
> When grass is dry at morning light,
> Look for rain before the night.'

DICE

Playing dice may well be the most popular game in America today, and it is interesting to discover that the term 'crap shooting' actually developed from the French. Apparently small boys wishing to play dice but discouraged from doing so by their parents, would crouch out of sight in the attitude of toads and their activity was given the name, *crapaud*, the French word for toad. In America the term was shortened to 'crap'. There are, of course, many superstitions attached to dice, including blowing on them and snapping the fingers to keep away bad luck. You can, though, achieve success by rubbing the dice on a red-headed person, and if you always have a pair on your person you will never be short of money! The omens to be drawn from the numbers on the dice are as follows. One spot indicates a letter of great importance, while two spots signifies a forthcoming successful journey. Three spots means you are in for a big surprise – and you will probably be sleeping in a strange bed! Four is unlucky and indicates trouble on the way, while five signifies a change in your family affairs, or if you are single your lover will prove unfaithful. Finally, the six is lucky and will bring you unexpected money. Like winning the crap game perhaps?

DIMPLE

In most parts of the world, a dimple is considered lucky and the British believe this is so because the mark was made by the impression of God's finger. In certain parts of America, though, the reverse is said to be true, as summed up in an old rhyme: 'Dimple on the chin – Devil within.'

DINING TABLE

An old phrase 'Sing at the table, die in the workhouse,' still repeated to noisy children waiting at the table for a meal, has its origins in superstition. To do so, it was said, was to engage the attention of evil spirits who might well strike down the providers of the family, leaving nothing for the hapless orphans but to be committed to the workhouse with all its sad implications.

DOCTOR

In Britain, before the introduction of the National Health Service which obviated the need, it was considered unlucky to settle a doctor's bill completely for this implied confidence that a total cure had been effected. It was thought better to retain a small portion of the bill to avoid the misfortune of having to summon the doctor in again when the offended fates started up the illness once more. Superstition also decrees that the first person to be seen by a doctor in a new surgery is sure to be cured, while to call a doctor to see anyone who is ill on a Friday is very ill-omened.

DOG

Because the dog has traditionally been thought to possess the ability to see ghosts and 'smell' death it has been surrounded by superstitious beliefs over the centuries. It may well be that the animal is sensitive to some chemical change in human tissues, for there are many instances on record of dogs showing great distress hours before the death of a beloved master or mistress. A dog is always said to 'know' the difference between a good person and a bad one, and show it in his reaction by tail-wagging or growling. A dog howling at an open door for no apparent reason presages death, while a dog which howls when a child is born signifies an unhappy life for the infant. Many people including the Hindus and American Indians believe that a dog can be used for transferring evil or illness from human beings by ritually applying the sufferer's complaint to the animal and then driving it from the house or community. The gypsy people believe that if a dog gets into your garden and digs a big hole it is a sign of a death in the family. The Irish say it is unlucky to meet a barking dog first thing in the morning while in many places in the British Isles it is claimed that if a strange dog should suddenly start following you it is a sign of good luck, and if a black and white dog crosses your path on the way to a business meeting, you will be successful in your dealings. A dog howling outside the house at night is an omen of death or some coming misfortune, and if it is driven away but still returns this makes the unhappy event all the more certain. If a dog howls once, or three times, and then falls completely silent it is a sign that a death has actually occurred. In America, a dog falling asleep with his paws all drawn up round him and his tail outstretched is said to be a death omen. The death may not necessarily be in the family, though, but the direction in which the animal's tail points will indicate from which direction the news will come. If a dog runs between a courting couple they will certainly have a quarrel and may well not marry, while if a dog actually runs between a woman's legs it is an omen that her husband – or father – is going to punish her for some offence. The animal is also a weather omen, for if it eats grass, rolls for some time on the ground or scratches itself for a long time, then rain is on the way. Should a particularly bad storm be on the way, long before it is evident the dog will have retreated under a table or into some safe corner.

DONKEY

The poor old donkey which tradition says earned its reputation for stupidity in the Garden of Eden when God asked it its name and it could not remember, has nonetheless served man well as a beast of burden and weather omen. For when the creature takes to braying incessantly and twitching its long ears, then no matter how clear the skies may be, rain is on the way. There is also a superstition attached to the cross mark on the donkey's back that it appeared after Christ had ridden on one of its kind into Jerusalem on Palm Sunday. As a result of this some country people believe that a child suffering from whooping cough will be cured if it is sat on the mark and the donkey walked in a circle nine times. In Britain and Europe it is also still claimed that a donkey knows when it is about to die and hides itself away for this purpose. This has given rise to the saying, 'You never see a dead donkey', and the perhaps understandable superstition associated with it that to see one will bring you particularly good luck.

DOOR

The superstitious importance of doors being opened when either a child is being born or a person dying, to ensure the processes take place smoothly is found worldwide. There is also a superstition that it will bring bad luck to leave a house with all the doors open inside and out, and similarly never to open a front door unless the back door is closed. Both these beliefs stem from the ancient fear that evil spirits would thus have easy access to the house. The Romans thought that misfortune would be brought into a house by anyone entering with his left foot first – hence a manservant was placed there to prevent this eventuality and became the forerunner of the modern footman. In Germany, country people will go to great pains to avoid slamming a door in a house where someone has died in case they strike a soul, while in Africa many natives will not sweep out a dwelling through a door for a year after a death in case the dust harms the delicate soul.

DOUBLE FRUITS

It is lucky to find any fruit growing double, and if you take such and share it with a friend then you can both have a wish answered. This British superstition is complemented by an Austrian one that if a pregnant woman eats such a fruit she can expect twins!

DOUBT

There is a delightful Jewish superstition that if you are in doubt about any matter count the number of buttons on the coat you are wearing at the time. If there are an even number, then you are right; if an odd number, wrong.

DOVE

Tradition says that the dove is the one bird into which the Devil cannot turn himself, and consequently it has been re-garded as sacred since the earliest times. If one is seen flying near the window of a sick room or actually knocks upon the pane, then this is a sign of death, while no miner would dream of going down a mine if a dove was seen near the pitshaft. It is also credited with being the messenger of Venus, and as such is a bird of good omen – particularly to lovers. According to Indian tradition the bird actually contains the soul of a lover and great misfortune will follow the killing of one.

DRAGONFLY

The dragonfly will serve as an omen for a fisherman but only if he is a good man and not one given to bad habits. According to superstition if such a man casts his line and a dragonfly comes along, the creature will hover over the spot where fish are plentiful and aid him to success. To the fisherman of poor character, though, he will only indicate the empty reaches of the water.

DREAMS

Superstitions and omens regarding dreams are indeed legion and people from the very earliest times have been convinced that images seen while asleep foretell the future. The subject is one which warrants a book to itself and in fact has been very fully covered in a companion volume to this entitled *The Dreamer's Dictionary* by Lady Stearn Robinson and Tom Corbett, in which there are over 3,000 entries to help you interpret just about every dream you may have had! Perhaps it should be added here that according to certain people such as the North American Indians, dreams are caused by the soul leaving the body during sleep and wandering over strange lands. In both Britain and America it is said to be lucky to forget your dream of the previous night, but if you have the same dream three times in succession it is sure to be fulfilled. In several countries (India and Japan are two particular examples) dreams are interpreted as meaning the opposite of what you experience, but most people seem to agree that if you have a bad dream you can rid yourself of any possible after-effects by simply spitting three times as soon as you wake up!

DRESS

It is believed to bring bad luck if you put your left arm first into any item of clothing, as the left is always associated with the Devil. Similarly to button up on the wrong buttonholes will bring bad luck unless you undo them all and start again. To ensure good luck when you first put on a new item of clothing, people in the north of England believe you should ask a friend to pinch you! Of course, it is also universally felt to be lucky to accidentally put on any dress inside out – although you should ensure the luck by keeping it on that way! If a girl breaks a needle or pricks her finger while making a new dress it is an omen that she will be kissed while wearing that dress.

DRINK

When enjoying a drink, whether alcoholic or not, remember the old superstition that it should never be stirred with a knife or else you will get stomach ache!

DROWNING

The superstition that a person about to drown sees their whole life flash before them seems to be discredited by those who have just avoided such a fate, but nonetheless the act of drowning is surrounded by a number of strange beliefs. Many coastal dwellers claim that a person cannot drown until they have been under the water and surfaced at least three times, and further that drowned bodies will always reappear seven, eight or nine days after sinking. There is also a widely held superstition that a body lying drowned on the bottom of a river can be brought to the surface by firing a gun across the surface of the water. The report of the gun, it is said, will break the victim's gall bladder and thereby cause the body to rise. Two other methods of locating a corpse are to float a lighted candle over the likely area and it will go out directly over the body, while the American Indians prefer to take a rooster in a boat over the spot and it is said the bird will crow when it reaches the right place. Perhaps the cruellest belief – and it does still persist in some parts of the world – is that one should never attempt to rescue a drowning person for if it is the will of the water gods that the person should die and if they are defied, then the rescuer himself must expect to fill the same role at a later date. Finally, an interesting but grim statistic from an American police report says that men who have drowned float face down, while women float on their backs with their faces upwards.

DRUNKENNESS
There are many remedies which people have devised over the years with the purpose of putting a stop to drunkenness, most of them based on some unpleasant ingredient slipped into the imbiber's glass. Certainly the most startling is the suggestion of dropping a live eel into the drink (enough to put anyone off for a while at least!) although superstition believes that an owl's egg cracked and mixed secretly with the alcohol will prove most effective in the long run. Should you want to go on drinking and not become the worse for wear, the Welsh recommend roasting and eating the lungs of a pig – a recipe which will apparently give you immunity for twenty four hours!

DUCK
A duck's eggs can be an omen of great misfortune for its owner if they are dun coloured and many people believe the only way to avoid this is to destroy the creature immediately it has laid such unusual eggs. The unfortunate duck must also be hung with its head down after it has been killed so as to ensure that all the evil spirits, which rural belief maintains it harbours, can fall from it.

DUNG
Dung placed around a house will bring good luck, according to a British superstition, and do the plants a power of good, too! In India it is believed to be a curative for many illnesses and to ward off ghosts – due in no small degree to the cow being considered a sacred animal.

DWARF
In Britain, Canada and India particularly it is considered very lucky for a man to meet a female dwarf, and for a woman to meet a male dwarf.

EAGLE

The eagle is now a protected bird in most parts of the world, but it also has the immunity of a superstitious belief that anyone who steals its eggs will never thereafter enjoy peace of mind. It is said, too, that when the bird is seen hovering over plains for any length of time it is presaging disease and death for those below. The sound of its screeching is also a death portent.

EARS

Superstition throughout Europe maintains that small ears indicate a mean person while large ones are the outward sign of a generous nature. It is also widely believed that a tingling in the ear signifies somebody is talking about you. According to the tradition, if your right ear tingles they are saying good things, while if it is the left they are pinpointing your faults. The Dutch believe it is possible to get your own back on the speaker when your left ear tingles by biting your little finger and at that moment the person will find himself biting his tongue! There is also a common superstition that earrings worn in pierced ear lobes will cure bad eyesight – though why this belief should have developed, or why it should persist when there is not a shred of evidence to support it, is quite beyond explanation. Similarly many sailors believe that wearing gold earrings will protect them from drowning, although again the reason for the belief is impossible to determine.

EASTER EGGS

The practise of giving chocolate Easter Eggs to children is another custom rooted in superstition which goes back to the days of the Egyptians and the Romans, both of whom used to give each other presents of eggs as symbols of resurrection and continuing life. Later, Christianity adopted the egg as an emblem of the Resurrection of Christ. Prior to the chocolate eggs, it was common practice to give infants hard-boiled eggs dyed red in memory of the blood of Christ. These, it was believed, would also keep them healthy and well for the coming year. Of Easter Sunday itself, there is an old superstition that the sun 'dances' when it rises on this morning, and that a lamb and flag appear on it although no one should attempt to check this superstition without wearing the proper protective glasses. The custom of wearing new clothes on this day also originated because once it was the first day the clothes which had been put on for Lent could be removed – and as they were invariably dirty and worn, replacing them with something completely new was quite natural.

EATING

There are one or two superstitions relating to the act of eating. For instance, the pleasant diversion of dining out is merely a visible sign of faithful dealing between host and guest, in effect forming a 'living connection' between the two people. In some primitive parts of the world there are still peoples who treat the act of eating together as such a sacred occasion that a husband and wife will only eat at the same table during their marriage feast. As to food itself, it is said that when eating fish you should always remove slices working *towards* the head; and after eating a boiled egg always break the shell or witches will use it for their evil machinations. If you cut a loaf of bread in uneven slices this is an omen that you have been telling lies, and if the loaf crumbles in your hands then an argument is brewing.

EGGS

There are a number of good and bad luck superstitions associated with ordinary chicken eggs. It is said to be an omen of death to find a very small egg, while there is an old British superstition that the tenth egg of any batch is always the largest. You will certainly be courting bad luck if you collect eggs and bring them into the house after nightfall. Eggs with no yolks are considered unlucky and are believed to have been laid by cocks; while double-yoked eggs were said to indicate a death in the owner's family. Sailors do not mention eggs by name while at sea – the usual term is 'roundabouts' – and it is believed in many farming communities to be unlucky if a hen sits on an even number of eggs. The chances are they will not hatch out at all, but if any do they will all be cockerels. You can be sure of good luck, however, if, after eating a boiled egg, you knock a hole through the bottom of the shell with your spoon. Do not, though, on any account throw the shell onto the fire for this will prevent the hen who laid it from laying again. The safest way to avoid any trouble is to completely crush the shells, for the Scots believe that witches collect up those left whole and will use them to sail to sea and sink the ships of honest seafarers. (This association of witchcraft with egg shells goes back to Roman times.) On a more cheerful note it is possible to divine a future lover by hard-boiling an egg, removing the yolk, putting salt in its place, and eating it alone for supper. When you go to sleep, says the superstition, you will dream of the person who is to bring that special love into your life. Finally, one must not overlook the extraordinary Japanese superstition that if a woman steps over an egg shell it is likely that she will go mad!

ELBOW

An itching elbow according to superstition in both Britain and America indicates you will be sleeping in a strange bed shortly. The Bostonians go further and say there will be a stranger of the opposite sex in the same bed with you! In Britain and India if you accidentally knock your elbow you are in for some bad luck unless you quickly bang the other one as well. There is also a strange belief recorded in parts of rural England that if you want to get your own back on someone who has been making life hard for you then just bite your elbow and he will get drenched in a thunderstorm. But having said that, just try and bite your own elbow!

EMU
The New Zealand emu is believed to be a harbinger of good luck and its flesh a cure for many illnesses. However, it is also said that to kill one of these birds is a prelude to misfortune.

ENGAGEMENT
American superstition claims that the day on which a couple buy their engagement ring holds important omens about their future. If it is on a Monday, for instance, they can look forward to a busy, exciting life; on Tuesday a peaceful and contented existence. Wednesday indicates a good-tempered relationship, while Thursday will enable you to achieve all you wish from life. Friday is a day which will demand much hard work, but there will be rewards in time, while Saturday is a day which will give much pleasure. Nice to know that there isn't a bad day among them! As for the ring itself, it is said to be unlucky if the one which is chosen has to be altered for any reason, and should the ring wear badly or become loose before the wedding ceremony this is an omen that the match is not going to be a happy one. Perhaps there is no need to add that it is very unlucky to lose or break an engagement ring. A British superstition says that it is unlucky for an engaged couple to hear their banns read in church together, and an old rural custom proposes that after two people have become engaged they should take a twig of laurel, break it in half, and retain a piece each – and as long as they keep these so will their love flourish. Interestingly, popular superstition even has a method for a girl

to break off an engagement – she should present a knife to her discarded suitor. To cut his throat with, the cynic might ask?

EPITAPHS

Despite the increasing popularity in collecting epitaphs from tombstones in old graveyards, an American superstition declares that by doing so you run the risk of losing your memory.

EVIL EYE

This is another very ancient superstition that has invariably been associated with witchcraft, and people with different coloured eyes, or ones set close together or deep in their head, were often suspected of having the Evil Eye. Many a country-man or woman has complained of being 'overlooked' by someone with the Evil Eye with the result that they, their family or livestock have suffered in some way. The history of the witchcraft trials and persecutions from the sixteenth to eighteenth century is packed with instances where some unfor-tunate old soul was condemned to death merely because their accuser believed they had fallen ill or their cat had been blighted by the glance of this person. An antidote to the Evil Eye was to spit in the eye of the 'Overlooker' three times, or else if an animal had died from such attentions to burn it, where-upon the person who had laid the curse would suffer the same agony. The sign of the cross was also said to be effective. The use of a clay image, or witch poppet, made in the likeness of the person suspected of having the Evil Eye and then stuck with pins, was also said to have the power to lift the spell. There are two other less unpleasant methods of removing the Evil Eye if it has been applied to a child: you may either hold the infant upside down by its clothes for a few moments each morning, or else borrow a silver coin from a neighbour, place it in a basin full of water, and then wash the child with the 'charmed' water. It is also interesting to learn that in the East, many parents believe their children can be protected from the Evil Eye by keeping them ragged and dirty – for it is believed the Eye will only fall on those who are attractive and well-kept.

EYEBROWS

There is an old saying that 'meeting eyebrows never know trouble' and that anyone whose eyebrows do join across their nose will always be lucky – although in some countries of Europe such a person is accounted as being untruthful and perhaps even a vampire or werewolf as well!

EYES

In many countries itching eyes are looked upon as good and bad omens – if the right eye feels ticklish then you are in for some good luck, but if it is the left then things are not so good. A cure for this affliction should it continue is to bathe the eye or eyes in rainwater collected from the leaves of the teazel plant. It is also widely held that if a man's right upper eyelid twitches then it is a sign of good luck while the left is unlucky. Strangely, for women the reverse is true! Many English country folk believe that a stye in the eye can be cured by rubbing it gently nine times with a gold wedding ring or any other small piece of gold. And, finally, the Americans have a delightful old verse indicating the old superstitions about different coloured eyes:

> 'Blue-eye beauty, do your mammy's duty,
> Black-eye, pick a pie,
> Run around and tell a lie;
> Grey-eye, greedy-gut
> Eat all the world up.'

F

FALSE DEATH

There is a European superstition, perhaps most strongly held in Germany, that if a person is quite unintentionally reported to be dead when he is not, then he will gain an extra ten years of life.

FEATHER BED

Despite the fact that a feather bed should be comfortable at all times, superstition maintains that if one of these beds is turned on a Sunday whoever sleeps in it thereafter will have bad dreams for a week. Devonshire people further believe that this turning on a Sunday will also bring death into the house. The folk of the north of England claim that no one can die happy and painlessly in a feather bed – particularly one made from pigeon or game bird's feathers – and in many places it has been the custom to take a dying person from his or her bed and lie them on the floor for their last moments.

FEET

If you accidentally scrape your right foot on the ground while walking along the street there is a British superstition that you are shortly going to meet a friend; if it is the left foot, the omen is that you are in for a disappointment of some kind. Throughout much of Europe it is said that if your feet begin to itch for no apparent reason, you are shortly to make a journey somewhere you have not been before. To possess an extra toe is an indication that you will be lucky in life according to a general superstition, while in Scotland it is said that any man with a second toe longer than his first will be of a bad tempered disposition. And there is a bit of snobbery about the belief which is still heard in Brookline, Massachusetts that if your bare instep is high enough to let water flow underneath it, you are of good descent. In contrast people with flat feet are said to be ill-omened and to meet such a person when setting out on a Monday would lead to a bad week. Finally, it is always unlucky to enter anywhere new with your left foot first.

FERNS

In England, ferns are sometimes known as 'Devil's Brushes', although it is said that if they are hung in the house they will protect it from thunder and lightning. If they are cut or burnt, however, they will bring on rain, and in parts of Britain there is a belief that to tread on the plant will cause you to become confused and lose your way. The spores of the fern, known as brackenseed, have for centuries been said to contain curative properties and at one time it was claimed that if they were carried in the pocket they would make a person invisible! To this day, though, it is still believed that brackenseed found growing on a tree and crushed and mixed with water will relieve stomach ache, or carried in the pocket or handbag will ensure that the owner's loved one never loses that love for him or her.

FERTILITY

There is a delightful superstition in parts of America that if a married couple throw cow peas across the road near their home the woman will become fertile, no matter how long she has been barren.

FINGER

Superstition has attributed numerous qualities to the fingers, some of which are still in common usage in many countries of the world. For instance, a child with long fingers is said to be destined to be a musician and will always be unable to save money, but if the forefinger is as long as the second finger, or longer, then this is a sign of dishonesty. This forefinger is sometimes referred to as the 'Poison Finger' and should never be used for applying any medication, while the third finger of the left hand (on which the wedding ring is worn) is believed to be lucky and have healing powers when used for such a purpose. A crooked little finger is a sign of wealth. Anyone born with more than five fingers is said to be very lucky and probably a prodigy in the making. If you are forced into the position of telling someone a 'white lie' to avoid hurting their feelings, then cross your first and second fingers behind your back and no harm will come to either of you. And, of course, crossing the fingers has always been a way of avoiding any impending bad luck. According to a European superstition, if you pull your finger joints and they make a cracking sound then you can rest assured that *somebody* loves you.

FINGER NAILS

There have always been strong superstitions associated with finger nails, and nail clippings are widely believed to be an essential ingredient in any witch spell. The nails were said to contain characteristics of the man or woman to be spelled and would therefore ensure that it operated on the right person. Clippings have also been utilized in healing. They are taken from a person who is ill and ceremonially burned or buried in the hope that the illness is similarly removed from the sufferer. In a more general context, crooked nails are said to indicate a greedy person, while if they project in the middle this is an omen of an early death. The size of the 'half moon' shapes at the base of the finger nail are an indication of the time a person has to live – the larger they are the longer he has to go. It is widely believed to be unlucky to cut your nails on Friday or Sunday, though Monday and Tuesday are good days. A baby's nails should always be bitten off and not cut until he is a year old or else he will grow up to be a thief, and in the north of England it is said a woman who is able to cut her right-hand nails with her left hand will always be the boss in a marriage. In many superstitions, white spots on the fingers are generally held to be omens of good fortune, although black spots presage misfortune and yellow specks indicate death. The Germans have a superstition that the number of white spots found on a person's nails indicate the number of years he or she has to live. And in Britain a white spot on each nail has a different meaning as this verse indicates:

> 'A friend, a foe,
> Money to come, a journey to go.'

More fully explained, this means that a white spot on the index finger indicates a new friend; on the middle finger a new enemy; on the ring finger some wealth or a new lover; and on the little finger a forthcoming journey. Although not mentioned in the verse, it is said that a white spot on the thumb promises a present. In addition, the Japanese reproach any girl who bites her nails with the threat that she will have a difficult time giving birth to children.

FIRE

The fireplace has always been the centre of numerous superstitions, dating from the time when fire itself was regarded as the flame of the gods and should be treated with the utmost respect. For this reason it is said to be unlucky for anyone other than a member of the family or a long-standing friend to poke the fire, or else they show disrespect to the gods. There is a curious belief that a fire will not light in direct sunlight; this would seem to originate from the idea that the first flame used by man was stolen from the sun and that great orb is still jealous of all attempts at imitating his power. If a fire which has been laid catches alight quickly without any artificial aids it is said that the household will receive unexpected visitors very shortly. If, though, it draws badly evil influences are at work (or rain is on the way) and the poker should be placed at right angles to the grate, thus forming a cross and driving off these influences. A fire that burns at one side of the grate indicates a wedding in the offing, while one that crackles indicates frost. Once the fire is well away, however, if it is poked and shafts of flame leap upwards you can be assured that if a loved one – a husband or wife – is away from home, then they are well and happy. On the other hand, if the fire roars up the chimney then there will shortly be a fierce argument in the house or a storm outside. Should a hollow develop in the fire as it burns, say the Welsh, then a grave is going to be dug before long for someone in the family. Sparks at the back of the chimney indicate important news on the way, and there are signs to be read from the cinders of the fire, which are divided by tradition into two categories – oblong cinders are called 'coffins' and oval shapes 'cradles'. 'Coffins' leaping from the fire presage a death in the family, while 'cradles' naturally enough indicate a baby is to be born into the house before long. Although it is probably rare nowadays to find a household where it happens, there was a widespread belief that bad luck would fall on any family that did not clear the grate of embers before going to bed. And similarly in disfavour is the superstition that a fall of soot at any time indicates a 'great disaster' on the way. In America, if a fire burns brightly on Christmas morning then you are in for a good year, but if it only smoulders then times will be hard. Finally, never let children play with fire before bed-time because, apart from the obvious dangers, a Scottish super-stition says they will wet the bed in their sleep.

FISH

Long before the true nutritional value of the fish was known, mothers urged their children to eat up their helpings and grow strong and wise – just as they do today. Indeed right from the earliest times the fish was believed to be a harbinger of wisdom and knowledge and to eat its flesh was to acquire these qualities

93

for oneself. In America, the tench has for generations been particularly credited with these qualities and also the ability to cure sickness – hence its nick-name, 'Doctor Fish'. The river fisherman generally is subject to a number of superstitions, of which the most widely held is that if he stops to count the number of fish he has caught at any time he will catch no more that day. It is also said to be unlucky for any naturally right-handed fisherman to cast his line with his left hand, and vice versa. To spot an earwig on your way to fish is a good omen, and the Scots maintain that the only way to remedy the situation when the fish just will not bite is to throw a fisherman himself into the water and then haul him out as if he were a prize catch! After this performance, says the tradition, the fish cannot resist following the man's example! In this context too, American fishermen have the following saying:

> 'Fish East means fish bite least,
> Fish West, fish bite best.'

One of the strangest sea fishing superstitions says that if a fisherman and his wife have a quarrel and fight just before he goes to sea then he can expect a good catch. The argument though, must develop naturally, and not be staged deliberately, and if a man actually draws blood from his wife then he can expect an especially large haul. Many coastal folk say it is unlucky for a fisherman to meet a cross-eyed person or a woman wearing a white apron as he is going to his ship, and he can only avert the misfortune by returning home and waiting for the next tide. Fishermen everywhere believe that fish are aware of times of trouble and will desert a strife-torn coast, but it is an omen of a good catch if the first fish examined from the first haul is a female. The Scots have a number of superstitions about the sea, including it being very unlucky for a fisherman to swear using God's name unless every man then touches a piece of iron. They also believe that the words pig, sow and swine should never be used when the nets are being lowered or the catch will be lost. Again the antidote is for the fishermen to touch the iron studs on their boots. In a number of other places in the world it is thought to be unlucky while at sea to refer to things on land by their real names and some most ingenious, not to say unlikely, substitutes have resulted. In Yorkshire it is felt the best way to ensure a good catch is to slice a small cut in one of the cork floats as the nets are being played out and insert a small coin in the slit. This, says the old tradition, will be taken by King Neptune in payment for the fish he allows into the nets. And there is another belief of great antiquity that it is unlucky to fish on every day of the week for this is a sign of greed and will be punished by the gods of the deep.

FLEA

Although considered unpleasant, the Germans say a flea foretells that you will either be kissed or receive some good news if it bites you on the hand, and there is also a quaint European superstition that fleas will never enter a bed if it has been carefully aired on the Thursday before Easter. The claim that fleas desert the body of someone near death is very well-known.

FLOWERS

Apart from the pleasure it brings, the custom of giving flowers to people is also a good luck token, and folk as far back as the ancient Egyptians have believed that such gifts are harbingers of fortune. Many country people, however, claim that it is unlucky to take flowers which have bloomed out of season into the house, as plants that should flower in the summer but bloom in the winter will bring misfortune on all who come into contact with them. When giving flowers to someone who is ill, it is as well to remember the superstitions attached to flower colours which hold good throughout much of the world. White flowers are absolutely taboo for any sick person, while red (and roses in particular) denote blood and life and are very acceptable. Never, though, give a bunch of the two mixed together, especially to a hospital patient. Violet shows goodwill on the part of the giver, and yellow and orange as the colour of the sun will please anyone whatever their state of health. It is unlucky for a sick person to place flowers on their bed, and never pick a flower from a grave and throw it away lest the place where it falls become haunted. These grim superstitions are perhaps lightened by a German belief that if you take a flower to the dining table with you, wipe your lips with it after you have drunk some wine, and then give it to your lover you can be sure of his or her undying love. Rather more serious is the claim that flowers planted during the time of the new moon will bloom best and that sunflowers bring good luck to a whole garden. According to the month of your birth, these are your lucky flowers according to a very general superstition.

> January – carnations and snowdrops
> February – primroses
> March – daffodils
> April – daisies
> May – lilies of the valley
> June – roses
> July – water lilies
> August – gladioli
> September – asters
> October – dahlias
> November – chrysanthemums
> December – holly

Finally, in Britain there is an old saying that if you imagine you can smell flowers, it is an omen of death.

FLY

That old joke about the fly in the soup and the waiter's instant response, actually evolved from an omen that a fly which falls into a glass or dish from which someone is about to drink is a sign of prosperity. There is, though, no indication that this happy future will be affected in any way if you change the drink or soup for a fresh one!

FOG

The people of New York State still repeat this delightful verse (which is probably of British origin) when a fog clouds a particular district:

'Fog on the hill,
Brings water to the mill;
Fog on the moor
Brings sun to the door.'

FOOTBALL

Football is another sport beset with personal superstitions, of which the most evident is the use by a great many clubs of a mascot – often a small boy or girl – to bring them luck. In the dressing room, a number of teams place great store by seeing the oldest player in the team bounce the ball to the youngest who must catch it on the bounce for the luck to hold. By and large players put their left boot on first (the good luck going on last with the right), and usually like to go out onto the pitch in a certain order. Many a centre forward will bounce the match ball on the centre spot three times before the kick off, and not a few goalkeepers touch or kick both of their goal posts as the match begins. The dislike certain players have of being watched by their wives or girl friends is probably subconsciously rooted in the old belief that a woman can put the evil eye on a man's activities! It has also been suggested that the banners and personal adornments displayed by supporters – plus their singing and chanting – have all evolved from the ancient idea that such things drive away the spirits of bad luck from the object in question – on this occasion, the supporters' team!

FOX

The Welsh believe that if you see a lone fox then good luck is in store, but for a pack of several to cross your path bodes nothing but misfortune. Foxes running close to a house are said to indicate that disaster and even death will follow in their wake.

FRIDAY

Friday is an ill-fated day in superstition and it is generally believed to have earned its unhappy reputation because it was on this day that Adam was tempted by Eve. Among the activities which are said to be unlucky if they take place on this day are births, weddings, beginning a new job, the sailing of a ship, moving house, and cutting your nails. Says an old verse: 'Whoever be born on Friday or its night, he shall be accursed of men, silly and crafty and loathsome to all men, and shall ever be thinking evil in his heart, and shall be a thief and a great coward, and shall not live longer than to middle age.' Both the Scots and the Germans consider Friday a good day for courting but in many places it is the night of the witches' sabbath, and in both England and America it was the custom to hang criminals on Friday which earned it the reputation as 'Hangman's Day'. If you are born on Friday, the Hungarians say the ill-luck can be removed by putting a couple of drops of your blood on a piece of cloth cut from an old piece of your clothing and then burning it – this will apparently 'destroy' the bad luck. The criminal fraternity believe that a burglary committed on a Friday is rarely successful and will probably lead to arrest. Similarly, they think to be brought to trial on a Friday is an ill-omen. There is also a widespread belief that if it rains on Friday then Sunday will be fine. About the only Friday activity that offers some promise of better things is sleeping – for if you dream during that night and then repeat your dream the next morning to someone in your family then it will come true. That is assuming, of course, that you dreamt something you would want to come true!

FROG

It is widely believed to be unlucky to kill a frog as they are said to possess the soul of a boy or girl who died in childhood – and indeed country people often compare the cry it makes when injured to that of a child. A frog croaking during the day is an omen of rain, while if one of these creatures comes into your house of its own accord then it is a sign of good luck. Young frogs are said to be able to cure several illnesses and promote love; and warts can be removed by spearing a frog and rubbing it over the blemishes. When the unfortunate creature breathes its last, says the superstition, the warts will disappear.

FUNERAL

Naturally enough the funeral, as the final act in a person's life, has its fair share of superstition. The tradition among men of raising their hats when a funeral procession passes is not just simply out of respect for the dead, but because of an old belief that a person who did not bare his head and then follow the cortège for a short distance would himself die shortly afterwards. It is equally foolhardy to throw a rose into the grave or run at any time during a funeral. The belief that a funeral procession must never be broken or halted lives on to this day, and whether on foot or in vehicles, ill-fortune will overcome the mourners if they are interrupted in any way for this will present the spirit of the corpse with the opportunity to escape from its earthly form and become a ghost to haunt the living. In America it is believed to be unlucky to count the number of vehicles in a funeral procession for the number will indicate the years the person who counted them still has to live. It is also held to be unlucky to be the first person to drive a new hearse – for the omens are that your own death is not far off. In Scotland it is maintained that if the sun shines brightly on the face of one of the mourners then it is an omen that he will be the next among those present to pass on. There is also a belief that at least one door in the house of the deceased must be left open during the funeral, or if not when the family mourners return a terrible quarrel will break out among them. It is considered very unlucky to postpone a funeral for any reason, and the aftermath can be another death in the family or neighbourhood. It is even more ill-omened if the postponement covers a weekend for this means the body will lie unburied on a Sunday and in the words of the old tradition 'the dead man will go looking for someone else to take with him'. The Americans believe it is very unlucky to attend a funeral unless specifically invited, although the burials of famous men and women are excluded from this. Also they maintain that if any kind of difficulty is experienced in lowering a coffin into the grave, then this is either a final struggle on the part of the soul to escape or a last attempt by evil spirits to gain this same soul. In either case only if the coffin cannot possibly be fitted into the grave will any misfortune come to the mourners. In some states of America it is still believed that unless someone from a different town to the deceased is present as he is buried then his soul will never rest in peace, and at a Jewish funeral no animal should ever be allowed near the coffin because of a superstitious fear that the departing soul will try to enter the creature's body. The giving of food to mourners after a funeral also ensures you good luck, for this shows that you appreciate the honour they are doing to the dead person. Interestingly, in some places the origin of wearing black mourning clothes is believed to have been in an attempt to trick the Devil who is always looking for more souls and apparently cannot see black. Among many primitive peoples it was traditional at funerals to paint themselves black to make themselves invisible to evil spirits, while the Australian aboriginals reverse the process by plastering themselves all over with white clay! Perhaps the strangest of all funeral superstitions is that which says the first body laid in a new cemetery or graveyard will always be claimed by the devil. Yet there are many instances on record of country people refusing to have relatives buried in such a place until some unfortunate and totally friendless soul is found to fill this unenviable role.

FURNITURE

Items of furniture which fall over for no reason are believed to be omens of death, in particular pictures dropping from the walls or blinds suddenly rattling down over windows. In many parts of Scotland it is believed that if furniture makes a creaking sound it presages a change in the weather.

GAMBLING

Gamblers are literally plagued by omens and superstitions as they pursue lady luck in search of a fortune. Whether in a plush casino or playing a quiet game indoors, the gambler looks for signs in everything he does. Perhaps two of the most popular beliefs in the world of gambling are that a novice at the tables cannot lose the first time out and that it is impossible to lose with borrowed money. A gambler should not, though, ever lend money to an opponent as he is to all intents and purposes playing *against* himself and can hardly expect to be successful. Some gamblers believe it is unlucky to play in their own homes or if a dog is in the room, and that cards should never be played on a bare or polished surface. The bad luck here obviously occurs if the cards slip or are reflected in such a way that the other players can see what a person is holding – hence the universal popularity of the green baize cloth. Another super-stition which seems to smack of male chauvinism says that a man should never allow a woman to touch his shoulders before he sits down to play, and indeed he should try and avoid meeting any female on his way into the casino. These seemingly impossible instructions bear the hallmark of having been devised by some frustrated male loser many years ago! (The

Edwardians, on the other hand, believed that they could ensure themselves luck merely by having a pretty girl standing behind their chair while they played and a great many actually hired beautiful chorus girls to do just that!) The most popular good luck charms carried by gamblers today are locks of hair, small animal charms, 'holy' relics, four leaved clovers, tiny horseshoes and coins with holes through the middle. It is said to be unlucky to see a cross-eyed man just before you play, to pick up the cards before the dealer has finished, or to allow your chips to lie scattered about rather than in neat piles. Now to a few superstitions that may help you change bad luck. When playing cards you should blow through the pack while shuffling or else walk around your chair or the table, or even turn your chair around and sit astride it. If these might cause too much embarrassment, just slip your handkerchief onto your chair and the mere act of sitting on it should change everything. When playing, avoid picking up the cards with your left hand (the association with left and evil again), and it is unlucky to sit cross-legged according to many gamblers. It is an ill-omen to let a card fall on the floor during a game, particularly a black one, but should you have a favourite card try and touch it with your index finger before you sit down to play. Card players believe that they will never get a good hand if they are dealt the four of clubs – particularly if they get it in their first hand – and indeed the card is nick-named the 'Devil's Four-Poster Bed'. Similarly, in poker two pairs consisting of aces over eights is considered unlucky for this was the famous 'Dead Man's Hand' Wild Bill Hicock was holding when he was shot. The nine of diamonds is also unpopular with gamblers and referred to by many as 'The Curse of Scotland' as it was the means used by the Earl of Stair to give instructions for the infamous Glencoe Massacre to begin in 1692. A run of black spades is also regarded as an omen of bad luck, and indeed there are several cases on record of famous card players who turned up two or more of these cards in a run and died shortly thereafter. In partnered games you can bring luck to your partner by sticking a pin on their lapel or dress, says a widespread superstition, while nothing but misfortune will come to either of you if one of you inadvertently whistles or sings while playing. Remember, too, never to get into a temper for according to an old belief 'the demon of bad luck always follows a passionate player', and if nothing goes right take comfort from that other long standing tradition, 'unlucky at cards, lucky in love'!

GARLIC

Superstition has always credited garlic with great power, and in particular of driving away evil spirits from the house. Every fan of horror stories and films knows that strands of the garlic hung over the doors and windows will keep any marauding vampire at bay. In France the pods of garlic are often roasted on Midsummer Eve and given to rural families for protection, while in the Far East the plant is also believed to contain the power to bring back lost souls and is used in special religious ceremonies.

GARTER

The girl who wishes to be sure and have children can be aided by superstition by wearing a garter made of straw (in some parts of Europe a garter of shells is said to be just as effective). She can even determine the child's sex – if the garter is made of wheat straw then she will have a boy, while oats will bring a girl. Interestingly, the garter is most effective if worn just prior to the girl's wedding, but it will have no effect whatsoever on a bride who is no longer a virgin. The association of straw with fertility is believed to date back to the story of the Nativity when the baby Christ was laid on a straw manger in Bethlehem and thereby conferred special qualities on it. Brides, of course, often still wear garters and if one of these is secured by any man at the wedding feast he can expect plenty of good luck thereafter. Men once used to compete for these garters, actually trying to pull them off the legs of the bride before she went off on her honeymoon! A garter tucked under a pillow is said to make a girl dream of her husband-to-be, and red garters have always been considered a good cure for rheumatism.

GAS WORKS
There is a superstition recorded in several localities in Europe that if a child is carried through a gas works – and in particular close to the plant where the gas is actually manufactured – then this will cure any respiratory trouble it may be suffering from.

GEESE
Despite the fact that legend calls the goose the silliest creature on earth (hence the expression 'a silly goose'), the bird is said to give warning of a death by flying around a house. Among some English country people there is still a tradition to have goose for dinner on Michaelmas Day, September 29, for as this rhyme explains:

> 'Whosoever eats goose on Michaelmas Day,
> Shall never lack money his debts to pay.'

Superstition also maintains that if the breast bones of a roasted goose are found to be brown, then the next winter will be a mild one; if they are white or bluish then it will be severe.

GEM STONES
Certain gems are traditionally believed to bring good luck when given as presents to those whose birthdays correspond with the appropriate stone. The full list with their meanings is as follows:

> January – Garnet (Constancy)
> February – Amethyst (Sincerity)
> March – Bloodstone (Courage)
> April – Diamond (Purity)
> May – Emerald (Hope)
> June – Pearl or Agate (Health)
> July – Ruby (Contentment)
> August – Sardonyx (Fidelity)

September – Sapphire (Repentance)
October – Opal (Loveableness)
November – Topaz (Cheerfulness)
December – Turquoise (Unselfishness)

There is a superstition that an engagement ring containing pearls will 'bring tears to the marriage' (which one would have thought inevitable anyway!) while the opal 'the stone of tears' has always been regarded as the unlucky stone unless it is worn by someone born in October or in combination with diamonds, according to the Americans. Some experts believe this superstition may have originated because the stone is very brittle and must be treated gently. Certainly, in the East, it was said to be a most lucky gem and of all others actually indicated the owner's state of health. Here are a few more of the qualities superstition attributes to various gem stones. *Amber*, for example, is considered lucky because it is among the easiest of gems to find on beaches and is therefore very much a stone of the people rather than just the nobility. The *agate* can cure fever and poisonous bites or stings. *Coral* is a powerful weapon against sorcery and the Evil Eye while *jade* is also lucky and particularly prized in the East where it is the only green stone other than *emerald*. Superstition attributes the *ruby* with changing its colour according to the health of the wearer whether or not the person is showing any symptoms of illness. The *topaz* is said to signify both money and friends and as such is regarded as a good luck stone. The *turquoise* with its dazzling colour is said to be an emblem of prosperity and given with loving hands removes animosity between giver and receiver and carries happiness and good fortune. The strength of its hue is believed to be an indication of the wearer's health, and any sudden change signifies danger awaiting the owner. It is also supposed to be good at rousing sexual passion! The *pearl* is said to resemble tears and for this reason is rarely found in engagement rings, rather as a brooch or string adornment. The *diamond* as the most popular of all gems symbolizes conjugal affection – courage in the man and pride in the woman. The sparkling colours that spring from its surface are said to represent imprisoned glories that will bring good fortune to the wearer.

GLASS

Never look through a piece of broken glass at anyone or you will be sure to have a quarrel with them, a British superstition says.

GLOVES

The glove was traditionally the symbol of love and authority, and although not worn as frequently nowadays still features in superstition. The most famous belief concerns dropping a glove; if you pick it up yourself this will bring bad luck, but if someone else does then you are in for some good fortune. The origin here clearly lies in the ancient tradition that a lover who picked up his mistress's glove could thereafter hope to enjoy her affections. To lose a glove is said to be unlucky, but to find a pair – especially on a Sunday – will give you a successful week at business according to a superstition reported in Britain and many countries of Europe. If you should leave a pair of gloves behind you when visiting friends you are advised to be careful what rituals you observe when you go back to collect them if you ever want to visit the house again. (Not for fear of offending the hosts, we hasten to add, but by tampering with tradition!) When you return to the house, sit down first before picking the gloves up and do not put them on until you have stood up again. This superstition is till very widespread and frequently seen in operation.

GLUTTON

There is an old superstition still repeated in Canada, particularly in the Province of Quebec, that unless you can make your thumb and finger meet round your wrist you are a glutton.

GNATS

Superstition insists that these annoying insects which we devote so much time trying to get rid of, are actually harbingers of good fortune. If someone is taken ill, then the windows of the sick room should be opened at sunset so that the tiny creatures may fly in. While they are in the room, they will attract the illness to themselves and on leaving take it away with them, so spare the insect spray if you will! The gnat is also said to be a weather omen; when they fly close to the ground rain is to be expected, but if they are seen in great numbers and particularly flying high then a period of fine weather is in the offing.

GOAT

The goat has a place in superstition because of his association with the Devil and in particular the god, Pan, who was supposed to be half man and half goat. It is said that the Devil can take the form of a goat when he wishes to move unnoticed and the idea that he has a cloven foot probably comes from this association. Some English country people say that it is never possible to see a goat constantly for twenty-four hours for at some juncture he has to visit his master, the Devil, and pay him homage, at which time his beard will be combed. But despite this belief, numbers of people throughout Europe regard a goat's foot and the hairs from his beard as talismans to ward off the Devil. Goat skins are believed by sailors to ensure a calm voyage when hung from the mainmast. And in parts of Europe and America it is held that a goat can remove sickness from a house by being lured into the grounds, and then after it has been encouraged to munch grass as near as possible to the room of the person who is ill, it should be driven away: thus taking the disease with it.

GOD-PARENTS

The Germans have two superstitions about God-parents. Firstly, that no pregnant woman should become a God-mother or her own child or the God-child will die; and secondly God-parents who have lost a God-child should not take on the task again for fear the same fate befalls the new child. In Britain, it is said to be unlucky for an engaged couple to act as God-parents, for it means they will never marry, while if a God-parent looks into the font water while the child is being christened it will grow up to look like him or her.

GOLDEN PLOVER

To hear the melancholy whistling sound of the golden plover is believed to be a death omen in Wales, and in quite a number of countries the birds are said to contain the souls of Jews who took part in the crucifixion of Jesus Christ, hence they are sad, wandering creatures.

GOLF

Golfers are another superstitious breed of sportsmen whose beliefs are mostly quite inexplicable. For instance, many of them carry an old club in their bag which they no longer use. It was successful for them in the past, and they now claim it is a good luck charm. Golfers everywhere say it is unlucky to approach a tee from the front, change a club once you have selected it, and clean a ball when the match is going your way. In Scotland, the home of golf, players can still be heard repeating that whoever wins the first hole will lose the match, and also paying deference to the idea of thirteen being unlucky by saying that anyone who reaches the thirteenth in an 18-hole competition and is 'two up and five to play' will be unlucky. This would appear to be brought about more by a fit of nerves with victory seemingly there for the taking, than the action of unseen elements of fortune! A good many golfers believe that certain colours of clothing will bring them luck, and a noted taboo is against using the word 'shank' because to hit a ball with this part of the club is about the unluckiest thing a golfer can do in terms of his shot, short of missing the ball completely, that is! In teeing off it is felt to be a good omen to use a ball bearing the odd number three or five (a higher number is said to encourage a higher score!) and the ball should be placed so that the maker's name is visible to the player. It is unlucky to unwrap a new ball during a round, this should always be done before approaching the first tee. And, finally, golfers do not like starting a game at 1 o'clock as this is the thirteenth hour of the day and bodes ill for their play.

GOOD FRIDAY

Perhaps the most extraordinary superstition about Good Friday is that bread or buns baked on this day will never go mouldy, and such items are not only said to be lucky but possess the ability to cure simple illnesses like colds and whooping cough. It is, though, an unlucky day for planting crops – because a much older superstition says no iron should enter the ground on this day viz. a spade or fork – and women are also advised not to wash clothes for they will never come clean. This latter belief apparently stems from the story that as Christ was being led to Calvary, he passed a washerwoman who waved a wet garment in his face. At this he responded, 'Cursed be everyone who hereafter shall wash on this day.' Good Friday is, though, a good day on which to start weaning a baby for he will invariably grow strong and healthy and prosper in life.

GOOD LUCK SYMBOLS

Taken on a world-wide basis, the following items comprise the 'top ten' good luck symbols and are most frequently found incorporated in charms and bracelets to bring the wearer fortune and happiness: dice, crossed fingers, a clover leaf, a shoe, crescent moon, a fish, a dog, wheel, toadstool and the famous three monkeys – hear no evil, see no evil, speak no evil. Unquestionably, though, the figure of St Christopher is the most popular of all good luck charms.

GORSE

The bloom of the gorse bush is widely believed to be a harbinger of death and to hang some in the house is to court misfortune for a member of the family.

GRASS

While it is generally agreed that cats and dogs eat grass to aid their digestion, a rural British superstition maintains that in both cases when this is seen happening it is an omen that rain is imminent.

GRAVEYARD

There is an old superstition that the body put in the first grave dug in a new graveyard is always claimed by the devil. It is also said to be unlucky to dig or plough any ground in which a body has been buried, and certainly no crops planted there will flourish. Because of a very ancient superstition that the south wind brings corruption, the south side of churches has always been regarded as the holiest and it was here for generations that people insisted on being buried. Only folk who had committed suicide or the corpses of stillborn children were buried on the north side. Graves should, of course, always be dug running east to west, so that the corpse may lie with his feet to the east and his head to the west and thereby be ready to rise when the call comes from the east on the Day of Judgement. People in many European countries believe it is unlucky to step over a grave, and particularly over one in which lies a stillborn baby or unbaptized child. Despite the long history of grave robbing, it has always been considered unlucky to disturb a grave (you may well release a ghost), and no good will ever come of using tombstones or any other objects from a graveyard in the construction of a new building. Such a construction is said to run the risk of collapsing because it has 'death built into it'.

GREEN

The colour green has for many years been regarded as an unlucky colour in Britain and America and certainly no bride hoping for a happy future would dream of wearing it as any part of her ensemble. The origin of this superstition is that it was the colour of the fairies and little people and they had such power over it that they could easily steal away anyone they found wearing it. Many actors and actresses also believe it is an ill-omened colour, and that to wear a green costume on stage is to bring misfortune to both the play and its players. It has been suggested, too, that the use of green on postage stamps is an ill-omen and that whenever the Post Office have employed it on any new issue the country has immediately suffered unrest and great social problems. In contrast, it is interesting to note that in several European countries green is regarded as lucky because of its association with the spirits of the trees, and superstition there says that to hang green branches over doorways not only keeps away misfortune but drives witches and demons off.

GREYHOUND
Welsh sporting enthusiasts believe that a greyhound with a white spot on its forehead is a lucky animal.

HADDOCK

The Scots believe the haddock is a lucky fish, and that the black spots on each side near the gills are the impressions of Christ's finger and thumb made when he used one of its kind to feed the five thousand. They also say the fish should never be burned, as the following verse explains:

> 'Roast me and boil me,
> But dinnah burn by behns.
> Or then I'll be a stranger
> Aboot yi'r hearth-stanes.'

HAIR

There are many superstitions and omens recorded regarding human hair, a number of which have disappeared with the passing of time, but several fascinating examples continue to thrive. Let us begin with the men first. One of the oldest of all superstitions says that a hairy chest is a sign of strength and men so endowed will be lucky in life. A bushy beard is similarly approved. Perhaps more lucky still are those with hairy arms and hair on the back of their hands for they are destined to become wealthy. The hair on a man's head can also indicate if he is going to have a long life, for if it grows down on his forehead and back above the temples then he will live to a ripe old age. A cowlick is also said to be a lucky omen. The ladies can assure themselves of good luck by having their hair cut only when the moon is on the increase: to cut it when it is decreasing will cause it to fall and lose its lustre. In Scotland it is said that if a bird uses a woman's hair which she has combed out and thrown away for its nest she can expect a headache soon after. A woman who has hair growing to a point down on her forehead will live to be a widow, for this is the ill-omened 'Widow's Peak'. And any lady who suddenly develops two curls on her forehead when she always has straight hair must watch out for her husband for this is a sign that he has not long to live. Although, in general, hairy people are said to be lucky, in India a woman who is hairy is said to be incapable of being faithful to her husband. The Indians also claim that a man without any hair on his chest either is, or will be, a thief. Lank hair is widely claimed to indicate a cunning nature, while those with curls are cheerful, peace-loving folk. There has always been a certain prejudice against red hair and those who have it are said to be invariably quick tempered. It is thought the feelings against red originated in England because of the red-haired Danes who once invaded the country, while in Europe the prejudice is ascribed to the fact that Judas Iscariot apparently had such hair. The day on which hair is cut is also subject to superstition according to this old verse which country folk in England still repeat:

> Best never enjoyed if Sunday shorn,
> And likewise leave out Monday.
> Cut Thursday and you'll never grow rich,
> Likewise on a Saturday.
> But live long if shorn on a Tuesday
> And best of all is Friday.'

It is said to be most unlucky to comb your hair at night, although no such superstition attaches to the use of a brush – and this may well have originated from the earliest times when

113

the hair scattered by a comb might alert the senses of some prowling night creature. Apart from putting hairdressers out of business, no one should cut their own hair – not that this act will bring them bad luck but it will make them an unlucky person for anyone else to meet! There is also a curious superstition that if by any chance a clipping of your hair fails to burn when thrown on a fire then it is an omen that you will meet your death by drowning. If it burns brightly you are in for a long life. To suddenly lose a lot of head hair is said to presage loss of health and financial security. Should you find a stray hair on your shoulder this indicates an important letter is on its way to you, but if you drop your comb in the process of adjusting your hair then it is an omen you are in for a disappointment. The belief still persists among many men in America that thinning hair is caused by an overtight hatband, a variation of the old European belief that evil spirits can find their way into the body of a person through the hairs on the head. In the same country there is another widespread belief that baldness can be cured by shaving the head very closely, and that the hair will lose its 'vital fluid' unless it is singed after cutting. That curse of advancing years, grey hair cannot be combatted by pulling out the offending strands, for country folk believe that for every one pulled out, ten more will grow in its place.

HAIRPIN

Several superstitions about the hairpin which seem almost universal are headed by the claim that finding a hairpin will lead to making a new friendship – and you can increase your good luck by hanging it on a hook. If you lose one, though, you will make an enemy, but if it merely slips out of your hair and you are able to retrieve it then someone is thinking of you. In German tradition, though, this portends that you will lose a lover.

'HAIR OF THE DOG THAT BIT YOU'

This curious expression much used today between people having the first drink of a new day after recovering from a hangover induced the previous night, actually originated as a widely-held so-called medical cure. It was said that the only way to cure the bite of a mad dog was to take some of its hairs (after it had been caught and killed, of course!) and either eat them with a slice of bread or lay them across the wound with some pieces of herb and bind up the lot with a bandage. Although such cures have long since been discredited, the idea of utilizing what caused the pain to relieve it has not been abandoned but transferred to drinking alcohol!

HALLOWE'EN

Hallowe'en, the last night of summer, October 31, is traditionally the time when the spirits of the dead are allowed a last fling before winter sets in. It is an important night in the witchcraft calendar, and in Ireland it is said that if you hear footsteps behind you never look round for it is one of the dead following you and if you turn and see him or her you will soon join them. Today, of course, the night has become one for parties and games, particularly in America where girls still retain two Hallowe'en love traditions. The first instructs them to go to a spring of water carrying a lamp and if they peer into the depths they should see reflected their future husband. If they are nervous of going out when it is dark, however, they can go to the same spring during daylight, carrying a broken egg in a glass, and pour some of the fresh water into it. Shortly after, says the superstition, they should get a picture in the mixture of the man they are to marry and as a bonus a vision of the children they are to have as well!

HAND

An itchy palm is still as widely referred to in superstition today as it has been for untold generations. The belief is that if your right palm itches then you are about to receive money or get some important news, while a tickle on the left means you are going to have to pay out soon! (You can break this spell, though, by rubbing your hand on wood.) It is also said to bode ill if two people wash their hands together in the same basin of water – for this will lead to a quarrel between them during the same day unless they quickly spit in the basin. In Devon it used to be said to be unlucky to wash a baby's hands before it was a year old or it would never have any money but today most mothers put hygiene before a fortune! There is also a widely held belief that a moist hand is a sign of an amorous disposition, while a cold hand indicates a warm heart. It is bad luck to shake hands with the left hand, and if two couples cross hands while shaking hands there will be an unexpected marriage. Should three people begin shaking hands simultaneously it is an omen of good luck for all of them! In Jewish tradition it is said that on the night of Hosha'na Rabbah, anyone who attempts to read his future from his shadow and does not see his right hand will lose a son during the year, and if he fails to see the left hand, he will lose a daughter. If a finger is missing, then it is a friend who will die.

HANDKERCHIEF

Tying a knot in one's handkerchief to remind one of something is actually a variation of a much older superstition which maintained that such a knot was a charm against evil. Apparently, should any demon or spirit be around when you tied the knot it would be so intrigued by the formation that it would quite forget any ideas it had of causing you ill. Engaged couples should beware of handkerchiefs, according to a European superstition, and never give them to each other as presents for to do so, it is said, will cause a break-up and ensure no wedding ever takes place. In the Ozark Mountains region of America, young girls use handkerchiefs as a love omen – hanging them on bushes on May Eve and expecting when they return at dawn to find the initials of the man they are to marry traced in dew on the linen surface.

HARE

The hare is generally regarded as an ill-omen in many countries although perhaps strangely a black hare is sometimes lucky, and a white one unlucky! To see one, or more particularly

116

have it cross your path, means trouble in store. A hare running along a road is said to presage a fire in the vicinity, while any sailor who sees one near his ship knows he risks misfortune by putting to sea that day. A hare crossing the path of a bride and groom at a wedding also bodes ill for the couple. And pregnant women used to fear seeing one as it would give their unborn child a hare-lip. The fears about the hare stem from the ancient belief that witches can disguise themselves as these creatures, and there are numerous stories on record that following the wounding of a hare an old man or woman suspected of witchcraft has been found suffering from the self-same injuries. Two extraordinary beliefs about the hare which are still repeated though no longer held are that it is so timid that it never closes its eyes, even in sleep; and that once a year the creatures change their sex! The left foot of a hare, like that of a rabbit, is also considered a good luck charm in some places, though in others it is said to be best suited to keeping away rheumatism.

HAT

If you wear a hat, be careful how you put it on – for an old superstition decrees that you are in for a day of bad luck if you should put it on the wrong way round. There is though, a rather expensive way of countering the bad luck – buy a new hat! In America it is said that if a lady puts on a gentleman's hat then it is a sign – unconscious or not – that she wishes to be kissed!

HAY

If you should get held up by a vehicle carrying bales of hay coming towards you along a country lane, do not despair – English superstition says it is a good luck sign and a wish made as you patiently wait to get by will be granted. If, however, you come upon the hay cart from *behind*, this is not so good, and you had better look for another route, for apart from the inconvenience of being held up, you will suffer great misfortune if you should actually watch it disappear from sight.

HEADACHE

There is a superstition still prevalent in several of the rural states of America that a headache can be cured by putting your thumb in your mouth and pressing it against the roof of the mouth. There is probably as little chance of this working as following the formula for curing a head cold which is summed up by the phrase 'feed a cold and starve a fever'. In both instances there are medical prescriptions much more likely to do the job, and what success there is that can be ascribed to these 'old wives' tales' is probably mostly due to auto-suggestion – the mind wanting the cure to work and nature taking its course.

HEALTH

In rural parts of Britain there is a superstition that it is unlucky to say you are 'very well' in reply to a query about your health – there should always be a qualification of some kind or else you are courting trouble.

HEARSE

It is believed in several districts of Britain that it is lucky to see an *empty* hearse coming towards you but unlucky if you turn round to watch it go by.

HEATHER

White heather is said to be lucky because it is the only variety which is free of the bloodstains of the Picts who were so brutally slaughtered over heath and moorland. Its association with bloodshed is also referred to in Scotland where it is maintained that 'heather will never grow over the graves of the clans'.

HEDGEHOG

The hedgehog is another creature believed to harbour bad luck, and if you should see one, superstition says you should kill it to avoid misfortune striking you. Some European farmers hold to an old tradition that at night hedgehogs suck the milk of cattle lying in the fields and consequently do their best to be rid of them. The creature is also thought to be a weather omen, and an old saying has it that after his winter hibernation, the hedgehog emerges on Candlemas Day (February 2) to inspect the conditions. The creature is said to be able to tell if the harshest weather is over and Spring coming along. If this is so he does not return to his winter quarters, but should he go back, there are another six weeks or so of hard weather to come. British country folk have referred to this omen for centuries, and in America the same belief is applied to the groundhog or woodchuck. A further weather omen about the hedgehog is to be found in the eighteenth century American work, 'Poor Richard's Almanac' which says:

'Observe which way the hedgehog builds her nest,
To front the north or south, or east or west;
For if 'tis true what common people say,
The wind will blow quite contrary way.
If by some secret art the hedgehogs know,
So long before, which way the winds will blow,
She has an art which many a person lacks,
That thinks himself fit to make almanacs.'

HEM

If you find that part of the hem of one of your garments has become turned up, says an American superstition, you can take it as an omen that you will be getting a new and similar garment very soon.

HEN

'A whistling woman and a crowing hen is neither good for God nor men,' says one of the oldest of British superstitions whose origin is lost in the mists of time. The hen is, though, a somewhat ill-omened bird, and if one crows near a house or goes to roost at an unusual time this presages a death in the owner's family. Such a bird may have 'the Devil in it' according to tradition, and should be put down because it may also begin to destroy its eggs and teach the rest of the chickens to do the

119

same. It used to be a British custom for a hen to be taken to the home of a newly wed couple to ensure them happiness, and it is still felt to be true that if hens gather together on a mound and begin to preen their feathers then there is rain on the way.

HERRING

The herring fish will provide a glimpse of what the future holds for you, says an old superstition, if you eat one which has been salted, bones and all, in three mouthfuls. You must then go straight to bed without uttering a word to anyone and without taking a drink of any kind – and you will dream of your future. Or perhaps have a very uncomfortable night! Many fishermen believe that if the first herring of the season which they catch is a female they are in for a run of good catches, while a male will have the opposite effect.

HICCOUGHS

The old British and European superstition about the origin of hiccoughs is that someone is thinking of you. In Greece it is a sign that a person who dislikes you is complaining about you to someone else and the only way to stop the pain is to guess the name of that person! A German tradition says hiccoughs can be cured by soaking a piece of paper cut in the shape of the cross and placing it on the forehead, while the favourite British treatment is to hold your breath and count to one hundred!

HOLES

Natural holes formed in trees, rocks or stones have for thousands of years been believed to contain the power to rid any person who is passed through them of illness. The theory was that as the body passed through the hole the disease was left behind and the person emerged on the other side healthy again. There are innumerable cures to be found in countries throughout the world which feature the use of a natural hole and there are many stones to be seen which are claimed by people to have the most miraculous healing powers. Among the sicknesses it was said could be cured in this way are rickets, whooping cough, consumption and boils. In certain places, too, it was claimed that a childless woman could be made fertile by being passed through such a hole. It is interesting to note also that the superstition maintained that once a person had been cured in this manner he gained an affinity with the rock or tree and he should ensure thereafter it was never damaged or removed – for if it was, he was likely to suffer similar infirmities himself.

HOLLY

Holly, which plays such an important part in Christmas celebrations, derives its name from the word 'holy' and tradition says its evergreen leaves represent eternal life, its red berries are symbolic of the crucifixion, and its prickles make it an ideal deterrent against all evil spirits. Hence the reason for making displays for our doors, and decorating the rooms of our homes with it to ensure a happy and misfortune-free Christmas. Superstition does decree, however, that you must pick the holly before Christmas Eve, or be open to the evil intentions of any enemy you may have in either the real or spirit world. The prickly holly leaves are said to be male, and for this reason lucky for men; while the smooth variety are female and will bring fortune to the ladies. Aside from the good luck that the tree harbours, the holly is a weather omen for when the branches are heavily laden with berries this is a sign of a hard, snowy winter to come. The tree is also said to be a good protection against thunder and evil spirits – and a rather amusing cure for chilblains, the feet having to be beaten with a holly branch to 'let the chilled blood out'. Ouch!

HOOP

If the iron hoop around an ale cask or a water butt comes off for no apparent reason on Christmas Eve, this is an omen in Europe of a death in the family during the following year.

HORN

Although it is unlucky to keep a horn in the house, American tradition says that an ox's horn in particular is a very potent protection against the Devil. A stag's horn will ward off the evil eye in Britain and Spain.

HORSE

Because of the important role he has played in man's life from the very earliest times, it comes as no surprise to find the horse surrounded by superstitions. In the time of the ancient Greeks the animal was an object of worship and doubtless many of the superstitions have their origins in this fact. The British believe that a black horse is lucky, and a piebald is unlucky while in Europe the reverse is true. English country folk are very uneasy about white horses and if they meet one on a journey spit on the ground to avoid bad luck. There is a superstition repeated among race horse breeders that a horse with 'white stockings' on its front legs is lucky, while an animal with these markings on opposite front and back legs is very lucky indeed. Perhaps, though, the best combination of all is a horse with a white star shape on its forehead and a single white 'stocking' on a *hind* leg. (It should be added that the 'stocking' must only come a few inches up the horse's leg – further than this and it is prone to stumbling.) The custom of plaiting a horse's tail which is primarily done nowadays for style, actually has its origins in superstition – for throughout much of Britain it was believed that a horse with ribbons plaited into its tail was safe from the machinations of witches. A horse with a groove in its neck into which a human thumb can be placed is believed to be particularly lucky, for this is said to be the 'Prophet's Thumb Print' and shows that the animal is a descendent of one of the five brood mares which belonged to the prophet Mahomet. In parts of Britain there still persists a belief that there is a single word which when used will control any horse of whatever temperament. This 'Horseman's Word' is a closely guarded secret and only passed from one true horseman to another and not revealed to outsiders so, sadly, it cannot be revealed here! The most ominous sight for Americans is to have a red-headed girl on a white horse cross their path – an almost unlimited period of bad luck will follow such an

122

encounter. In the Ozark Mountains it is also believed that it is possible to arrange the colour of a colt before it is born by holding up a cloth of the chosen colour before the mare. Finally, if a horse snorts while on a journey it is a sign of good luck, while a group of horses seen standing with their backs to a hedge is an omen that a storm is brewing.

HORSEBRASSES

These beautiful items now enthusiastically sought by collectors to hang on walls or beside the fireplace, were originally designed to protect horses from the spells of witches and the Evil Eye in particular. The practice originated something like five thousand years ago, and shiny metal talismans (for such they are) have been found in civilizations as far apart as Scandinavia and China. The charms were invariably shiny so that the light would dazzle the evil spirits and drive them off, and the symbols believed to have most effect and carry most good fortune were acorns, birds, beasts, flowers, hearts and swastikas, all of which, of course, have mystical associations.

HORSE RACING

The omens and superstitions which are applied to horse racing are again very numerous, but almost invariably personal, and virtually everyone who has ever gambled on a horse has brought some particular hunch or 'feeling' to bear when making a selection. Choices are often based on the number a horse is carrying or the colours of his jockey, but as a tip if you use a pin in the list of runners, then one that has been used in a wedding dress is said to be the luckiest. Never bet on a horse whose name has been changed – he is sure to be unlucky – and also never wish a horse or its rider good luck before the start: that is very unlucky indeed!

HORSESHOE

The horseshoe is, of course, one of the most familiar items in superstition and there are few people who would defy the weight of public opinion that it is a harbinger of good luck. It is believed to be lucky if you find a horseshoe in the road and this will be redoubled if you take it home and nail it over the doorway. It is generally agreed that the points should be *upwards* – for if they are down the luck will 'run out' – although sideways has been said to be effective, for the shoe then takes on the form of the letter 'C' for Christ. The general shape of the horshoe is said to symbolize the heavens and a house roof, thus representing man's spiritual and secular life. The 'power' of the horseshoe superstition almost certainly developed because it was created in the sacred fire and made from the sacred metal, iron. To this was added the fact – which must have seemed truly miraculous to early man – that the shoe could be fitted to the horse with nails and apparently the animal felt no pain. In his scarcely developed intellect, man did not credit this facility to the constituency of the horse's hoof, but the amazing power of the horseshoe. From there it is only a step to realize that such a prized object, when it had completed its active life, was probably nonetheless powerful, and what more natural thing to do than hang it somewhere for protection from evil and to promote good luck? Scottish fishermen in particular believe a horseshoe fixed to the mast will protect a ship from storms (that great seaman Nelson had one on his ship the *Victory*) while in the North Country people say that if you find a horseshoe, spit on it and throw it over your left shoulder making a wish, and the request will be granted. The luck of a horseshoe with seven nail holes is obviously redoubled, and some folk believe finger rings made from horseshoe nails are luck bringers. Country people playing the old game of pitching horseshoes believe they can bring themselves luck by rubbing two of the shoes together before they throw. Finally, it is interesting to note that it has become an increasingly common practice in America for well-wishers to send floral gifts made in the shape of horseshoes to new business ventures, particularly those in the areas of entertainment.

HOSPITAL

At hospitals throughout the world, doctors and nurses believe that bouquets of red and white flowers are extremely unlucky, symbolizing death, and should such appear they are invariably quickly dispatched to the chapel. If a nurse knocks over a chair during the course of her duties then a new patient will soon be arriving in the ward. And should a nurse get her apron strings twisted while she is putting the garment on, she can expect to take on new duties shortly thereafter. Whether they are harder or more pleasant there is no way of telling! A nurse who carelessly places blankets over a chair while she is making a bed presages a death in the ward. Apparently, the origin of this particular belief lies in the fact that the dead were once wrapped in woollen blankets before being placed in their coffins. The colouring of pills has much to do with super-stition, too – red and pink being popular because of their association with blood and healthy skin: black, of course, being Death's colour has no place in such company. In some hospitals Saturday is believed to be an unlucky day on which to be discharged for if you are, you can expect to be back again before long.

HOT CROSS BUNS

These tasty little buns made especially at Easter actually originated before Christianity and took the form of cakes made from wheat which were used in the pagan Spring Festivals. The buns are credited with several special properties including curing certain illnesses and the power to last almost indefinitely without going mouldy. Hung in the house they are said to protect it from evil and fire, and sailors used to believe that taken to sea they prevented shipwrecks. In some parts of England farmers even credit them with the power of keeping rats out of a granary!

HOUSE

If you are about to move into a new house, you can ensure good luck for yourself and your family by walking into every room carrying a loaf of bread and plate of salt. This, it is said, will propitiate any spirits who might be there, and show them you mean them no harm; they, in turn, will not bother you.

There are also superstitions attached to the plants which are sometimes found growing on the roofs of houses, particularly old ones, the seeds of which have obviously been carried there by the wind. Flowering plants are said to be an omen of good luck while grass and such-like should be removed to avoid misfortune. Strangely, while the Welsh believe that if the small house leek is found growing on the roof of a house it will protect the family inside from illness, the English maintain it will lead to your house being struck by lightning! When visiting a house, always leave by the same door as you entered says an American superstition, otherwise you will take the owner's luck away and probably bring bad luck on yourself. And should a door in any house open by itself, then expect an unwelcome guest. Finally, if you forget your key and find yourself locked out, according to an English superstition there is a very definite procedure you must observe to avoid bad luck. Once you have got in through a window, go round to the front door, open it, and then go back to the window and climb out again and enter the now opened door in the normal manner. Although this may seem unnecessarily complicated, there are still many country folk who would never dream of doing otherwise!

HUNCH

The expression 'Backing a hunch' comes from an old superstition that to touch a hunchback would bring good luck. According to tradition, deformed people were considered evil by nature, and in return for being so cruelly misshapen they returned nothing but evil to humanity. So by touching such an evil object, it was thought a person received aid in warding off the unseen forces of nature. Indeed the reason for kings of the past keeping a hunchback as court jester was not merely to entertain the courtiers but also to ensure good luck. Today, still, hunchbacks can be seen in the vicinity of certain famous casinos demonstrating the continuing impact of the superstition – and getting a good living in tips into the bargain!

IDIOT

Although it may seem rather bizarre and unfeeling today, many people believed it was a good omen to meet an idiot when on some important task. Fishermen in particular held that to cross the path of anyone who was mentally unbalanced when going to their boats would ensure a safe and successful voyage. The origin of this superstition is that all such people are 'God's Poor' and despite their limitations are blessed in their own way. It is interesting to note, too, that in old English the word silly meant 'blessed'.

INITIALS

In the states of Massachusetts and Ohio in America it is said that if the initials of your name spell a word, regardless of what it is, it is an omen that you will be rich. Except P.O.O.R. perhaps?

INK SPOT

It has been a superstition in the British Isles for several centuries that to spill some ink while writing a letter is an omen of good luck – even if it may somewhat spoil the look of the correspondence!

INVALID

When you go out of doors for the first time after an illness you would be well advised to first walk around the house in the direction of the sun to ensure a speedy recovery. To walk in the opposite direction, says an old English superstition, is to court a relapse in your condition.

INVISIBILITY

There were once quite a number of superstitions which offered invisibility if you were prepared to carry out some rather gruesome rituals (including digging up a body and changing shirts with it), but today only two ever seem to get mentioned in Britain and then without much conviction. The first requires you to simply wear an agate, while the second says you can come and go unseen by carrying the right eye of a bat in your pocket or handbag!

IRON

Although superstition has long credited iron with the power of driving away witches and evil spirits, it is nonetheless unlucky to bring *old* iron into the house as this can only lead to misfortune. Tradition says that the brightness of new iron blinded evil spirits and drove them away, but rusted or old iron had no effect on them at all and they could take up residence as they pleased. For this reason any antique piece of iron-ware which is found should be thoroughly cleaned before being put on display anywhere indoors.

ITCHING

The superstitions surrounding those irritating little tickles which suddenly arise on the body for no apparent reason have some very intriguing explanations according to tradition. Under the heading HAND is mentioned the monetary rewards to be expected when your palms itch, and if your right ear suddenly tickles, for instance, then someone, somewhere, is speaking well of you. The reverse is naturally true if it is the left ear. If your nose itches then you are shortly to be either annoyed or kissed by someone, while if your feet get un-comfortable you are going to make a difficult journey some-where. Should your knee trouble you, says superstition, you'll be kneeling in a strange place before long – although in Boston, U.S.A., they say it is a sign you are jealous of someone! A head itch is said to be generally lucky, and if it is your right ankle that requires a scratch, do so with pleasure for you will be receiving some money. But not so the left – you will be paying out before long! Perhaps, an elbow itch promises the most – for this is an omen that you will be sleeping with someone new before long!

IVY

Because of its association with the Roman god Bacchus, ivy has often been hung outside inns and is naturally considered a good luck plant. If it grows on the walls of a house it will protect those inside from misfortune and the ministrations of evil spirits, but should the plant die then those inside are in for misfortune, probably of the financial kind. The ivy leaf is one of the few items which will enable man to see his future love – if he gathers ten leaves on the night of Hallowe'en, throws one away, and sleeps with the rest under his pillow then he will dream of his wife-to-be. Similarly a girl can find out who her mate will be by plucking several leaves of the plant and reciting the following verse:

> 'Ivy, ivy, I love you
> In my bosom I put you,
> The first young man who speaks to me
> My future husband shall he be.'

JACKDAW

In Britain the jackdaw is believed to be an omen of ill-luck when it is seen perched on a building, and if it should come down the chimney then there will be a death in the family. Strangely no such superstition applies to a group of jackdaws, and in parts of Europe a flock of these birds alighting on a house presage both an addition to the family and financial reward for those living inside. Should a group of them fly around continually making their 'cawing' sound, then there is rain on the way; and if they are late settling down in the evening this is also an indication of bad weather.

JANUARY

A British superstition among farmers says that a mild January will result in wintry weather from February right through to the end of May, and as a result cause poor crops.

JAPONICA BERRIES

Some English country people believe these large green berries were the original 'Forbidden Fruit' of the Garden of Eden, and naturally to eat them is to court misfortune. Nonetheless, they are eagerly harvested and used in jam making in a great many other parts of the British Isles!

JEWELLERY

In America it is said that bad luck will result for the owner if jewellery is redesigned without following the original design as closely as possible.

JOCKEY

Jockeys are yet another superstitious group of sportsmen who take particular care observing omens and other signs before each race meeting. Many of them have favourite riding crops which they consider lucky, and certainly all share the belief that to drop one of these before a race begins is an omen of a bad ride. Even when dressing before a ride, no jockey likes to see his boots standing on the floor – they should always be kept on a shelf or else he will have no luck with his mount. And no one engaged in this profession likes to be referred to as a 'jockey' before he is due to ride – unless his proper name is used he feels he is destined to lose.

JOURNEY

Despite the fact that a great many people always look back to wave as they set off on a journey, according to superstition it is actually a bad thing to turn in the direction of your house once you have left for it will bring misfortune. Equally you are better off continuing with your journey if you have left something behind, for to go back will put all your day's business in jeopardy. If it is absolutely imperative to go back, sit down and count to ten before starting off again. It is said to be bad luck to watch a person journey completely out of sight and if you do you may never see him or her again. These superstitions appear to be connected with the story of Lot's wife who looked back at the destruction of Sodom and was turned into a pillar of salt.

K

KETTLE
Young girls are warned by superstition not to turn a boiling kettle around so that the spout faces the wall or they will never find a husband. Apart, of course, from the damage the steam might well do to the paintwork!

KEYS
If a woman possesses a ring of keys which continually get rusty despite her efforts to keep them clean, this is a good omen for it means that someone among her family or friends is planning to leave her money in their will. This superstition, prevalent through much of the industrial Midlands of England, is claimed in several recorded instances to be absolutely true! In Europe it is said a child can be protected from all evil spirits by sleeping with a key under his pillow.

KINGFISHER
The kingfisher is claimed to have obtained its wonderful plumage because it was the first bird freed from the Ark by Noah, and as it flew up into the skies its previous dull grey colour was transformed into sky blue. It is also interesting to note that another name for the kingfisher is the halcyon, after

the Greek legend of the faithful lover Halcyon, who was turned into one of these birds, and it is from this that we get the expression for particularly pleasant times as 'Halcyon Days'. It is naturally enough a lucky bird, and tradition says that when the bird is sitting on its eggs there will be no storms at sea. It used to be said, too, that a dead kingfisher hung on a ship would show the direction of the wind. There is a more general belief that to hear the sound of a kingfisher coming from the right is an omen of success in business, while from the left bodes ill. In parts of Europe it is believed that if a few of the bird's feathers are sown into a person's clothing they will protect both his life and health.

KISSING

Primitive man believed that the air he breathed possessed some magic power and thus kissing became looked upon as a sacred act – an act in which men and women mingled their souls. According to two British superstitions if a dark complexioned man kissed a girl she could expect a proposal, but if a girl kissed a man with a moustache and got a hair from this on her lips she was destined to die an old maid! Among many people it is still held that children should not be allowed to kiss each other before they can speak or they will grow up foolish and give their affections indiscriminately. It is also said to be unlucky to kiss anyone on the nose as this will cause trouble between the two people involved, and that misfortune will come to anyone who is kissed by someone leaning over their shoulder to give them a peck on the cheek. In the olden days it was said that such a kiss was followed by a knife in the back! There is also an old English saying that 'When the broom is out of season, kissing is out of favour' – but perhaps even those who are not country folk by birth will be aware that this plant is actually found flowering all year round!

KNIFE

The oldest superstition connected with knives is that to cross them at table is an omen of bad luck and indicates hostile intent. Similarly the custom of laying knives and forks carefully side by side on the table has come down to us from the time when man habitually held his knife in his hand while he ate and the only way he could show that he harboured no evil intent to anyone at his table was if he laid it down beside his plate. It is also unlucky to toast bread with a knife or spin it on the table top. Always be careful that you do not let a knife drop from the table if you are involved in a love affair for this will surely break it; although if you should already be married it is a sign that someone will come visiting you shortly. Should you be given a knife as a present it is as well to give the donor a small coin to ensure that no bad luck strikes you, claims another widely found tradition. A knife made of iron is said to be a good form of protection against witches and evil spirits, and in Scotland you are advised to put a knife under your pillow at night to prevent the fairies carrying you off in your sleep. In Southern England, too, it is said that a knife hidden under the window sill will keep the Devil at bay.

KNOCK

In Ireland if a knocking sound is heard three nights running on or about midnight then it is said to be a death omen for someone in the house. Similarly in Scotland, three knocks at regular intervals of one or two minutes foretells the same thing. Any knocking noise near the bed of a sick person is also said to be a death omen throughout the British Isles. In Virginia in the United States there is a quaint superstition that if you knock on the door of a house and receive no answer it is a sign of death, though a more likely explanation is that there is no one at home!

KNOTS

Knots play a part in both birth and death superstitions: people in many countries believe that all knots on the clothing of women giving birth (including those purely for decoration) should be undone to make the passing of the child easier. Similarly, at death all the knots on a dying person's clothes should be eased so that the soul may pass without hindrance. In Scotland it is believed that no body should be put in a coffin with knots on any of its clothing or the spirit will never rest in peace. The knot also plays a part in weddings, and in several European countries a bridegroom will go to the altar with one of his shoes unlaced lest witches deprive him of the power on his wedding night of 'untying' his bride's virginity. Country people throughout Britain still like the old superstition that if two folk are pulling a piece of cotton with a knot in it and the thread breaks, whoever holds the piece with the knot may make a wish and have it granted.

LADDER

The superstition that to walk under a ladder propped up against a wall or building will bring bad luck can be seen in practise everywhere, though few people probably realize that the origin of this tradition is linked with our old friend the Devil once again. The ancients maintained that a leaning ladder formed a natural triangle and as the triangle was the symbol of the Holy Trinity to walk through it showed a lack of respect and an affinity with the Evil One. Should you do so inadvertently, though, all is not lost, for superstition says you should immediately cross your fingers and keep them crossed until you see a dog. You may also try the more unlikely remedy of spitting on your shoe and leaving the spittle to dry. According to another tradition if you are a single person and commit this offence you have no chance of marrying for at least a year! The same superstition also exists in many non-Christian countries, where all actions which cover the head can lead to misfortune: for example some Japanese have a fear of telegraph wires and believe if they walk underneath them they will be possessed by devils. In a number of European countries it is believed to be bad luck to reach through the rungs of a ladder for anything, and some Dutch people still claim that walking under a ladder is an omen that you will be hanged. The Americans also believe that if a black cat should pass under a ladder, then whoever next climbs up it is in for some bad luck. Finally, if you want to be successful in life climb up a ladder with an odd number of rungs, but be careful. Apart from the obvious danger to life and limb, to slip is an omen that you are going to lose some money.

LADYBIRD

This pretty little insect got its name from a very old belief that it in some way represented the Virgin Mary, and consequently ill-fortune will strike anyone foolish enough to kill it. It is said to be lucky if one lands on you, but for the luck to be effective you must not brush it off. English country folk say that the number of spots on the ladybird are also important, for if you count those on the insect which has alighted on you, each one represents a happy month to come. The superstition that the insect understands the human tongue also has a simple explanation. Country people will tell you that if the creature is placed on the hand and the following lines are recited it will do as you say:

> 'Ladybird, ladybird, fly away home,
> Your house is on fire, and your children are gone.'

In fact the ladybird takes to the wing to get off your hot and sweaty palm!

LAMBS

Despite the famous phrase that any unruly member of a family is the 'black sheep', in many rural parts of Europe the birth of a black lamb is regarded as an omen of good luck to the flock. In parts of England, though, such lambs are believed to herald misfortune, and twin black lambs presage disaster for animals and humans alike. On the other hand, if the first ewe to give birth produces white twins the flock will enjoy a prosperous year. Omens can also be drawn from the first lambs you see in the Spring: country people say that if the first of the tiny creatures you see is facing away from you then your year will be hard, while if the lamb is looking in your direction expect twelve months of plenty.

LAMP

The folk of Massachusetts believe that an oil lamp should never be held directly over a sleeping person, or this will cause their death. In Europe, a burning lamp keeps evil spirits away from a new born baby and its mother; while in Greece a spluttering lamp is an omen of misfortune.

LAPWING

The Scots believe that to see a lapwing flying overhead making its peculiar screeching noise is an ill-omen. They say that the souls of men doomed never to find rest live in the bodies of these birds, and that their call is actually the word 'bewitched' repeated over and over again.

LARK

The pretty little lark, along with a number of other wild song birds, used to be caught and sold in little cages throughout Europe. As a result of this unpleasant practise – now banned by law – a superstition developed that these birds would sing better if they were blinded with a red hot needle, and consequently many were mutilated in this horrible fashion. Once, too, it was said that if you ate three lark's eggs on a Sunday morning before the church bells rang you would have a sweet voice. In Scotland it is claimed that the words the lark sings may actually be distinguished if you lie on your back in a field and listen without making a sound. Whether you do catch a word or not, it is still a pleasant way of spending some time on a hot summer's day!

'LAST PIECE'

British and German girl children have been told for generations that if they eat the last of anything remaining on a plate they will live to become old maids – the prime objective, though, was probably good manners! Little American girls are much better off – for they learn that whoever gets the last piece of cake at tea-time will be the first to marry.

LAUGH

Among many country people excessive laughter is still looked upon as an evil-omen, for the person is held to be 'possessed' by his mirth and cannot hope to live for a great deal longer. In parts of Britain it is said that to laugh before breakfast will lead to tears before nightfall.

LAUNCHING

The custom of launching a new ship by breaking a bottle of champagne across its bows is actually the continuation of a much older tradition. The vessel was symbolically given 'life' when human blood was smeared over it. Later the blood was replaced by red wine, but nowadays champagne almost invariably serves.

LEAF

The leaves of the oak and ash trees are regarded by many country people as omens of summer weather. If, they say, the ash is in leaf before the oak then we can expect a very wet summer, while if the position is reversed the rainfall will be light. Leaves in general are a weather omen, for if they make a sudden rustling noise then rain is on the way – and bad weather is also imminent if they turn their undersides upwards. It is said to be an ill-omen if trees shed a large number of leaves before the autumn; and a bad sign, too, if fresh leaves taken into a house wither quickly. There is also a widespread belief throughout Europe that if you can catch a leaf falling from a tree in the autumn you will not have a cold all winter. And British children say that every leaf that is caught fluttering down between Michaelmas (September 29) and Hallowe'en (October 31) will result in a happy day in the coming year.

LEAP YEAR

Superstition tells us that Leap Years are good for important undertakings, and anything started on February 29 is sure of success. Such a year also allows girls to propose to their chosen men with no sense of embarrassment and every hope of success. The Scots take a particular delight in this old tradition – though there is one condition that the girls must all observe, or the men can reject their advances without fear of bad luck. Every girl must wear a scarlet flannel petticoat which is at least partly visible below her dress! Perhaps this was the origin of the term a 'scarlet woman'?

LEATHER
The popularity of leather owes much to the superstition which arose in early times that it possessed the power to scare demons and evil spirits away.

LEEK
The power of the leek is a long established tradition in Wales and from the earliest times Welshmen would rub the plant all over their bodies because they believed it gave them extra strength in battle and prevented them getting wounded. It is probable that the wearing of this plant today – especially at sporting occasions – is an unconscious continuation of the old superstition.

LEFT-HANDED PERSON
There is a European superstition that it is unlucky to meet a left-handed person on a Tuesday morning. At any other time of the week, though, it is a good omen. The origin of this idea is believed to be Scandinavian and related to the god of war, Tiw, whose name was the origin of Tiw's day – the modern Tuesday.

LETTER
For letters from friends to cross in the post is said to be an ill-omen, and to presage a quarrel or trouble between them, according to American superstition.

LETTUCE

An abundance of lettuce plants in the garden is claimed by some country people to prevent a wife from conceiving – surely the most unlikely method of birth control one is ever likely to meet! The Romans, however, believed that the lettuce had aphrodisiac and child-bearing powers and fed heartily on it at feasts and weddings – they also said it prevented drunkenness!

LIGHTNING

Lightning is certainly one of the most feared forces of nature, and from the time of the Ancient Greeks it has featured in superstitious beliefs. Perhaps the most widely quoted statement about it is that it never strikes twice in the same place – a belief which persists for no good reason as there are numerous instances where it has! (The Empire State Building in New York, for example, is struck as much as fifty times each year!) In early days the force was believed to signify the anger of the gods, and that probably accounts for the superstitions associated with it. It is said that no one is ever killed by lightning when asleep, and that it is a good omen to be awakened by a flash. However, it is unlucky to mention lightning immediately after such an event, and it was once believed that to look at lightning would drive a person mad. There are several methods of protecting yourself from this danger – including winding a snake skin around your head, sleeping on a feather bed, keeping a fire burning in the grate, or even taking account of this old rhyme:

> 'Beware of the oak, it draws the stroke.
> Avoid the ash, it courts the flash.
> Creep under a thorn, it can save you from harm.'

In addition, the Americans say that wood taken from a tree which has been struck by lightning should never be used as firewood as this exposes the house to a similar attack. And all mirrors should be covered with cloths, and all scissors hidden when lightning is about or the omens are bad.

LIGHTS

The old belief that it was bad luck to have three lamps or candles together in a room – surprising because three is considered a lucky number – has now been applied to electric lights, and there are many people who would not challenge the fates by having such an arrangement in their homes. The most likely explanation for this idea seems to lie in Slavonic tradition: that only a priest could light three candles at the altar without incurring the wrath of God – for an ordinary layman to do so would lead to the greatest misfortune.

LILAC

The lilac is regarded as one of the 'drowsy-scented flowers' and as such ill-omened. White lilacs in particular should not be taken into a house – and especially not a hospital – while the purple and red varieties are also regarded with some suspicion. The only luck associated with this flower is to find one of the rare five-petalled lilac blossoms of any colour.

LILY

The lily has always been regarded as the symbol of virginity – 'pure as a lily' – and people in many countries believe that it is unlucky to break or spoil the plants: particularly for a man, as the action is said to threaten the purity of the female members of his family.

LION

There is a curious superstition recorded in several countries that a lion will not injure a royal prince – the reason being that the king of the animals believes in showing respect to his equal in the human world. However in parts of Africa it is said that the lion both fears and is jealous of the game cock because it wears a crown (its crest) and spurs, and seemingly does not show due deference like all other creatures. Women in many African tribes also believe that a piece of a lion's heart given to their baby sons will make them grow up to be strong and brave.

LIPS

An itching or tingling sensation of the lips is an omen that someone is going to kiss you soon, says a superstition noted on both sides of the Atlantic.

LIVING TOGETHER

Many societies used to consider that any man and woman who lived together without being married were harbingers of bad luck for the whole community. Such couples were said to be in league with the Devil, and it was not unusual for effigies of them to be burnt or for them to be kept awake all night by a group of local people shouting and banging drums or playing horns outside their house. This was said to drive away the devils which the couple harboured – although it was probably more likely eventually to drive away the unfortunate and sleepless couple!

LIZARD

The lizard is a creature of ill-omen for a bride, for if she sees one on her way to church her marriage will be unhappy, says a superstition still noted in Britain and Europe. In France, though, if a lizard runs over a woman's hand it is said she will become a good needle-woman.

LONGEVITY

Soup manufacturers will doubtless be pleased to hear an old European tradition which says that plenty of soup eaten slowly produces longevity!

LOVE

The majority of superstitions relating to love seem to concern themselves with the young lady and ways in which she might find a lover – quite a number of them will be found under other specific headings. Here, though, are a few more worth noting and still heard from time to time. In the Southern States of America it is said that if a young girl holds a mirror over a well she will see on it the image of her future husband,

143

while in Britain if a girl sleeps with a mirror under her pillow she will dream of her lover. The American girl can also spot her future husband if she is prepared to carry out this rather complex ritual. She must first stand by the roadside and count ten red cars, and then look for a red-headed girl wearing a purple dress. After this she just needs to keep her eyes open for a man with a green tie, and the very *next* young man she sees after him is her intended! It is rather easier for the American male, though, for he merely needs to eat the last slice of bread from the tea table and the next girl he meets will be his – plus a bonus of ten thousand dollars to boot! During the early days of photography it was said that if an engaged couple were photo-graphed together, the wedding was in danger of never taking place. Equally strange was the idea that if a girl sat on a table while talking to her sweetheart, she would never marry him. Country people also claimed that a girl who did not look towards the north the first time she left the house in the morning would always be single, and the same fate awaited the young woman who read the marriage service to herself. In contrast to all these pitfalls for young lovers, superstition says that if a twig of laurel is plucked from a tree by a young man and divided equally with his sweetheart, as long as they both keep their halves, their love will flourish. If your lover is proving untrue to you, though, and yet you still wish to retain his affections, the Germans recommend lighting three candles by the wrong ends and repeating the Paternoster three times. This should bring him back with redoubled passion! While neither a long nor a short courtship is said to be lucky, tradition decrees that a courtship of one year with a three month engagement will stand a couple in best stead for their life ahead. It is said to be unlucky for a man to propose marriage on a train, bus or in any public place, but a girl who is proposed to at a dance and refuses will, for some extraordinary reason, be in for a great deal of luck! If, while he is proposing, a young man is interrupted by another girl, it is an omen that one day she will be his second wife. And, finally, a man who has been refused three times is best advised to stay unmarried!

LOVE LETTERS

There are numerous omens and superstitions associated with the practise of writing love letters, and here is a selection of some of the most widely held. A love letter should always be written in ink – to write in pencil or type it is ill-omened for the courtship. Postcards are acceptable means of communication, but no lover should ever ask his or her intended a favour on one, or the affair will break up. It is a good sign if your hand trembles as you write to your loved one, for it means your love is reciprocated; while if you make a blot while you are writing the omen is even better – for this means the one you adore is thinking of you at the same moment. It is not a good omen, though, to propose by mail, and if a girl receives two letters from different lovers at the same time then she will marry neither of them. A love letter that arrives either insufficiently stamped or with the flap open means the affair is cooling off. And beware of posting love letters on three particular days, for, according to Scottish superstition, they will bring an end to your affair – Christmas Day, February 29 and September 1. (In some countries any Sunday is also said to be ill-omened and will lead to a quarrel.) Finally, to find out if your lover is true, set fire to one of his or her letters – if the flame is bright and full the love is true; if it is small and blue you are not destined for each other. It must be added, though, that you do this at considerable peril, for it is said to be very unlucky to burn love letters. If they must be destroyed, they should be torn up.

LUCKY FINDS

Superstition says that the luckiest things you can find are horseshoes, four-leaf clovers and teeth!

M

MADNESS

Although the superstition is rarely heard nowadays, in Britain, much of Europe and in several Mediterranean countries, it was held to be lucky to live in the same house as a madman. The Japanese, however, still believe that you are quite likely to go mad if your hair is set alight, and because of the recent rabies scare throughout Europe an old superstition about how to cure the bite of a mad dog has been voiced again in certain rural districts. This requires that you catch and kill the mad dog, remove and burn its liver to charcoal, then powder this and eat it in a bread and butter sandwich! This cure is, though, certainly neither guaranteed nor recommended!

MAGPIE

There are several omens associated with the magpie, which is said to be an unlucky creature because it was the only bird which refused to enter the Ark, preferring to perch on the roof of Noah's craft. It is unlucky to spot two magpies flying together, while if a group of them are seen chattering this is also an evil omen. The Germans have specific ideas about the implication in the number of magpies you see – viz. one is unlucky, two denotes merriment or a marriage, three a successful journey, four good news and five company. And the Scots put this and more into a little rhyme:

'One means anger, two brings mirth.
Three a wedding, four a birth.
Five is heaven, six is hell.
But seven's the very Devil's ain sell.'

To be fair to the creature, though, there is a superstition that if a magpie perches on your roof then it is a sign that your building will never fall down. However, if one of these birds flies around your property croaking, then this presages the death of a member of the family. It is also unlucky to see a magpie when you are setting off on a journey, and if one of the birds flies before you on your way to church it is a death omen. In effect, it is best if you treat the bird with respect and many people believe it is as well to cross yourself when one flies by. To be absolutely sure of avoiding trouble, the folk of some parts of Britain take their hats off to the magpie as he passes and give a little bow! (Incidentally only the Chinese consider the magpie a bird of good omen, and they believe that misfortune will strike you if you kill one.)

MAKE-UP

It is said to be an ill-omen to spill face powder, according to American superstition, for this presages a quarrel with a friend.

MANDRAKE

The mandrake plant, a member of the potato family and so named because its strange shape rather resembles that of a human being, has a history steeped in superstition and has been much used in witchcraft spells – primarily because it has opiate properties. For many years it was believed that to pull one from the ground would cause a person to fall dead (for this reason dogs were always made to dig them up), and that the plant actually made a shrieking sound as it was torn from the soil. If this sound did not drive you mad, the superstition went on, then the plant could be used in curing many skin diseases,

147

as a purgative, or as a love charm to make barren women conceive.

MARCH

An old weather omen still repeated in country districts regarding March goes as follows: 'A wet March makes for a real bad harvest. A dry and cold March will never beg its bread'.

MARIGOLDS

These pretty golden flowers are not to be treated lightly if you wish to avoid becoming a heavy drinker – for to pick them, even look at them, will doom you to a life on the bottle, says an extraordinary superstition from the West Country of England, where the flowers are actually called 'The Drunkards'. The Welsh, though, hold no such superstition, but do believe the plant is a good weather omen, for if blooms are not open before 7 o'clock in the morning they say a storm is in the offing. The marigold has also been used in wedding garlands and as a love charm, and many country folk say that if its head is rubbed on a wasp or bee sting this will immediately relieve the pain.

MARRIAGE

The taboo against marrying someone from your own family or clan predates social or Christian ethics by many centuries, and arose among primitive men for two reasons. Firstly, he saw that by introducing 'fresh blood' into his herds of animals he improved the stock, and so did likewise for himself; and, second, it was considered unmanly, even cowardly, to take a woman of your own people rather than seek one from elsewhere. It has always been held to be unlucky for two sisters to marry two brothers – there is only so much luck to go round, says superstition, and one of the couples is going to lose out. Although it is unlucky to be married on your birthday, it is particularly lucky if you and your wife share the same birthday – although you must be a year or two apart. An old British almanac writer drew on local superstitions to devise the following rhyme about the most suitable month of the year in which to marry, and it embodies several ideas which are still widely held today:

'Married in January's hoar and rime,
Widowed you'll be before your prime.
Married in February's sleepy weather,
Life you'll tread in time together.
Married when March winds shrill and roar,
Your home will be on a distant shore.
Married beneath April's changing skies,
A chequered path before you lies.
Married when bees over May blossoms flit,
Strangers around your board will sit.
Married in the month of roses – June,
Life will be one long honeymoon.
Married in July with flowers ablaze,
Bittersweet memories on after days.
Married in August's heat and drowse,
Lover and friend in your chosen spouse.
Married in September's golden glow,
Smooth and serene your life will go.
Married when leaves in October thin,
Toil and hardship for you gain.
Married in veils of November mist,
Fortune your wedding ring has kissed.
Married in days of December cheer,
Love's star shines brighter from year to year.'

Apart from the fact that the weather is often very good in June, the popularity of this month is rooted in the fact that it is named after the goddess Juno, the adored and faithful wife of Jupiter, who is the protector of women and marriage and said to bestow especial blessings on those who wed in her month. The previous month, May, is the unluckiest as it is named after Maia, the wife of Vulcan, who was the patroness of the aged. Superstition even has something to say about the best days of the week for getting married on: Monday is good for wealth, Tuesday for health, Wednesday is said to be the best, while Thursday will doom you to a life of struggle, Friday, too, is not an easy day, and strangely, while Saturday is said to be the one day without any luck at all, it is still by far the most popular with most people! The marriage ceremony itself developed as a formal social acknowledgement by two people to their friends of their establishing a life together – and that much used phrase about 'tying the knot' was an actual occurrence among the Babylonians who would take a thread from the bride's and groom's clothes and then symbolically 'tie the couple together'. The old adage 'Happy is the Bride the Sun shines on' is not so much a superstition as a throwback to earlier times, when it was the custom for marriage ceremonies to take place at the door of the Church, and doubtless no bride would be pleased to make her vows in the pouring rain! An American belief claims that as raindrops symbolize tears, a wet wedding will lead to a bride crying through her married life, and they add: 'Marry in Lent – live to repent'. Finally, there is one further piece of advice offered by superstition in this old British rhyme:

'Change your name and not the letter,
You change for worse and not for better.'

MARTIN
The martin is a lucky bird because of the old tradition that it serves as God's 'bow and arrow', and it will bring good luck to any house where it nests and successfully lays its eggs and rears its young.

MAY
May is generally believed to be an unlucky month, and particularly unfortunate for beginning any new enterprise or getting married. This belief is of very ancient origin and dates back to the time of primitive man who knew the month to be the best for planting and sowing his crops, and having no mechanical aids, needed every pair of hands that were available: hence there was no time for anything else, and certainly not time for mating! As old country folk still say, 'Marry in May – and you'll rue the day!' A lot of rural people also believe a child born in May will always be sickly, while cats born in this month are both unlucky and incapable of catching mice or rats!

MAY BLOSSOM

The May blossom is said to be a very unlucky flower and to bring it into the house presages misfortune. Suffolk people, for instance, believe it is particularly unlucky to have the flower in a bedroom, while others claim that to use a brush made from broom in the month of May will 'sweep away' the head of the household.

MEAT

While you are busy cooking the Sunday joint (or preparing meat on any other day for that matter) keep an eye on what happens to it, for there are omens to be read from it. If it shrinks then it is unlucky for the household; but if it swells, says the superstition, then all who eat it may look forward to prosperity. And a good meal too, one would imagine!

MEDICINE

It is advisable never to sell empty medicine bottles – they should always be returned for re-use – for according to a superstition prevalent throughout much of Europe, if you ignore this you will find you will want them filled again for yourself before very long.

MICE

In several traditions mice are said to be the souls of murdered people, and should one of these creatures nibble either clothes or a bag of flour during the night, this is a sign of some impending evil. The mouse has also been an ingredient of countless old folk cures over the years, and is credited when fried, roasted or baked with being particularly good at clearing up measles, whooping cough and bed wetting. As an omen a mouse is said to be a bad sign if encountered on a journey, and if one is heard squeaking behind the bed of an invalid, then that person is not going to recover. People in many parts of England also believe that if mice swarm into a house where they have not previously been noticed, then it is a sign of a forthcoming death in the family. In parts of Germany, however, a white mouse is said to be lucky, and to kill one will bring misfortune on a home. The Scots say they have a foolproof method of clearing mice from a house – one should be caught and held by its tail before a fire, and as it roasts all the others will flee the premises.

MILK

It is believed to be a very good omen to see some milk immediately on waking up in the morning, according to an Indian tradition – but throughout Europe spilling milk must be avoided, as it is a favourite drink of the fairies who will plague any household where they once find some on the floor.

MINCE PIES

In many households at Christmas even the most bloated diner is urged to round off his meal with a mince pie or two, for each one is said to presage a month's happiness. The original superstition, however, said that for a year's good luck a mince pie should be eaten on each of twelve consecutive days – and indeed to have more than one at a time completely defeated the object of the exercise. In the South of England it is actually felt to be best if each of the twelve pies is eaten in a different house. Strangely, the mince pie, which was probably first baked in Roman times with very different ingredients from those used today, was originally oblong-shaped, and it may well have earned its lucky reputation when it was adopted by the Christian religion because its shape was seen as symbolizing the cradle in which Christ was born on Christmas Day.

MINERS

It is perhaps not surprising, because of the danger inherent in the work, that many of the old superstitions about mining have remained. Perhaps, though, one of the oldest still widely held by miners is that a dove seen hovering around a pithead is an omen that there will shortly be a disaster below ground. Some older miners, particularly in Southern England, believe that to mark anything with the sign of an 'X' is to court disaster, because there are evil spirits which dwell in some mines and if they were to see this symbol of Christianity they might well become furious and cause a tragedy. Miners throughout Britain and Europe were for generations convinced that bad luck would result if they should see a woman or a cross-eyed man while on their way to the pit for the night shift, and in many communities the womenfolk would never stir from their homes at such times. An equally strong belief which still persists is that it is very unlucky for a miner to return home for anything he might have forgotten once he has set off for work – if he must go back, he should knock three times on the window for it. No miner would ever whistle below ground, and it is also thought unlucky to have a cat anywhere near a mine. Among older miners, too, it is said to be a mistake to wash the back too often for this will lead to a general weakness of the spine. These same men also still tell stories of how would-be criminals used to beg lumps of freshly hewn coal from them, for there was a general belief among the criminal fraternity until the turn of this century that a piece of coal secreted on their person would prevent them from being caught by the police!

MIRROR

Another of the oldest and still most widely held superstitions is that to break a mirror will result in seven years' bad luck. Although the origins of this belief have become obscured over the years, it seems to stem from the ancient idea that the reflection of a person seen in a glass was actually their soul, and if this reflection should be shattered the soul was similarly broken and the person would either die shortly afterwards, or at least be unable to go to heaven when he did pass on. There is a strange variation on this superstition to be found among Yorkshire people, who believe that if you break a mirror you will lose your best friend. (Although it is not widely known, the English have a way of preventing the bad luck caused by breaking a mirror. All the splinters of the glass should be carefully collected together and taken to a river or fast running stream and hurled in – this will then carry away all the misfortune.) In America, however, it is not considered unlucky deliberately to break a mirror, and even if you break one accidentally, the seven years' bad luck can be quickly avoided by taking out a five dollar note and making the sign of the cross at the same time. This particular note is said to have inherited the good luck qualities previously associated with the gold piece. In Europe, a number of people say that it is unlucky to see yourself in a mirror by candlelight, and that no child should be allowed to gaze in a glass until he is a year old or he will stutter or not live to a ripe old age. In many countries it is not unusual to find the mirrors in a room where someone has died covered with cloths, as it is believed that anyone who sees their reflection in this mirror at this particular time is similarly doomed to death. Equally widespread is the claim that if a mirror falls and breaks for no apparent reason, then someone in the family is going to die, while if a mirror glass inexplicably shatters while still hanging on the wall then a relative or close friend is near death. Although, as is mentioned elsewhere, it is unlucky for a bride to see herself in her full bridal outfit before she goes to her wedding, a newly wed couple who stand and admire themselves in a mirror while still in their marriage outfits will ensure themselves long life and happiness.

MISTLETOE

The mistletoe, which provides such a delightful excuse for stealing a kiss at Christmas, is said to have earned its status for some unfortunate misdemeanour as a result of which the Old Gods condemned it to look on for evermore while pretty girls were kissed! A more likely explanation lies in the fact that the plant was held to be sacred by the Druids, who called it the 'Golden Bough' and featured it in their religious worship. The tree is also said to be a 'thunder plant' and can protect a house from storms, and when chopped up and boiled is an antidote for poisons. Interestingly, in some rural areas of England it is still said that if a girl is not kissed under the mistletoe before her marriage she will be barren all her days. The reader might also just like to note that while it is perfectly permissible to cut down a few branches of mistletoe, never take the whole tree for this will result in the most dire bad luck. Finally, a warning about a piece of mistletoe which has been much kissed under – unless it is burned on Twelfth Night, says a superstition found in many European countries, all those who kissed beneath it will be quarrelling before the year is out.

MOLE

That rather attractive creature the mole is generally said to be a good luck sign, but in certain parts of England, if he digs up earth close to the house, this is a portent of a death in the family. Should this mole hill appear near the kitchen or wash house, then the person doomed is the wife. In many places, too, it is said the paws of a mole carried on the person will protect anyone from illness, and they are particularly good at relieving cramp and toothache.

MOLES

Moles growing on the body are indications of both good and bad luck, according to where they are positioned. As a general guide, those on the left hand side are unlucky because of the ancient association of the left with the Devil. Round moles are said to be signs of luck, while those oblong in shape indicate misfortune. To have a mole in the middle of the forehead presages wealth, while one on the forehead just above the temple shows a person of wit and understanding. Moles on the chin, ear and neck are lucky, although the Irish believe that one of these marks on the back of the neck shows the owner may well hang. Similarly lucky are moles on the elbow and wrist, and one placed between these two points indicates prosperity in later life. Perhaps most fortunate of all is the girl with a mole on her left breast for, says superstition, she will be irresistible and have the choice of any man she wants!

MONEY

To make sure you always have money, an old tradition requires you to carry a bent coin or one with a hole in it on your person – never, of course, using it for any purchase. You should also never have coins in more than one pocket or else you will lose the lot. Superstition also offers several other money making hints. For example, that little golden-coloured creature the money spider (*Arenea Scenica*) actually got his name because of an old belief that if one was carried in the pocket the owner would never be poor, and it is also an omen of forthcoming wealth if you find one on your clothes. Similarly, the old custom of spitting on the first coin taken during the morning's business was based on the belief that this would help it to 'stick' to its new owner and thereby make him or her wealthy. Probably one of the oldest superstitions concerning money is the belief – still found in a number of places – that you will never be rich if you mend your clothes while still wearing them. Quite why this should be no one has ever been able to explain!

MOON

Moon superstitions are innumerable and it can only be hoped here to give a fair cross section of those most widely held – beginning perhaps with the claim, substantiated in some medical circles, that madness can be engendered by the full moon, a belief which was first held by ancient peoples who derived the word lunatic from the Latin word for the moon, *luna*. By and large, though, man has always held the moon in respect (even worshipped her), and anyone seeking good fortune is advised to bow to the new moon, and turn over any silver coins in his pocket. By the time of the next new moon the amount will be doubled. The time of the full moon is said to be a good time for curing many illnesses and for a young girl to learn whether she is to marry. One way of doing this is by holding a silk handkerchief up in front of the moon, and the number of moons which show through represent the number of months she must wait before she will go to the altar. In Tennessee in America, a new moon can be used as a love portent if you glance at it over your right shoulder, take three steps backward and then repeat this verse.

'New moon, new moon, true and bright,
If I have a lover let me dream of him tonight.
If I am to marry far, let me hear a bird cry;
If I am to marry near, let me hear a cow low;
If I am to marry never, let me hear a hammer knock.'

To see the new moon for the first time through a window (or any glass) is an ill-omen, although if you view it first in the open and over your right shoulder then luck is coming your way (you can also make a wish). According to an ancient document in the British Museum (*The Cotton MS.*), the first ten days after the full moon are those most affected by superstition, and the advice the anonymous writer offers is as follows:

First Day. The first day of the new moon is the best on which to begin any new venture. If you fall ill on this day, though, you will be sick for some considerable time and probably have to endure much discomfort. Any child born on the first will live a long time and be happy and prosperous.

Second Day. This is a good day to buy or sell anything, and particularly auspicious for taking a sea voyage. It is also an excellent time for farmers to plough the land or for seeds to be sown in the garden.

Third Day. A generally ominous day – and a child born on the third will not live long. Criminals should also beware for they are most likely to be caught for any crime committed on this day.

Fourth Day. The right day of the month to start any construction operations in connection with houses and buildings. If politics are your chosen profession, adds the superstition, this is a most fortuitous day on which to have been born.

Fifth Day. The weather on this day will be fair indication of what is to follow for the rest of the month, and a good day for a woman to conceive.

Sixth Day. The best day of the month for anyone to go hunting or fishing.

Seventh Day. An ideal time for a boy and girl to meet and fall in love.

Eighth Day. Beware of falling ill on this day above all others, says superstition, for a sickness begun on the eighth will almost certainly end in death.

Ninth Day. Do not allow the moon to shine on your face on this night or you will have your features distorted and perhaps go mad. (In some places it is believed that to let the new moon shine on your sleeping face during any of these early days will result in insanity.)

Tenth Day. Anyone born on this day is destined to be a wanderer and restless of spirit.

Most countrymen believe plants and seeds are best sown when the moon is waxing – except for plants like runner beans and peas, which twine themselves around poles in an anti-clockwise direction and should be sown when the moon is waning. These same folk look at the new moon for weather omens – for if the 'horns' of the moon seem to point slightly upwards then the next twenty-eight-day cycle will be fine; while if they turn down then the period will be wet. Rain can also be expected when a giant outline of the full moon can be seen between the 'horns' of the new moon and if there is a halo round the planet at any time. Two new moons in one month are said to presage a month's bad weather, and any new moon on a Saturday or Sunday leads to rain and general ill-luck. When the moon is waning, superstition says that anything cut will not grow, and it is an unlucky time for a marriage or for a child to be born. On the other hand it is a very good time to move house, for the old belief says it will ensure you never go hungry. Finally, although man's journey to the moon has dispelled many of the old superstitions about it (including that lovely idea it was made of cheese), the idea has not quite died in country areas that the spots on the planet's surface represent the 'Man in the Moon'.

MOTH

People in many nations believe that white moths are actually the souls of dead people and it is unlucky to kill them. Black moths, though, are ill-omened, and if one should fly into a house this is a sign that someone living there will die within the year. However, if one flies out of the darkness at you, then an important letter is on its way to you.

MOTOR CAR

Although the car is a comparatively recent invention, this has not prevented it acquiring a number of superstitions which appear to be becoming more widely held with the passing years. For instance, only the most foolhardy motorists would talk about accidents, or boast of a trouble-free record, before setting off on a journey. It is also believed to be a good omen to transfer a few old items, such as a lucky coin or St Christopher medal, from a car you are parting with to your new model – in this way transferring the good luck. Many motorists have come to believe that certain cars are jinxed and, no matter what you do, they will go from one mechanical failure to the next, or one accident to another. Such cars may well have been purchased on Friday the thirteenth or have a number which adds up to the ill-omened thirteen. It is felt to be lucky to stay with the same make of car after enjoying a trouble-free period with such a vehicle, and many car dealers say that motors which have belonged to wealthy people are in demand for it is felt that some of their luck may be transferred to the next owner. Perhaps, though, the most widely held of all car superstitions is that if you clean your vehicle, no sooner have you finished than it will rain. This, of course, is only a continuation of the ancient belief that by performing any act nature will follow suit – in this instance by 'raining' water over his car, the motorist invites the rain gods to do the same. And more often than not they oblige!

MOTOR RACING

Like several other kinds of sportsmen, racing drivers have many good luck charms which are personal to themselves, and one of the few superstitions that appear to be universal is that it is unlucky to get into the car on the side of the exhaust pipe – if it only has one, of course. Before the advent of television, which now pursues them relentlessly from the pits to the starting grid, the old school of motor racing drivers also believed that to have their pictures taken or to sign autographs before the race was unlucky.

MOUNTAINEERING

There has been a superstition in the Alps since time immemorial that mountain climbing will be made much easier if the climbers wear the tongue of an eagle sown into the collar of their coats.

MOUSTACHE

The Americans have a quaint superstition concerning moustaches which is summed up in this delightful verse:

> 'Beware of that man
> Be he friend or brother,
> Whose hair is one colour
> And moustache is another.'

MURDER

It comes as no surprise to learn that it is a bad omen to see a murder or to pass a dead body lying on the ground, but in Germany it is said that the spirits of those who have been murdered must wander about the earth for as long as the natural lives of the victims would have been had they not been murdered.

MUSIC

According to the American Indians, if you imagine that you can hear music then you are in the presence of some benevolent spirit. Some African tribes also claim that a person bitten by a tarantula can be cured by having soothing music played to him!

MUSICIANS

It is fairly common to find among musicians the belief that it is bad luck to recommence a piece of music they have been practising if they have been interrupted for any length of time. They should apparently take up another piece – if only for a few bars – before going back to the original. It is also believed to be unlucky for a musician to keep a violin in his home if no one in the family plays it. Although this is credited as superstition, there is actually sound commonsense in the belief, for a violin – particularly a good one – will deteriorate and lose its tone if not regularly played. Several particular tunes are also said to be ill-omened, and many musicians and singers believe that bad luck will strike them if they play or even whistle the tune 'I Dreamt I Dwelt in Marble Halls' except in a performance of *The Bohemian Girl*, the light opera for which it was written. Similarly the singing of Tosti's 'Goodbye' outside its usual context will have dire consequences on the performers and theatre concerned. The music from *Macbeth* is also ill-omened and should never be hummed during rehearsals.

MYRTLE

Myrtle is held to be a lucky plant, especially if it grows on either side of the front door, for the house and those who dwell in it will always be happy and peaceful. Allow it to wither and die, or dig it up, at your peril. However, in Germany a girl engaged to be married should not plant myrtle as this will cause the wedding to be broken off; while in most of Europe a profusion of the plant growing in a garden presages a wedding in the household.

NAIL

In Britain it is said to be lucky to find a nail in the road, for nails have been looked upon as a form of protection against evil since at least Roman times when iron was regarded as the sacred metal. A rusty nail which is found is more lucky than a shiny one, and proves most effective when carried on the person or, to serve the whole household, by being driven into the lintel of the kitchen door.

NAMES

There is a grim and widely held superstition that if a child in a family is named after another child who is related and died in infancy, then the new baby is similarly doomed. Many country people also believe that if a child is given the same name as a pet animal then misfortune will strike both the baby and the creature. For years, too, it was said to be unlucky to tell anyone outside the immediate family what a child's name was to be before it was christened. It has always been considered lucky to name a child after someone famous in the belief that they might acquire some of that person's good fortune. And in the Midlands of England there is a curious belief that any person named Agnes will invariably go mad; while in various other parts of the country any boy named George will never be hanged – though records show quite a number have! Finally, it is lucky to have initials that form a word, but all young women should beware of using their married name before they are actually wed, or it will never come to be.

NAPKIN

Although good manners dictate that one should always roll or fold up a napkin after use, an English superstition maintains that to do so if you are visiting a house for the first time means that you will never go there again. Should you be staying longer, though, it is quite in order to leave the napkin tidy and there will be no repercussions.

NAVEL

The Turks have an unusual superstition about the origin of the navel. This claims that after the first human being had been made, the Devil spat on him in disgust, but Allah quickly tore out the contaminated flesh so that it would not spread, and thus the navel originated.

NECK

A stiff neck used to be an omen among many people in Europe that the sufferer was going to be hanged at some later date.

NEEDLE

It is said to be unlucky to mention the word needle when you wake up in the morning, and in Germany it is thought to be equally unfortunate to find in the street a needle complete with a thread of black cotton. To break a needle while sewing portends a wedding, according to British tradition, while country people in many places believe it is unlucky to lend a needle to anyone they know as this will 'prick' their friendship.

NEST

If a bird uses a person's hair in the making of its nest, says a European superstition, then that person will suffer a headache as a result. In parts of Austria the belief claims the person will get a boil or some other skin eruption.

NETTLE

The phrase 'to grasp the nettle', widely used when referring to tackling some difficult problem, actually originated in superstition as a result of a belief that a person could be cured of a dangerous fever if a relative were to take hold of a nettle and pull it up by the roots, at the same time repeating the name of the sufferer and his or her parents! Despite its sting, the nettle has been much used in folk medicine, and for generations it was believed that if a person carried some of it on his person he would be safe from lightning.

NEW HOUSE

The custom of taking a gift to someone when visiting them in a new house is found all over the world and has superstitious origins. Once it was believed that spirits not only lived on the land, but also inhabited buildings as soon as they were built – so the act of taking a present is actually to propitiate these beings. Indeed, the superstition decrees that the gift should be a present *for* the house, rather than for the people, and the most acceptable are those that can be used in maintaining the building. The tradition is related to the ancient practise of burying a living creature in the walls of any new building to keep the spirits happy – and is also the unconscious reason why we often put little caches of newspapers, coins and other objects in the foundations of a new house before it goes up. Many people also hold to the other very old superstition that the family cat or dog can be prevented from running away from a new home by putting butter on its paws. Seemingly, once they have licked the tasty butter off they lose the urge to go off and seek their previous surroundings.

NEW YEAR

If the first man to cross the threshold of a house after midnight has struck on New Year's Eve (the 'First Footer' as he is called) is dark haired and carries a shovel full of coal, then a year of good luck will follow. This widely known superstition originated in Scotland, of course, but now seems to be much more widely observed by partygoers all over the world. Conversely, if the first person to enter the house is a woman or a fair-haired man, then bad luck can be expected – and it is perhaps not surprising to find in many places a tall, dark haired man is specially recruited to make the necessary entrances at the homes of all his friends and neighbours. Not a few people also believe that empty pockets and empty cupboards on New Year's Eve portend a year of poverty – which might perhaps account for the way some merrymakers stock up for this particular night! Throughout Britain and Europe, too, it is felt to be bad luck to let a fire go out on New Year's Eve, but you could ensure yourself good fortune by draining the last dregs from a bottle of drink on this night. Cheers!

NIGHTJAR
In parts of England the nightjar is known as the 'Corpse Fowl' and it is widely regarded as a bird of misfortune. To hear its eerie cry at night is an ill-omen, and should one perch on a house or building then there will be a death inside before long.

NIGHTMARE
Although nightmares scarcely fall within the scope of this book, there is an interesting old superstition related by country people that you can avoid having nightmares by hanging your socks or stockings over the end of the bed with a pin stuck through them. (Yorkshire folk say putting them on a coal-rake will do just as well!) The 'nightmare' was originally believed to be a huge spirit which settled on people while they slept and gave them a feeling of being stifled – and in Europe an old preventive for this was to place a knife or something similar at the end of the bed, as it was well known that the denizens of darkness feared iron and steel.

NIGHTSHADE

Deadly nightshade has always been regarded as an ill-omened plant and over the years it has been much used in witches' spells. Nonetheless, it is an important ingredient in several folk cures, and a number of old almanacs consider it a most effective weapon against evil spirits when garlands of it are placed about any threatened person, animal or dwelling place.

NIPPLES (MALE)

According to a strange middle-European superstition, it is possible to tell from a man's nipples whether or not he has fathered children. If they are pink in colour, then he has not – while if they are brown, then he has!

NOSE

In Europe an itching nose indicates you are in for a fight, in Scotland a letter, and in America it is a sign someone unknown is in love with you. The Canadians, for their part, sum up all nose itches thus:

> 'You'll be mad,
> See a stranger,
> Kiss a fool,
> Or be in danger.'

NOSE BLEED

A sudden nose bleed is said to be an ill-omen, although should the person be in the presence of a member of the opposite sex to whom they are attracted, an old English superstition says this is a sign that they are in love. A single drop of blood from the left nostril is an omen of good fortune to come, but more than one from either side foretells a serious illness for someone in the sufferer's family. Nowadays, as many of the old cures for a nose bleed were so involved and unpleasant, it comes as no surprise to find that even country people have discarded them. (For instance, one cure instructed a sufferer to spear a toad with a knife and then wear the corpse in a little bag around the neck!) Perhaps the most widely believed superstition still extant suggests dropping a key down the back of the neck, but the advice that the head should be held back while doing this reveals the real secret of the cure – to help the flow of blood to cease by its own means. Some rural Americans claim a nose bleed can be stopped by poking a cat's tail up the nostril, but should this fail they also suggest placing a small wad of newspapers beneath the upper lip!

NOVEMBER

A hard frost in November before St Martin's Day (November 11) is said to be an omen that the winter will be a wet rather than a very cold one. A rhyme often heard in rural Britain illuminates the superstition:

'Ice before Martinmas enough to bear a duck,
The rest of the winter is sure to be but muck!'

NUMBERS

Numbers play a significant part in superstition and are to be found in many entries throughout this book. Since earliest times man has utilized them to divine the future. This science, known as Numerology, is rather beyond the scope of this work – and indeed has formed the basis of several books already – but it is interesting to note that the Romans first devised their system of counting based on the appearance of the fingers, with 'V' representing the whole open hand, and the 'X' two hands crossed. From among the many superstitions associated with numbers, here are a selection of some of the best known. A person born on the first day of the month is said to be lucky, while the number is an unlucky one for a house. The same goes for the second, although this is not true for a woman because the figure 2 has a feminine aura. There are countless examples of the power of three and hence it is held to be a lucky number, while four has a sinister reputation in the Far East and is associated with death. Five is a magical number, while six is of doubtful virtue although those born on this day have the power of prophecy. Seven is another sacred number and held to be a day on which success will greet any special venture. Little regard is paid to eight, while nine is another lucky number and much used in healing and the making of spells – hence every doctor makes us say 'Ninety nine'. Ten has no associations other than the Christian Commandments, while eleven is decidedly unlucky. Twelve has always been something of a puzzle, and perhaps its only reason for being thought more lucky than otherwise is its significance in several religions. Thirteen, of course, is universally held to be unlucky and there is even a term for those who avoid its influence at all costs: *Triskaidekaphobics.* Each nation seemingly has its own reason for fearing the number and the ways and means for avoiding it are legion. Even now – as we see at school – the multiplication of figures goes as far as twelve times twelve and no further. There is no reason why we should not go on to the thirteen times table, but we stop at twelve, and this may be an un-conscious throwback to the early times when thirteen was part of the unknown and therefore full of possibilities – and omens. Finally, numbers are also said to be sexy – one of the oldest superstitions of all claiming that odd numbers are masculine and even numbers are feminine.

NUN

There is a superstition noted in America that it is unlucky to look at a nunnery. At one time all over Britain it used to be held unlucky to see a nun, while fishermen still think it is an ill-omen for their catch to see a nun, clergyman or priest while going to their ships. They should turn back and not go to sea that day. Nuns are also said to be a bad sign if they join the passengers of an aeroplane, although of late groups of three or more nuns seen in the street are said to bode well. In some areas it is said that the good luck may be increased by spitting as the nuns pass!

NUTMEG

The humble nutmeg is said to be lucky, and if one is carried on the person it will protect against rheumatism and boils.

NUTS

Before rice was thrown at weddings, an old superstition claimed that if a bride was presented with a bag of hazel nuts as she left the church by an older married female relative who had already had children, then the young woman herself would be similarly blessed. Rice has replaced hazel nuts, of course, because it is much easier to come by, and maybe the ever increasing population of the world has something to do with the fact that rice grows much more prolifically than nuts! A good crop of nuts in a district is said to presage a larger number of births than usual, and it is believed to be lucky to find a nut with two kernels in a single shell. If one of the nuts is eaten, the other thrown over the left shoulder, and a wish made, it will be granted.

OIL

In these days of ever escalating oil prices, there is probably a lot of commonsense in the Greek tradition that it is an evil omen to spill oil for this portends poverty.

ONION

For centuries it has been believed that an onion hung in a room will keep away disease, and indeed modern research has shown that this superstition does have an element of truth in it, for the onion will attract germs when cut and left open. An onion placed under your pillow is supposed to give you dreams of a lover to be – if you can get to sleep with the aroma, that is! There has long been a tradition among schoolboys that an onion rubbed on the right part of anatomy will prevent the strokes of a cane being felt. Better still, if the onion can be rubbed on the cane, the stick will split at the first blow! Young girls can also use the onion as a method of love divination if they cannot decide between several lovers. If the name of each man is scratched on a separate onion, and these are left in some warm place, whichever sprouts first denotes the strongest love!

ORANGE

The orange is a lucky fruit and when given as a gift between boy and girl is said to help induce love between them. Orange blossom is, of course, a must at any wedding. While most regard it merely as a good luck charm, it is also because of its original association with fertility, an insurance that the bride will have children.

OVEN

Jewish superstition says an oven should never be left empty or you may not have anything to cook or bake in it when you want to. Merely leaving an empty basin or tray in it, though, is sufficient to avoid the repercussions.

OWL

Despite the fact that we often refer to the 'wise old owl', the owl is widely regarded as a bird of ill-omen and many country people say that to see one flying or hear it hooting by daylight will bring misfortune. The origin of the superstitions about the bird obviously emanate from its solitary, night-time existence and mournful cry. Indeed there is a belief that anyone who looks into an owl's nest will become unhappy and morose for the rest of his life. If the bird is seen perching for any length of time on a house, or flaps its wings against a window-pane, it presages a death or sickness therein. Some country people claim that whenever one hoots somebody, somewhere in the district has just died. Perhaps, though, the strangest superstition about the bird comes from Wales, where it is believed that if an owl is heard hooting among houses, it is signifying that an unmarried girl has just lost her virginity! In France, if a pregnant woman hears one, it is an omen that her child will be a girl; while in Germany if one is heard hooting as a child is born, the infant will have an unhappy life. In the Southern States of America there is a popular rhyme still repeated about the owl and its cry:

'When you hear the screech owl, honey, in the sweet gum tree,
It's a sign as sure as you're born a death is bound to be;

171

Unless you put the shovel in the fire mighty quick,
For to conjure that old screech owl, take care the one that's sick.'

OYSTERS

Along the Eastern seaboard of America it is believed that you will always be lucky if you carry a piece of oyster shell in your pocket or handbag. And anyone who eats oysters on St James's Day (August 5) will never go hungry, according to a British superstition.

P

PALM

If you get an irritation in the palm of your right hand you can look forward to receiving some money, while if it happens to the left then you will lose some, according to an almost universal superstition. The one place which is the exception to this rule is America, where the reverse is said to be the case.

PALPITATIONS

According to an old English superstition palpitations of the body – in particular of the heart, the eye, or any of the muscles – are omens of good and bad luck. If they are felt on the right side of the body they are signs of good fortune, but on the left nothing but bad, which, considering this is where the heart is located, is perhaps to be expected!

PANCAKE

The pancake is regarded as a harbinger of luck throughout much of the world, and it has been suggested that this may originate from the fact that it contains so many different kinds of herbs and food stuffs of which a goodly number embrace lucky qualities.

PANCAKE DAY

Shrove Tuesday, or Pancake Day as it is more popularly known, was once blighted with superstitions, but today the sole remaining one in Britain declares that to eat a pancake on this day will ensure a year's good luck and you will not go short of food or money. However, there is a rider that the pancake must be eaten before eight o'clock at night or it will have the reverse effect. The origin of this custom goes back several centuries when the day was observed as a last festivity before the austerity of Lent set in. The word 'Shrove' derived from *shrive*, meaning confess, and it was part of the festivities – apart from eating special pancakes – to hound out prostitutes from their quarters and indulge in the vicious sport of cock 'throwing'. When the authorities finally came to clamp down on such brutal occupations, the people turned to 'tossing' their pancakes instead of the luckless prostitutes and fighting cocks!

PANSIES

Superstition warns against picking these plants when the weather is particularly good, for, says the old belief, this will cause it to rain before long.

PARSLEY

Time has virtually confined to oblivion the superstitions that once used to be observed by country people about this plant – that to give pieces away was to give away your luck, and to transplant it would leave your garden vulnerable to the attacks of the Devil. This latter belief would appear to be of Roman origin, as the Romans used to line their graves with the plant. Some country women still repeat an old saying that to sow parsley will sow babies, while in certain parts of England it was believed that a girl with an unwanted pregnancy could get rid of it by eating lots of parsley! And not so long ago in parts of Britain children were told that they originated in a parsley bed – an interesting variation on the old saying that all infants were found under gooseberry bushes!

PARTING IN THE HAIR

A woman who washes her hair and then finds a parting where there is not normally one, can take this as an omen that she will be a widow some day, according to a European superstition.

PEACH

A sprig of peach blossom placed over the front door will keep all evil spirits away, says a Chinese superstition.

PEACOCK

Like the cat, the peacock is seen as only partly domesticated and basically still an independent creature with a mind of its own. Because of this, and its undeniable beauty and demeanour, it is not hard to see why it has always been looked upon as a royal bird. However, superstition is quite firm that the bird's feathers are unlucky and to have them on display in the house or wear them as adornment, will bring bad luck to the owner and his family. Experts believe this superstition originated in Ancient Greece when the bird was kept in the temples of worship – and to remove one, or even some of its feathers, was a crime punishable by death. Another view maintains that the eye-like pattern on the feathers is symbolic of the Evil Eye, one of the worst forms of bad luck. The bird does, though, have its use as an omen of rain – for when it sets up its harsh calling sound then this indicates an imminent change in the weather.

PEAS

A pea pod found to contain only one pea is said to be an omen of great good fortune. Similarly, if you discover a pod with nine peas, then throw one over your right shoulder and make a wish – it will come true.

PENNY

Always be sure to keep at least one penny coin on your person for luck; and to ensure a safe sea voyage, toss one over the ship's bows as it leaves port to propitiate the gods of the deep.

PHOTOGRAPH

There are still many people around the world who dislike intensely having their photograph taken because they believe it will bring them bad luck. The origin of this superstition lies in the ancient idea that the face mirrors the soul, and to take a picture of it somehow takes away the soul from its owner. Whoever then has this photograph has power over the person concerned, and may if he wishes use it to work evil against him. Although there are many more people who would laugh at the mention of such an idea, they may well feel disinclined to tear up a photograph of a living person for fear of doing them some harm.

PIG

Several of the pig's activities are said to be omens of events to come. For instance, if a pig is seen running about its sty or field with some straw in its mouth then there is a storm on the way. The animal can also signify a death in the family of its owner by making a peculiar whining noise. In Ireland it is said that a pig can actually see the wind – but this sounds rather like another Irish tale! Fishermen are particularly superstitious about the use of the word 'pig' and believe that to say it before casting your line will result in a poor catch. A pig crossing your path is believed to be unlucky in many countries of the world and you would do well to turn your back on it quickly until it has gone. On the other hand, to meet a sow with a litter of piglets bodes well for whatever mission you are on.

PIGEON

The pigeon is another bird widely associated with superstition, and it has been so since the earliest times. A group of pigeons seen sitting huddled together on the top of a roof presage a storm, while if a lone white pigeon perches on the chimney of a house then there will be a death in the occupier's family shortly thereafter. Also a sign of death is a pigeon flying into a house, or suddenly becoming tame after living in the wild. If one of these birds settles on a table in the kitchen then someone is going to fall ill. In some parts of Britain it is also believed that a pillow of pigeon feathers placed under the head will prolong the life of someone who is dying.

PIMPLE
In many parts of Britain, superstition still maintains that a pimple on the tongue is a sign that a person has been telling lies.

PIN
Probably many readers will have heard the superstition about good luck arising from picking up a pin lying on the ground: 'See a pin and let it lie, Sure to rue it by and by'. But there is an older tenet to this – the point should be pointing away from you to make sure of the good fortune. It is said to be bad luck if the point is facing you (though you can always walk round to the other side, of course!) Many folk in the North of England believe it is bad luck to lend a pin to someone, although they would never refuse the request, merely turn their back while the borrower seeks it out for themselves. It is unlucky to use black pins on any item of clothing, similarly any pins used at a funeral are ill-omened if used again. A bride would also be tempting fate if she went to the altar with a pin anywhere on her ensemble – this would be her 'undoing' in later life. Finally, bent pins make ideal offerings at wishing wells to obtain good luck.

'PINCH ME'
The expression 'Pinch me in case I'm dreaming' almost certainly evolved from an old superstition. In times past when men set off on long sea voyages they would often be away for years on end, and their families at home would have little idea of what was happening to them – or even whether they were alive – until they appeared again. When a man who had been at sea suddenly reappeared the initial reaction might well be that he was a ghost. The only way the sailor himself could convince his family to the contrary was to suggest, 'Pinch me and see!' Interestingly, it was still a custom among coastal dwellers in

Britain until quite recently to pinch sailors newly landed from the sea, as it was said to be unlucky if you did not!

PINE CONES

Pine cones are another means of predicting weather, for they will stay open when the omens are fine, but as soon as they close then rain is on the way.

PIPE SMOKERS

Pipe smokers should never light their pipes from a lamp of any kind, for if they do they will have troublesome, even unfaithful, wives, says a French superstition.

PLANTS

In some rural districts of Britain it is still the custom when a person dies to whisper news of this death to their favourite plants, or they too might wither and die. Indeed, to ensure plants' continued health, the superstition says they should have pieces of black material tied around them for a few days.

PLAYING CARDS

Despite their universal popularity as a game, playing cards are treated with suspicion by miners and fishermen who believe it is bad luck to have a set with them when they are working or at sea. A popular name for cards is 'The Devil's Picture Book', which accounts for some of the apprehension about them, just as it helps explain why they are so popular in fortune telling. Another interesting superstition about cards is that thieves rarely steal them when making a haul, for they believe this will turn fortune against them. As to the many beliefs which still persist about particular cards, a selection of these are included in the entry on GAMBLING.

PLOVER

The plover may well be considered a bird of ill-omen, for according to an English superstition if you have no money in your pockets or handbag when you hear the bird's first call of

Spring, then you will be hard up for the rest of the year. It is not a good sign, either, to see a group of seven of them together.

POKER

Many country people insist that the poker and tongs should never be put together at the same side of the fireplace or else there will be a quarrel between the husband and wife. There is also an old belief that a fire that will not draw can be remedied by placing the poker upright directly in front of the grate, forming a cross-shape. This would seem actually to work, if the poker is first placed in the glowing embers so that it gets warm: when it is put in front of the grate its heat will draw down a draught from the chimney and so bring the fire to life.

POINTING

Pointing at anything has always been considered unlucky, apart from being bad mannered, and it is especially ill-omened to point at a ship leaving harbour (for fear it will sink) and at anything in the heavens (in case you offend the gods).

POODLE

For some years there was an extraordinary superstition heard in parts of Germany that a black poodle was to be seen on the graves of priests and clergymen who had somehow failed in their calling or actually broken their vows. Why the animal should have been a poodle, or what its presence resulted in, was never explained.

POPPY

The poppy is thought to be an ill-omened flower in much of Britain, and many school children have heard of the belief that they may go blind (although only temporarily) if they stare into the very centre of one. It is also said to be an unlucky flower to bring indoors because it can cause illness. (This belief is no doubt based on the well-known narcotic properties of some varieties of the plant.) In its favour, though, the plant has now acquired a somewhat happier reputation as a symbol or remembrance for men killed during World War One, when artificial poppies are sold each year to raise money for charity on 'Remembrance Day'.

PORPOISE
Sailors believe that porpoises are luck-bringers and, when seen leaping and chasing one another in the vicinity of a ship, a good omen for the voyage. If they are viewed going in a northerly direction this is a sign of good weather, while to the south presages a storm.

PORTRAIT
Like the mirror superstition, if a portrait or picture of someone falls from a shelf or from its hanging on the wall for no apparent reason, this is said to be an omen that the person will die shortly thereafter. The Americans believe it is very unlucky to turn a portrait upside down, for this will bring disaster to the person concerned. The Dutch, for their part, believe that a picture of a sweetheart stuck to the dashboard of a car will protect the driver from misfortune.

POTATOES
A great many people still subscribe to the old superstition that the best cure for rheumatism is to carry a potato in your coat or trouser pocket. It should, though, be a new one that has been kept until it has turned black and is as hard as wood. In many parts of Europe it is said that potatoes should never be planted on Good Friday, for they will fail to grow, and to ensure a good crop, every member of the family should taste the first bunch of new potatoes pulled from the ground. Always remember, too, to make a wish when eating new potatoes for the first time. In America there is a further superstition that if a pan of potatoes boils dry, this is an omen of rain.

PRAM
Superstition claims that it is very unlucky to bring a new pram or baby carriage into a house before the arrival of the

infant. This idea is based on the ancient tradition that it challenges the fates by assuming that everything will go according to plan with the birth. It is interesting to note, too, that this superstition has derived directly from the older one that it was an ill-omen to bring a cradle into a house before the birth of a child.

PRECIOUS STONES

Precious stones are discussed in detail elsewhere in the book, but two general superstitions about them might just be mentioned here. Firstly, that all such stones put into honey become more brilliant; and, secondly, that a setting consisting of diamonds, sapphires and loadstones will make a man invincible and a woman quite irresistible!

PREGNANCY

There are superstitions associated with pregnancy which would appear to date from centuries gone by, when evil spirits were believed to accompany women at this time. Apart from the natural hazards which any woman faced, the rest of society believed that her touch carried misfortune and so she was barred from dealing with food or livestock. (A similar belief is also held in Japan and among North American Indians about a woman at the time of her menstruation.) In some European countries it is said to be unlucky for a woman to spin (though not knit or sew) during the time of her pregnancy, as this will doom her child to hanging; while in Britain country people say it is an ill-omen for her to step over a grave as the baby will die prematurely. In several countries women are told that to wear appropriate colours during their pregnancy will determine their baby's sex – viz. blue if she wants a boy and pink for a girl. An associated idea is that a healthy baby will be guaranteed if the child is produced as a result of sexual intercourse at midday when the sun is at its height; and to ensure an intelligent child, the mother-to-be should engross herself in scholarly books. A Scandinavian superstition says that a pregnant woman who

181

drinks from a cracked cup will have a child with a hare-lip; while should she step over a cat she will give birth to a hermaphrodite. Jewish superstition says that a pregnant woman who has been frightened by an animal or insect should not touch her face, or she runs the risk that her child will be marked in some way. There is an old German superstition that a pregnant woman should never look at a dead body or she will give birth to a still-born child. Nor should she look directly at the moon or her child will be 'moon struck'. The Germans also say that a mother can avoid a premature birth by always carrying one of her husband's socks with her as a safeguard. There is still a surviving superstition in certain of the middle European countries, including Hungary and Czechoslovakia, that if a woman who has just become pregnant wishes to have a baby boy she puts poppy seeds on the window sill of her house, while if she wants a girl she places sugar there. In Britain a pregnant woman who steals anything runs the risk of her child growing up to be a thief; and in America if a pregnant woman looks for any length of time into an empty sack, then her child will have to suffer hunger. American superstition also says that if an unborn child kicks on the right side of the womb this is a sign that it is a boy; while on the left it is a girl. The Welsh, though, believe they have an infallible way of determining the sex of an unborn child. It requires a shoulder of mutton which has been completely cleaned and then held before a fire until the blade bone is thoroughly scorched. The man of the house should then force a hole through this blade with his thumb and pass a small length of string through it, which can be used to hang the shoulder over the back door. Then whoever first enters the house under the bone – other than a member of the family – will indicate by their sex whether the child will be boy or girl. Finally, perhaps space should be made for the most bizarre and unlikely of all pregnancy superstitions – which does apparently still get repeated in parts of the Mediterranean – that if a pregnant woman inadvertently swallows the egg of an octopus while she is bathing she will give birth to an octopus and not a child!

PREGNANCY (MALE)

This heading is not a misprint – but refers to the age-old superstition that a man suffers in unison with his wife during the birth of their child. The belief is of great antiquity and is to be found among the customs of people all over the world, and indeed in some African groups the men actually take to their beds for much of the nine-month period while the women go about their normal tasks until only hours before the actual birth. The origin of this superstition is believed to be that men are stronger and cleverer than women and thus better able to fight the evil spirits who prey on unborn children. Sympathy pains are also well known in this context and tales of men suffering from stomach upsets during their wife's pregnancy are now explained by psychological means rather than superstitious ones. Some folk will tell you, though, that if a man develops unexpected toothache this is a sign that his wife is pregnant. The pains which the man is said to suffer while the birth is actually taking place are claimed in some northern areas of England to be a useful method of locating the father of an illegitimate child when the mother will not reveal his name. Merely look for a man confined to his bed with pains of the stomach and there you have your culprit, says the superstition!

PRIESTS

There is a strange and quite inexplicable belief in France that priests are more liable to be struck by lightning than other folk. In America it is said that to dream of a priest is an omen of ill-luck.

PRIMROSES

The Welsh believe that the Primrose brings bad luck if it blooms in June, and many other rural folk insist that a gift of primroses should always be a very full bunch. Just one or two of the flowers given as a present or taken into the house will bring misfortune to the recipient, and particularly imperil any poultry he may have. The flowers are, though, good as a protection against evil spirits when used in abundance, and have served in many folk cures, particularly for insomnia.

R

RABBIT

In many parts of Britain it is believed that to say the words 'white rabbits' very quickly three times on the first day of the month will ensure that you enjoy good luck for the rest of that month. Along several coasts fishermen say it is unlucky to mention the word 'rabbit' before going to sea, and if a reference to a rabbit is unavoidable then some other word should be substituted. Some miners believe that to see a pure white rabbit while on the way to the pit is an omen of disaster, while in parts of England, if a white rabbit is seen near houses, it is said to presage a death in one of them. Any rabbit running up a street of houses heralds a fire in one of them, just as to see or kill a black rabbit is very ominous. Superstitions about the rabbit seem to go back to very early times, when rabbits were regarded as symbolic of the moon god because of the way they played at night time. The foot of a rabbit is, though, a very well known *good* luck charm around the world, particularly in America, and has its origin in the fact that young rabbits are born with their eyes open and thus are able to 'see off' evil from their first moments. (Another explanation that has been offered is that, as the creature is such a prolific breeder, it possesses an extraordinary creative power and has thus become associated with prosperity and success.) The Easter Rabbit is another American good luck symbol, and children are told that it is he who brings their Easter Eggs. There are many parents who believe a baby will be protected by brushing it with a rabbit's foot – preferably the left hind one – soon after its birth, while it is a common sight to see one of these items hanging above a child's cot or pram to protect it from harm. Gardeners believe a rabbit's foot will make fruit trees flourish especially well when one is used to transfer pollen, and many a country poacher believes he will never be caught with one in his pocket. Naturally, it is very bad luck indeed to lose a rabbit's foot.

RAIN

Throughout this book are to be found many activities of animals and birds which are believed to be omens of approaching rain, and not a few of these are still held in high esteem by country folk everywhere. These folk also see rain portents in themselves when their corns or rheumatism ache, and indeed medical science has proved that changes in the weather *can* affect those who suffer from these complaints. There is also a weather prophecy concerning St Swithin's Day, July 15, that if it rains on that day then it will continue to do so for the next forty days. The origin of the superstition concerns the attempts of some monks at Winchester to dig up the body of St Swithin from its rather unsuitable resting place by the cathedral door (which the Saint had himself designated) and place it in a more reverent position. When work began on July 15 it started to rain and continued so for forty days, making the transference impossible – and the belief rapidly grew among the monks that the humble Saint had himself sent the rain as he wished to remain where he was. Throughout Europe there is a superstition that rain can be made to fall by dipping a holy relic such as the image of a saint or a crucifix into a river or lake. In Britain the same objective may be achieved by burning ferns, although in some districts heather will do just as well. Apart from the fact that it would obviously put a dampener on the proceedings, rain falling on a bride and groom as they leave the church following their wedding is said to presage an unhappy future for them, or else they will have a lot of children! There is also a rather delightful superstition to relieve the sombre occasion of a funeral, for if it should rain, say the people of Cornwall, this is an indication that the soul of the departed has safely reached heaven. Many old country people claim that rain water is a good cure for sore eyes, and that money washed in this water can never be stolen. The Welsh also claim that a baby bathed in rain water will talk sooner than its fellows. There is a somewhat bizarre superstition in rural England for stopping rain – a first born child should be sent out into it and told to strip naked and stand on his head! And children themselves have their own charm to put a stop to wet weather by simply chanting the following lines over and over again:

> 'Rain, rain go away,
> Come again another day.'

The more mischievous will substitute 'another day' with the words 'on mother's washing day'!

RAINBOW
The old superstition that there is a crock of gold to be found at the end of the rainbow is one that delights us from our childhood – despite the fact that we can never find the end! The beauty of the rainbow has, though, been a source of pleasure, and by implication good fortune, to mankind from the earliest times, although in Scandinavian mythology it is treated with a certain reservation because it is believed to be a path leading to the gods along which the souls of children particularly are called. Naturally the appearance of one was thought to be an omen that youngsters in the vicinity were about to die. Throughout the rest of Europe, though, the rainbow is said to be a good luck sign (make a wish when you see one) and a weather omen. For example, if one is seen in the morning then the following day will be wet, while if it appears in the afternoon the next day will be fine. The Irish also believe that if a rainbow is seen on a Saturday then the whole of the following

week will be stormy. Further, a rainbow in the west indicates there will be more rain, while if it is the east everything will soon be fine.

RAILWAY

There is a superstition still to be found in Wales and parts of England that ill-fortune will follow if you talk while passing under a railway bridge. This apparently applies if you are in a train or walking beneath the bridge at a station. The superstition may well have its origin in the fear of witchcraft and the belief that when you are in any way enclosed, except at home, you are in peril from witches who might lurk in the arch of the bridge.

RAKE

If a garden rake accidentally falls over with its prongs pointing upwards, old gardeners in Britain say this is an omen that there will be heavy rain the next day.

RATS

The superstition that if rats desert a ship, particularly while it is still in port, then it is an omen of disaster, is still found all over the world, although the creatures are much less common nowadays than they used to be. (On the other hand if rats go on board a new vessel this is a very good sign.) The origin of the belief lies in the old idea that rats contained the souls of men and were therefore ominous creatures whose actions should be noted and acted upon. Rats leaving a house for no apparent reason are said to presage its collapse, while if they suddenly come into the building then someone in the family is going to die. Should these creatures begin chewing the furnishings – particularly those in a bedroom – this is also an omen of death. There were many old charms and potions for ridding property of unwanted rats, but these seem to have fallen into disuse with the introduction of modern pesticides, although you might like to try the following verse, recited by old people in the North of England and Scotland, when all else has failed:

> 'Rats and mice,
> Leave this poor person's house,
> Go on away over to the mill
> And there you'll all get your fill.'

There is also a superstition noted around the world that if a child loses a tooth and it is thrown away with an appeal to the rats to 'send a stronger one' (the rat has, of course, enormously strong teeth), then the infant's adult teeth will grow all the tougher.

RAVEN

The raven is said to be the most prophetic of birds, with knowledge of both private and public misfortune; we still speak of having 'the foresight of a raven'. The American Indians call it the 'Messenger of Death'. Perhaps the most famous superstition associated with it is that if the famous ravens living in the Tower of London should be lost or fly away, then the reigning royal family will die and Britain itself will fall. The bird is indeed widely regarded as a creature of ill omen, and if one is heard croaking over a house then there will be sickness or death inside before long. An explanation has been ventured that the bird has a particularly acute sense of smell and can discern the odour of decay from some considerable distance. If the bird actually flies about the chimney croaking when someone lies ill inside, then that person's fate is sealed. Scottish deerstalkers, however, believe it bodes well for the hunt to hear one before setting out. Ravens facing the direction of a clouded sun are said to presage hot weather, while if they are seen busy preening themselves, there is rain on the way. And if they are seen flying towards each other then this is an omen of war.

RAZOR

It is unlucky to give a friend or relative a razor as this may 'cut' the friendship, and in Europe and America to find a razor is an omen of bad luck and disappointment.

RECOGNITION

To have the feeling that you know someone as they are approaching you, and then find you are mistaken when they get close, has an ominous explanation in British superstition. Such an experience is said to be an omen that the person you imagined the stranger to be will shortly die.

'RED HOT POKER'

The unmistakable flower known in Britain as the 'red hot poker', which looks exactly like its description, is an ominous plant in local tradition. Should one of these bloom twice in a year it is a sign of a death in the household.

RED SKIES

Red skies are said to be omens of forthcoming weather, according to an old verse which most of us learn as children and carry through our lives, often being made aware of how accurate it is:

> 'Red sky at night is the shepherd's delight
> Red sky in the morning is the shepherd's warning.'

The omens are likely to prove correct because of the following simple meteorological reasons: in Britain, with its prevailing winds from the west, if, as the sun sets in the west, the air is clear of moisture, the light will take on a red hue which is reflected on the clouds in the east – that is, on those that have already passed over us and can no longer affect us. In the morning the reverse is true, for the sun has changed its position and the light now falls on the clouds in the west, which are coming towards us. So if the red hue is to be seen watch out for rain! You may be comforted if this happens by another superstition that 'Rain at seven means fine at eleven.'

REED

The reed is said to be ill-omened if planted within the confines of a house, for it will speedily lead to a death, according to a British superstition.

REMARRIAGE

The Germans have a delightful belief that at the remarriage of a widower, the ghost of his former wife will attend the wedding and if she approves of the match will do no harm to the company.

RHEUMATISM

Superstition has provided an almost never-ending list of alleged cures for rheumatics, ranging from carrying in the pocket a potato or the right foot of a hare – to crawling through a gap in a bramble bush or having the affected joint stung by bees! Green peppers sliced into pieces and put under the finger nails are said to give off an odour which will drive the 'spirit' of rheumatism away, while the Welsh believe that the only way to relieve a sufferer is to strip him naked and bury him up to the neck in a churchyard for two hours at a time. The process must then be repeated daily until the cure is effected! For their part, the Americans believe in red string tied around the part of the body, while cotton thread is particularly good for ankles.

RIBBON

A red ribbon tied around a girl's head is said to be lucky, and to protect the wearer from evil spirits, according to a German superstition; while in Britain a silk ribbon around the throat will combat disease. In the East, though, coloured ribbons should not be worn on the head at night for they attract the Evil Eye.

'RINGING IN THE EARS'

The sudden sensation of ringing in the ears, according to certain superstitions, is an omen that death is somewhere near. It does not necessarily portend the death of the person concerned, though, or even of someone in his or her family, but in America particularly it is thought that the victim will live within the distance 'a small stone might be thrown'. A more cheerful belief, held in Britain and Europe, is that the sound indicates someone is talking about you – with praise if the ringing is in the right ear, or with annoyance if in the left. Further there is an English rhyme which actually defines who the person is:

> 'Left your mother,
> Right your lover.'

ROBIN
Superstition maintains that the robin received its famous red breast when it tried to pull the thorns from the bloodied crown on Christ's head as He hung on the cross. Naturally enough it is therefore the direst bad luck to kill or cage one of these birds ('A Robin Redbreast in a cage, puts all Heaven in a rage' says William Blakes's poem) and there is a widespread belief that if you do, the hand which actually did the killing will always shake thereafter. The Irish believe that killing a robin will cause a large lump to form on your right hand which will prevent you from working, while in Yorkshire if the person concerned owns a cow it will yield blood-coloured milk. Indeed, to harm the bird in any way is ill-omened, and should you break one of its wings the same will happen to your arm, and so on – while to break one of its eggs will lead to something valuable of your own being smashed. The robin is an omen of death if it flies through an open window into a house, and should one tap on the window pane of a room where a person lies ill, the sufferer is going to die. The bird also serves as a weather omen: if you see one sheltering in the branches of a tree or hedge then rain is on the way, while if it sits on an open branch chirping nervously, however gloomy or even wet it may be at the time, fine weather is imminent. Although to rob any bird's nest is an act of cruelty, to take eggs from a robin's is to court particular misfortune, many country folk believe. Even cats, it is said, respect the sanctity of the bird. Finally, when you see the first robin of the year, make a wish – but quickly, for if the bird flies away before you have decided what you want then you can expect no good luck in the next twelve months.

ROOK

It is an ill-omen if rooks leave an area where they have been settled, and it can mean some misfortune to the owners of the land: even that no heir will be born to the family. By contrast, in several European countries the rook is regarded solely as a harbinger of good luck, and prosperity and health will be enjoyed by anyone on whose land a group of these birds settle. The birds are believed to be able to sense when a tree in which they are nesting is about to fall – though there may be no visible evidence – and hence provide an omen when they suddenly move to another. Country folk also claim that if rooks build their nests high up in trees then the next summer will be fine, while if they are low down watch out for wet, cold weather. And if they perch close together at any time, facing the wind, then a storm is on the way.

ROSE

If while someone is holding a rose the petals fall, leaving only the stem, it is believed to be an omen that the person will shortly die. It is also said to be unlucky to scatter rose leaves on the ground. If roses bloom in the autumn then this is a sign that misfortune of some kind will strike in the following year. Like many of our modern superstitions, those associated with roses have come down to us from the Romans, who believed that the rose could protect the dead from evil spirits and so decorated their tombs with the flower. Not all beliefs about the rose are grim, though, for it can be used as a means of love divination by a young girl. If on Midsummer Eve she wraps a rose carefully away in a piece of clean white paper and keeps it until Christmas Day, and it is then found to be still intact, she can wear it in her buttonhole, and whichever young man first admires it will become her husband.

ROSEMARY

Rosemary has by ancient tradition a protective barrier against witchcraft when allowed to grow near the door of a house, and in Europe it is also an essential ingredient in various rituals for driving out suspected witches. In the North of England there is a superstition that a sprig of rosemary worn in the buttonhole will give the wearer success in all his tasks, and particularly help his memory. Among the more curious superstitions about the plant are: that it will only grow where a woman is head of the household (either literally or by domination); that spoons made of the wood cause even the most insipid food to taste good (just as combs made of it will make hair grow, according to the French); and that a small amount of crushed rosemary dropped into a barrel of beer will prevent all who drink it from getting drunk!

ROYALTY

Because kings and queens were once regarded as semi-divine, a number of superstitions grew up around the monarch, one or two of which are still repeated today. For instance, whenever a monarch dies it is said there will be a period of bad weather known as the 'Royal Storm'. The actual death of a king or queen is said to be forecast by the failure of the ash tree to disperse a crop of its winged seeds.

'RUE THE DAY'

The expression by one person to another that they might 'rue the day' they committed some misdemeanour, developed from the superstition that the rue plant symbolized sorrow and repentance. Once people in Britain would throw a handful of the herb at someone who had wronged them, with the curse, 'May you rue this day as long as you live'. Apart from this, rue is said to possess curative properties, particularly for the eyes; and, perhaps strangely in view of the above association, a sprig of it worn in the buttonhole is believed in many places to keep off evil spells!

RUSHES

The rush is said to be a lucky plant with special healing and protective powers, and in many parts of the British Isles it is believed to be a good omen to find one with a green top.

RUST

Although you may find it annoying if your keys or your knives get continually rusty, take comfort from the old superstition that this means somebody, somewhere is laying up money which you will one day inherit!

S

SAGE

Sage is believed in many parts of England to be a lucky plant, and able to impart wisdom and to strengthen the memory. For years, too, it was said that if sage grew profusely in any garden then a woman of strong will lived there – which probably accounts for why so many male gardeners always restrict its growth to one small corner of the kitchen garden! The plant is also said to be an omen of health, and if a sprig is hung in the kitchen when a member of the family goes off on a journey, then as long as it does not droop or waste then the absent person is happy and well. In many countries it is said that to eat sage in May is to ensure long life, and similarly widespread is the superstition that if the plant's flowers are allowed to bloom then ill-luck will strike the family in whose garden it grows.

SAILING

Several of the superstitions which beset seamen of old have been adopted by today's amateur sailors and yachtsmen, such as tossing a coin into the waves during a storm to appease the sea gods, and avoiding the colour green for any vessel. A coin is still often placed under the mast of a new boat for luck, and sailors in many countries would not dream of removing the mast while their boats are laid up for the winter without leaving a silver piece in its place. Many yachtsmen believe it is better to finish in second or third place in any heat of a competition, to ensure themselves the luck to finish first in the final!

SAILORS

Because of the very nature of their perilous profession, it is no surprise to find sailors beset with superstitions, and though modern technology has made most sea journeys comparatively safe nowadays, no one has quite been able to drive away all the old beliefs. The spirits of the deep have since time immemorial been the sailor's enemy, and seamen in the East particularly still pay regard to this by painting huge eyes on their boats to watch out for these terrors. In the West we still unconsciously propitiate these gods when we launch a new boat by breaking a bottle of champagne over the bows. In times gone by it was the custom to smear human blood over the prow so that as it dipped into the water it presented a 'sacrifice' to the gods – and this later became red wine. Perhaps no one needs reminding of the bad luck which is supposed to attach itself to a boat on which the launching bottle does not break at the first attempt. Sailors everywhere also still believe the superstition about rats leaving a sinking ship, for they are well aware that the rat hates to be wet, so if he is leaving a vessel it may well be leaking. A cat is believed to be lucky by sailors – particularly a black one – and no doubt useful in catching rats, too. However, a cat that becomes frisky at sea is said to 'have the wind in her tail' and to be an omen that there is a storm on the way. Seamen also believe bad luck will attach itself to any ship on which a dead person is carried, and this originally prompted the practice of committing the body of someone who had died at sea to the waves – apart from the obvious health hazards a decaying corpse represents. Some old sailors also believe that a body on board a ship will slow down its progress, just as they say to lose a bucket or mop overboard is an ill-omen. Misfortune has apparently often embraced ships which have had their names changed, and sailors are distrustful of putting to sea in such vessels. Equally most men of the sea do not like sailing on a Friday, nor do they like crossing any stretch of sea where a wreck has occurred in case they are haunted by the ghosts of the sailors who were drowned there. There is, of course, a popular superstition among 'landlubbers' – particularly girls and women – that to touch the collar of a sailor will bring good luck, and many a seaman has drunk long and well to satisfy such fortune-seeking! One of the most curious superstitions says that it is bad luck to strike a glass tumbler in such a way that it makes a ringing sound, for this foreshadows the drowning of a sailor. And in France it is believed that if a sailor drowns at sea, his wife will hear the sound of dripping water near her bed. On many cargo and mercantile boats, a woman on board is said to be an evil omen, and it is perhaps understandable that a lone female among a hot-blooded crew at sea for weeks on end might engender passions that would lead to trouble among the crew. In contrast to this, sailors consider that a child born on a ship is an omen of good luck – presumably a woman in this condition constitutes no sexual problems to the men! Any children on board a vessel are believed to be good omens. Sailors think it is unlucky to step on board a ship left foot first – and to leave it in the same way; and it is interesting to note that even the Navy have paid due regard to sea superstition by arranging for all salutes to be given in odd numbers. Whistling on board a ship is believed to be unlucky, for it can bring on a storm, although it *is* permitted when a sailing ship is becalmed as this is said to 'whistle up the wind'. (The popular British seaside pub name 'The Pig and Whistle' actually owes its origin to this superstition, for once back on land the sailor felt quite safe in whistling; and similarly, while the use of the word 'pig' at sea was said to presage disaster, no such problem existed on land!) The particular delight which sailors have in wearing tattoos has its origins in superstition too, in the belief that such markings warded off disaster and evil spirits. It is for this reason that lucky symbols are so popular. In the American Navy it is claimed that a pig and a cockerel tattooed on the left instep protects a man against drowning. Perhaps the most bizarre superstitions among sailors are that tattoos are a safeguard against catching venereal disease, and that a seaman can ensure his safety at sea before going on a voyage, by touching his wife or girl friend's pudenda for luck – a custom known as 'touching the bun'.

ST CHRISTOPHER MEDALS

These medallions have become increasingly popular in recent years, particularly for hanging in motor vehicles, for St Christopher is said to have been the patron saint of travellers and as such will protect from danger all those on the road. However, there is a real doubt among historians and ecclesiastical scholars as to whether St Christopher ever really existed.

SALT

Salt is of course famous in superstition, and few readers will not have heard the claim that bad luck will fall on anyone who, after spilling some salt, does not take a pinch and throw it over their left shoulder. Although this ritual is familiar throughout the world, its origin is obscure and it seems most likely to have begun because salt was regarded by the ancients as a sacred and precious commodity – it was not only essential, but often very difficult to obtain. Some authorities believe the superstition may have something to do with the fact that Judas allegedly spilt salt during the Last Supper, so by throwing some grains over the shoulder one is insuring oneself against misfortune. Others say that as evil spirits lurk on the left side, this action will blind their eyes and prevent them working evil. (Interestingly, in Denmark it is lucky to spill salt as long as it is dry, only wet salt is unlucky!) In any event, salt has a special place in superstition and many peoples present a new born baby with a small amount of salt to ensure that it wants for nothing in life. (The salt is further believed to protect the child from witches and evil spirits at this vulnerable period of its life, because these creatures are compelled to count every grain before they can work harm, and naturally never have enough time to complete the task!) There are also still people in Britain and Europe who always keep a small quantity of salt on their person to ensure that all their dealings are successful, and carry a pinch in their hand when out at night to protect them in the dark. It is further said to bring bad luck to a person to put salt on his plate for him – each diner must help himself. And to knock over a salt sellar is an omen that one of your friendships is about to be broken – the reason for this being that because of its lasting quality, salt is seen as a symbol of friendship. In several places in Europe it is still the tradition to sprinkle the steps of a new house with salt to ward off evil spirits, or to take in a small quantity of the stuff as the first item brought into a house by those moving in. Salt is naturally often associated with tears, and in America for instance it is said that every grain spilt means a day of sorrow. It is possible, though, to avoid crying after spilling salt – the grains must be collected up and thrown over the kitchen stove (rather than the left shoulder) to dry up the tears! In many places one can still hear the old verse, 'Help me to salt, help me to sorrow,' and in Russia and Italy in particular salt is never directly offered by one friend to another, or by a host to welcome a guest, for fear of bringing down misfortune. Salt can be used to divine the future if you have a strong nerve. On Christmas Eve leave a little pile of salt on the table, and if the next morning it is unchanged, then the future looks good. Should some have melted, though, this is said to be a death omen. Finally, there is a rather unusual superstition in Germany that if a girl forgets to put out the salt sellar while she is laying the table for dinner, this is a sign that she is no longer a virgin!

SANDALS

The Japanese believe it is unlucky to put new sandals on for the first time after five o'clock in the afternoon.

SATURDAY

There is a quaint belief about Saturday to be found in most European countries, that the sun always shines on this day – if only for a few moments. Unfortunately, though, this is almost impossible to substantiate! In Ireland it is said that a rainbow seen on a Saturday will be followed by a week of wet weather, while the Scots claim that anyone born on Saturday has the power to see ghosts. There are many rural districts throughout Europe where it is believed to bode ill to change a job on Saturday – or Sunday for that matter – and there is an old English rhyme which highlights this: 'Saturday servants never stay, Sunday servants run away'. In India it is an unlucky day because it is dedicated to Sani, the God of misfortune. Finally, though, Saturday is a good day to relate to your family or friends any pleasant dream that you may have had on Friday night – for if you do the dream will come true.

SCHOOL

A still common superstition in America says that if you drop your books while on the way to school or college, it is an omen that you are going to make mistakes in your lessons.

SCIATICA

Aside from some complex rituals which have now long since died out, country people still place great faith in carrying either the knuckle bone of a leg of mutton or a slice of raw potato as a preventive and curative for sciatica.

SCISSORS

A very widespread superstition says that it is bad luck to pick up a pair of scissors you have dropped – it is advizable to have someone else do it for you, or at least to step on them gently before picking them up. Should you be alone, however, and unable to summon assistance, the bad luck can be averted by rubbing the scissors in your hands until they are warm before using them to cut again. Scissors derive their power in superstition from the ancient tradition that steel is sacred and anything sharp may 'cut' your luck. If a pair of scissors fall and one of the blades pierces the ground then this is a death omen, while if they should break in half this is a sign of a great

200

disappointment to come. Dressmakers in particular believe it is an ill-omen to drop a pair of scissors as this presages an order for a funeral outfit. Many folk maintain it is bad luck to accept a present of a pair of scissors without giving a small coin in return to the donor. There is also a curious superstition in Africa that to open and close a pair of scissors during a wedding feast will render the bridegroom impotent.

SEA

Though most of the omens and superstitions relating to the sea have been classified under other more specific headings, it should perhaps be noted here that if while on land you hear the sound of the sea coming from the west, this is an omen that the weather is going to turn fine and continue to be good for some time to come. To kill one of those birds of the sea, the seagull, is believed to be unlucky, for they are said to contain the souls of dead sailors and those who know the sea claim that the sight of three seagulls flying overhead in a distinct group is an omen of death. If a seagull flies against the window of a house, then a member of the family who is at sea is in danger; and of course to see seagulls far inland is a sign of bad weather on the ocean. The petrel is an unlucky bird, said to presage storms, and hence its nickname of 'Storm Petrel'. The albatross, though, is a decidedly lucky omen when it is seen, bringing in its wake strong winds and fine weather – though, of course, to kill one is among the most unlucky things any seaman can do. Porpoises have become regarded as weather omens by the sailors of many nations, and it is said that if a school of them play near a ship then a terrible storm is on the way. On the other hand, if they appear while a storm is raging, then the end of the bad weather is not far off. Mention should also be made of Davy Jones, who is an important figure in sea superstitions, and is said to be a malignant spirit who has power over the sea itself – hence the nautical phrase for the sea as 'Davy Jones' Locker'. Finally, the Welsh believe that a spoonful of sea water taken each morning will help you live to a venerable age.

SEAWEED

Seaweed has for centuries been regarded as an excellent weather omen when hung in the porch of a house. If the weather is going to be dry and sunny it will shrivel up, but when wet weather is on the way it will swell up and feel damp to the touch. Many British coastal dwellers also say that dried seaweed kept in the house will drive away evil spirits and prevent the building ever catching on fire.

SELLING

Many rural trades-people throughout Europe believe that one of the coins given by the first person to make a purchase in the morning should be returned, to ensure a successful day's selling. In these times of rising inflation, however, the practice seems to have been varied so that the trader is merely required to give change for this first purchase. Spitting on the first money received each day is also a good luck omen.

SEVEN

The figure seven has numerous superstitions associated with it and is regarded as both a mystic and lucky number. The origin lies in the dim distant past and, of course, the creation of the world itself was said to have taken seven days: indeed one need only turn to the Old Testament to find numerous references to its importance. In everyday life, a seventh child is said to be lucky, while the seventh son of a seventh son will not only be doubly blessed but can cure disease and – according to the Scots – is possessed of second sight and has the ability to tell the future. There is also a widespread belief that if a person's birth date is divisible by seven then he will be lucky. In Britain there is a quaint superstition that seems to lend some weight to that phrase about the 'Seven Year Itch', for there are people who claim that every seven years a person's personality undergoes a complete change. This superstition is related to the expression often used by parents about troublesome offspring, that he or she will change when they are older – for example the difficult child of seven becoming a model fourteen-year-old! Interestingly, while this book was being written, the seventh day of the seventh month of the seventy-seventh year of the century took place, with a number of circumstances occurring which are worth recording. Aside from the quite considerable number of people who celebrated their seventy-seventh birthday on that day (including a Mrs Elizabeth Severn of Yorkshire), a child was born in Adelaide, Australia at 7.7 a.m. weighing exactly 7lb 7ozs. At lunchtime, the Financial Index in London was down 7.7, while a cricket enthusiast noted that the test match between England and Australia commenced on what was the seventy-seventh day of the Australians tour and in the seventy-seventh over, batsman K. D. Walters took his score to 77 and his partner was R. W. Marsh – batting number seven. And just to top the day off, the highest temperature recorded in London was 77 degrees Fahrenheit!

SEWING
   It is believed to be bad luck to sew anything on to a garment you are wearing, or to sew something new on to anything old. In Britain it is claimed that if a thread knots while it is being used, then the seamstress will shortly quarrel with someone; while in America if a seamstress loses her thimble then this will bring very good luck to the person on whose garment she was working – unless it was her own, of course, and then the omens are not so good. Around the Mediterranean there are old women who say that if the thread on the needle gets tangled while a garment is being mended, this will give health and prosperity to the owner.

SEX
   The fact that only in recent years has sex ceased to be a taboo subject and at last become openly discussed between the young and old, is the obvious reason why most of the extra-ordinary superstitions which surround the topic have survived for so long. Perhaps the most widely quoted of all such ideas is that men with large hands and feet have enormous penises, while

a woman with a generous mouth is sure to have a big vagina. Equally widely held is the belief that Latin men and those from hot countries have more sexual potency because of the generative power of the sun. Similarly, men whose bodies are covered in hair are more vital than those who are not. To such superstitions can be added the idea that too much sex weakens the heart and leads to blindness, just as masturbation is harmful. Interestingly, to these old myths have been added some peculiarly modern superstitions such as that sun lamps arouse sexual passion, that girls with contact lenses cannot take oral contraceptive pills, and that the wedding ceremony confers immunity to venereal disease! America, in particular, has become the home of some of the strangest sex superstitions to be found anywhere. For instance, blondes are said to be dumb but much more eager for sex than brunettes – although redheads have a still greater enthusiasm. Among men it is said that sex during a woman's period can lead to baldness, even impotence. Girls, for their part, have an idea that a Coca Cola douche will prevent pregnancy – apparently a modern variation on the old idea of a hot bath and lashings of gin. No doubt, though, as long as men and women enjoy sex, superstitions of one kind or another will manage to attach themselves to the act.

SHADOW

The idea that a shadow is somehow a part of a person has persisted in many places, and in most of these it is considered unlucky to walk on one – particularly to the owner of the shadow. In certain mountainous regions it is said to be a death omen if stones or pebbles fall on a person's shadow, while in parts of Europe where the shadow is seen as a manifestation of the owner's soul, to step on one is one of the worst insults that can be offered. In Wales if anyone sitting around the fireplace on Christmas Day casts a shadow with no head, it is said they will die during the coming year.

SHAKING HANDS

If by chance you should shake hands twice with someone before parting company, do so once more before leaving, because only this way can you avoid the ill-luck associated with carrying out this act more than once.

SHARKS

Sharks persistently following a ship – particularly in a group of three – are said to be an omen that there will be a death on board the vessel before long. The shark is credited by superstitious sailors with being able to 'scent' death, although a more likely explanation nowadays of the presence of these creatures is their hope that waste food of some kind will be dumped from the ship's galley. There is actually a stronger case for a creature being able to sense death in the instance of a vulture hovering over a desert traveller.

SHEEP

There are a number of superstitions associated with sheep which are described elsewhere, but to these should be added the widely held conviction that it is lucky to meet a flock of sheep when on a journey – even though they may hold you up for a while! The reason for attaching luck to this sight probably dates back to the times when people lived in scattered settlements without any real communication between one another, so that when a shepherd came into the view of a village the people could be sure of meat for their tables – surely a good sign! (The same argument also applies to the good luck associated with meeting a herd of cows on the road.) Many old shepherds throughout Europe carry a small bone from the head of a sheep in their pockets, as they believe this to be a harbinger of good luck, and a lot of these men also cling to an old tradition that on Christmas morning sheep bow three times to the east. This is obviously an association with the Christian idea of the 'Lamb of God', and accounts for the general good luck accorded to sheep. Some shepherds even continue to be buried with a tuft of wool in their coffins, so that on Judgement Day they may be excused attendance before God because no shepherd would leave his flock. Sheep are also said to be weather omens, and when they lie down on the grass then it will be fine, but if they bleat loudly and wander about then a storm is on the way.

SHIP

The ceremony of launching a new ship by breaking a bottle of champagne across its bows is a continuation of the old belief that a craft that had never put to sea was at the mercy of the sea gods unless they were propitiated with a sacrifice of some kind. Originally the sacrifice was a living creature – among some primitive peoples the victim would actually be a man or woman – or blood smeared on the bows, but this has now changed to the finest of drinks to show the deepest respect. The practice of flying flags from the mast of a ship dates from the earliest times, when boats were decorated with wreaths of flowers of the kind believed to be most pleasing to the gods. The ceremony of 'Crossing the Line', so beloved of people taking long sea cruises, actually originated as a genuine sacrifice, when the sea gods were propitiated by gifts of fruit and meat to allow the ship safe passage. These offerings were made not only at the equator, but whenever boats passed or crossed various important navigational points. Those beautiful figureheads of voluptuous women and mermaids which used to decorate the prows of vessels were also there for superstitious reasons – it was believed that naked women were luck bringers and would protect the ship from danger. (Interestingly, another superstition said that no ship could sink without her figurehead as this was somehow bound up with the 'life' of the vessel.) Some sailors still maintain that you should never point at a ship at sea with one finger, but always use your whole hand; that it is unlucky to carry as *ballast* any material that is wholly white, as white is a sacred colour and to treat it in this way is sacrilege; and that while one black cat on a ship will bring it good luck, two will have quite the reverse effect! It is also a well known nautical superstition that it is unlucky to alter the name of a ship, and particularly ill-omened to give any vessel a name ending in 'A' – with the *Lusitania* the most famous example of this.

SHIVERING

There are many countries in the world where the belief is held that if you shiver involuntarily then it is a sign that you have been touched by death, or that somebody is walking over the spot where you will eventually be buried.

SHOE

The tying of an old boot or shoe to the back of the bride and groom's wedding car is another of those indispensable traditions linked to the marriage ceremony, the origins of which are now almost impossible to establish accurately. For generations it has been believed that to attach a boot to the departing car would ensure good luck and happiness to the newly-weds – and before the invention of the internal combustion engine it was the tradition to throw the shoe after the couple to achieve the same ends. There are several mentions of this ritual in the Bible, and it is now felt among historians that the original act was not one to obtain good luck but to symbolize the passing of the bride from the care and authority of her parents into that of the bridegroom. With the throwing of the shoe by the girl's father, the bride became her new husband's 'property' and indeed in some cultures it was the practice for a husband to take a shoe belonging to his bride and place it at the foot of the bed on the honeymoon night, as a sign of his authority. It is interesting to recall, too, that although it is the custom for modern brides to throw their bouquets among the unmarried females in the belief that whoever catches it will be the next to wed, originally it was her right shoe that she used for this purpose! The old shoe as a symbol of luck is now associated only with weddings, but it was once felt to be lucky in other ways, and in some rural areas of Britain it is still said that to burn an old shoe will prevent infection in a house: certainly the smell might deter the less adventurous germs! In these same areas it is also held that ill luck will befall anyone who puts a pair of shoes or boots on a table, as this is symbolic of hanging. And even if, since capital punishment is abolished in Britain, such a fate is less likely than it once was, you may well be heading for a quarrel with someone close, say the old people. There is a contradictory superstition that it is unlucky to give someone a present of a new pair of shoes, but that on the other hand to do so will prolong the donor's life! In a number of countries it is said that unless you give a pair of new shoes to somebody at least once in your life, your spirit will certainly go barefoot after your death. It is also unlucky to walk in one shoe – which is almost certainly true for the chance of stumbling or twisting an ankle must surely be very strong! It is thought to be a bad omen to put a shoe on the wrong foot; for lovers to give each other a present of shoes; or to leave a pair crossed on the floor. Jewish tradition says that a person should never walk in one shoe or slipper, or one of their parents may die. In the Far East there is warning that if you leave a pair of shoes lying upside down you will quarrel with someone during the day, while there is a light-hearted superstition repeated in many English country districts that if a new pair of shoes squeak excessively this is a sign the owner has not paid for them. Quite recently it has been suggested by some experts that the superstitions relating to shoes probably originated from times when a shoe was used in many places to seal a bargain – the taking off and replacing of the shoe sealing the bargain between the two people.

SHOELACES

Superstition says it is lucky to find a knot in your shoelaces, but this is only the start of things. If your left shoestring comes undone it is believed that someone is saying unkind things about you, while if it is the right which is undone then they are flattering you. If you are asked to tie up someone else's shoelaces, then make a wish as you do so and it will come true. The Americans even have a popular verse on the matter of untied shoelaces:

> ''Tis a sure sign and true,
> At that very moment
> Your true love thinks of you.'

In addition, it is very unlucky to wear shoes with one brown lace and one black: for the brown symbolizes graveyard earth, and the black, death.

SHOOTING

There is an old tradition among shooting men in several countries that you can assure yourself of a successful day by having a girl who is still a virgin jump across your gun before you set out. And it is also widely held that if you miss your first shot, the omens are bad for the rest of the day.

SHOOTING STARS

Shooting stars are almost universally regarded as omens of good luck, and it is believed that a wish made before they disappear will be granted. Many people believe that each star in the sky is the soul of a man, and that shooting stars are on their way to earth to animate new born children. Similarly, say other old traditions, each time a person dies a new star lights up in the heavens. These superstitions are as old as man himself, and of course, associated with the belief that the heavens are the dwelling place of the gods.

SICKLE

There is a curious superstition recorded among many farming people in Europe that unless a man cuts himself with a new sickle the very first time he uses it he will never wield the implement successfully. The action seems to represent the idea that the man's blood on the sickle gives it 'life' to work effectively.

SINGING IN THE BATH

This is a favourite pastime with so many of us – until, of course someone knocks on the door and asks us to shut up and hurry out! In fact you should take note that throughout Europe it is held to be unlucky to sing in the bath *in the morning*, for a proverb says, 'Sing before breakfast and you'll cry before night.' In the evening, apparently, there are no such restrictions! Similarly, one is advised not to laugh before the first meal or the day will end in misfortune – 'Better the last smile than the first laughter' advises another equally enduring adage.

SISTERS

German superstition is sceptical about sisters who marry at the same time. Should they marry on the same day, or even within a year of each other, it says, then one or both of them will have an unhappy marriage.

SKULL

In the Deep South of America there is still a lingering belief in what was originally an old British superstition, that white moss taken from the skull of a murdered man has special magical and medical properties – particularly as a love potion. At first, the potion was said to be most effective in the curing of fits and headaches, but in the New World its attributes have been extended still further. The origin of the belief seems to be the idea that the skull of a man whose life had suddenly been terminated still retains much of the life force, and this can be drawn on for special purposes. It was also claimed in Ireland for many years that if a man took an oath on a skull and was lying as he did so, he would be struck dead soon thereafter.

SKYSCRAPER

There has recently emerged a belief in the United States that any single woman who witnesses the laying of the cornerstone of a new skyscraper – or any large building, for that matter – will not marry for a year thereafter. This belief may be connected with the old rural tradition that the woman who cut the first sheaf of the harvest *would* marry within the next year! Among some building companies it is felt that a single brick or similar item should always be left out of a new building, for according to ancient tradition a newly completed building is subject to the attention of hostile spirits – but as long as there remains even the smallest detail incomplete they will take no interest.

SLAMMING DOOR

A slamming door is an ill omen in parts of Europe, for it is believed that this action may well catch unawares a helpful spirit who is passing through, and trap it. The misfortune which follows is said to be all the greater if a thoughtless person was responsible for the slamming.

SLEEP

There is an old English superstition about the direction in which you lie when you sleep. If your head points to the north, the belief says, your days will be short; while if it points south your life will be long. Should you wish to be rich, point it east; while a westerly direction indicates travel. Interestingly, a good many modern doctors agree that the best night's sleep is to be had lying in a bed facing south – although they are at a loss to explain why. The Germans also have a superstition that a girl who falls asleep while at work will marry a widower. However, she can be cured of her lethargy by being made to take her shoes off and place them so that they face her!

SNEEZING

An accidental sneeze, as distinct from the sneeze caused by a cold, has, since time immemorial, been regarded as an omen. One of the most widely repeated rhymes says, 'Once a wish , twice a kiss, three times something better', while many country children still chant the following lines as one of their fellows sneezes:

'Sneeze on Monday, sneeze for danger.
Sneeze on Tuesday, kiss a stranger.
Sneeze on Wednesday, get a letter.
Sneeze on Thursday, something better.
Sneeze on Friday, sneeze for sorrow.
Sneeze on Saturday, see your true love tomorrow.
Sneeze on Sunday, the Devil will have you the rest of the week.'

Many people still regard the saying of 'Bless You' to someone who sneezes as superstitious, but in fact when 'God bless you' was said in Roman times, the sound of someone sneezing was very often the first indication that he had caught the plague, so the blessing might as well have been an expression of sympathy and despair, as those nearby hurried from the presence of the victim. (Interestingly, the Africans say the more fulsome, 'Health, wealth, prosperity and children', while Modern Italians for their part, say 'God be with you', believing that the 'soul' or 'self' leaves the body momentarily when someone sneezes, and this will ensure its safe return.) The Scots believe that a new born baby is under the spell of the fairies until it has sneezed, while folk in the Eastern Counties of England say that if you sneeze before breakfast it is an omen that you will receive a present before the end of the week. The Welsh, on the other hand, generally believe that sneezing is unlucky. In America, if you sneeze while speaking, it is a sign to everyone that you are telling the truth; while if you sneeze at table you will have a new friend before the next meal. The Americans also believe that if you sneeze as you set out on a mission, you will fail in it; but if you want to sneeze but cannot, it is a sign that someone loves you but dare not tell you. In Jewish lore, if anyone sneezes while a dead person is being discussed, misfortune will follow unless those concerned pull their ear lobes and recite the words, 'They in their world, we in ours.' The Chinese hold that a sneeze on their New Year's Eve means you will have bad luck throughout the following year. The Japanese, however, say that one sneeze is an omen that someone is speaking highly of you, but two mean someone is speaking ill of you. More generally, to sneeze first thing in the morning is good, but watch out last thing at night. To sneeze to the right is lucky, but to the left is unlucky. Finally, it is said to be very lucky for both if two people sneeze simultaneously.

SNOWDROP

Although this attractive little flower symbolizes purity by its whiteness, it is widely regarded as an omen of death and should not be taken into a house where anyone is ill. It is dangerous indeed to take a snowdrop into any house, for even if no one is

212

sick, a death will result in the family before the flowers next bloom. This belief probably came about because the snowdrop blooms only in the winter – a time when much sickness is about – and the association between the two was inescapable in the minds of earlier, unsophisticated people.

SODOMY

A recent report has indicated that there is an extraordinary superstitious belief, still expressed in both Persia and China, that sodomy is a cure for venereal diseases!

SONG

It is unlucky to sing before getting out of bed, and there are several superstitions about singing at the table. 'Sing at the table, die in the workhouse', says an old British tradition, while another version says that a young girl who does this will have a drunkard for a husband. The French claim it will lead to poverty, while the Americans feel it will merely lead to a disappointment. They also believe singing is an ill-advised thing to do in the street: 'Sing in the street, disappointment you'll meet.'

SOOT

An English superstition says that flakes of soot hanging from the bars of a fire grate indicate that a stranger will shortly be visiting the house; while if a volume of soot suddenly drops down the chimney there is money coming to one member of the household. It can also mean that bad weather is on the way!

SOW THISTLE

The sow thistle has long been believed to be good for the sight when boiled in water and the liquid used to anoint the eyes. The plant is also said to be a good preventive against witchcraft, and on a more commonplace level folk throughout Britain and Europe say that anyone who wears a sprig of it in their buttonhole will be able to run well and never grow tired! Beware, though, of running in partnership with anyone, for the leaf will drain his strength to keep you going!

SPADE

It is an ill-omen to try to attract anyone's attention by waving at them with a spade – for this will result in their death unless they throw a handful of earth at the person doing the waving. It is also bad luck to carry a spade on the shoulder into a house, for this symbolizes digging a grave for a member of the family.

SPARROW

The sparrow is said to be an ill-omened bird in much of Europe, because it was present at the Crucifixion and encouraged the Romans to torture Christ by continually chirping, 'He's alive, he's alive.' It is for this reason that sparrows hop rather than run, their legs seemingly tied together by invisible bonds as punishment for their lack of sympathy. Perhaps not surprisingly, it is said to be an omen of death if a sparrow flies into the house, but it is also very unlucky to kill one. Further one should never be caught and caged, or misfortune will follow. Sparrows serve as weather omens by chirping in a very agitated manner when rain is on the way. In many parts of Britain the sparrow is regarded as the symbol of the gods of the household, and as such is important to the wellbeing of the family, and much cherished.

SPEECH

Most readers will have had the odd experience of saying exactly the same thing at the same time as someone else. According to a British superstition this is a very lucky omen, and if the two people concerned made a silent wish before saying another word their desires will be granted. Linking little fingers and repeating the name of a poet will enhance the chances also. In Britain, too, it is said that if someone appears as you are speaking about him, this is a sign that he will live a long time. However, if you suddenly forget in the middle of a speech what you were going to say, this is a clear indication you are telling a lie. The Americans have a rhyme to be recited on such occasions:

'What goes up the window, smoke.
May your word and my word never be broke.'

SPIDER

The spider once featured in many old potions for the cure of illnesses such as gout, ague, whooping cough and asthma, and these involved either crushing and eating the creature with other ingredients, swallowing a portion of its web, or wearing a little muslin bag of live spiders around the neck! Today, though, it is regarded more as a good luck omen – particularly if one should drop from the ceiling on to your face. If a spider is found crawling on your clothes, you can expect to receive some money shortly, and the likelihood is enhanced if the creature is one of the little red type known as the 'Money Spider'. It is, of course, unlucky to kill one, and to do so will amost certainly bring on rain. On the other hand it is a good omen to see a spider actually spinning its web, as this is a sign that you are shortly going to get some new clothes. The good luck attached to spiders probably originated from the Middle Ages, when spiders, along with a great many insects, infested most homes. Because of its web and propensity for killing other insects, particularly flies, the spider played a major part in keeping down the carriers of disease and consequently became much favoured by the people. Their attitude was summed up in the lines, 'If you wish to live and thrive – let the spider run alive.' And the same is true today.

SPIT

Although the practice of spitting may be regarded as offensive and dirty by many people, it is deeply rooted as a good luck custom in the superstition of every country of the world. Although details of the beliefs vary, they appear to have a common origin in the idea that the spittle represents a man's soul, and to spit it out is to make an offering to propitiate the gods. Certainly in a great many different religious ceremonies, spittle is used to drive away evil spirits, exorcise demons and cure the sick. Also many people from the Romans onwards have regarded spittle as an antidote to contagion, as well as strengthener of the skin in battle. The origin of spitting on the hands before fighting – or threatening to fight – comes from the idea that the spittle will make the fist all the harder and stronger. Fishermen also often spit into their nets as they lower them, perhaps unaware that they are carrying on the ancient tradition of honouring the gods of the sea. Children, for their part, often stress the truth of something by spitting on their finger and repeating, 'Finger wet, finger dry, cut my throat if I tell a lie.' And just to round off this short list, in America it is said to ward off bad luck to spit when seeing a caterpillar or a cross-eyed person; that spittle will cure an insect bite; and that the quickest way to revive a foot that has gone to sleep is to spit on a finger!

SPLASHING

In both Britain and America it is said that if a young girl constantly splashes herself while she is washing her clothes, her future husband will be a drunkard.

SPLINTER

There is a quaint superstition repeated among country people throughout Europe, that if you get a splinter in any part of your body and have trouble squeezing it out, you should repeat a version of the following prayer. Not only will it slide out easily but the wound will not go sceptic afterwards:

> 'Our Lord was the first man
> That ever thorn pricked upon:
> It never blistered, nor never belted,
> And I pray God that nor may this.'

SPOON

There is a widespread belief that it is unlucky to stir anything with a spoon in the left hand, and that two spoons found in one saucer indicate a wedding in the family. In Scotland the hand with which a baby first picks up its spoon is said to be an omen for his future – if he uses the right one, good luck will bless him all his days, while misfortune will be his lot if he employs his left. If you drop a spoon on the table, you can expect a visitor – if it is a large spoon it may well be a whole family! If a spoon falls with the bowl upwards, then a surprise is forthcoming; while if it is found with the bowl facing down this indicates disappointment.

SPRING CLEANING

Many a housewife believes that it is unlucky to spring clean her home after the end of May, however inclement the weather before has been. But she probably does not realize that this superstition is actually Jewish in origin and based on the Hebrew rule that all houses must be clean and tidy before the Passover Feast.

SQUIRREL

Although the squirrel – or 'tree rat' as the authorities would have us describe it – is now hunted as a pest, the superstition does still persist in some parts of Europe that anyone who shoots a squirrel will have bad luck and lose his hunting skill. The superstition probably developed from the legend that the squirrel saw Adam and Eve eating the Forbidden Fruit in the Garden of Eden, and was so horrified at this affront to God's laws that he drew his tail – which was then small and thin – across his eyes, and as a reward was given the brush that now adorns all his kind.

STAIRCASE

Another of the most widely held superstitions is that it is unlucky to meet or pass anyone on the stairs, and that you are best advised to wait at the top or bottom until the other person has passed. If the passing is unavoidable, cross your fingers. It is believed that this superstition originated in the earliest times when staircases were mostly very narrow, so that if two people passed, one or other would be vulnerable to attack from behind. Many people also believe it is unlucky to trip while going downstairs – which is perfectly true if you should fall and hurt yourself! On the other hand, if you trip while going upstairs, this is said to be a good omen, and even a sign that there may be a wedding in the household before long.

STARS

The stars have featured in superstitions since the very earliest times, as the dwelling place of gods. For many years in Britain it was believed to be an insult to point directly at a star – to do so would result in your finger getting fixed in that position. The British and Americans regard it as lucky to see the first star of the evening – you will have a wish granted if you keep the wish a secret, and repeat the following verse:

> 'Star light, star bright,
> First star I see tonight,
> I wish I may, I wish I might,
> Have the wish I wish tonight.'

Shooting stars can also be wished upon as long as they are visible, and there is a delightful superstition (which the astronauts might like to think about) among people in the Middle East that these stars are actually missiles hurled by God to deter man from trying to invade his heavens. In England shooting stars are more happily looked upon as omens of the birth of a child.

STEEPLEJACKS

Steeplejacks have a superstition almost uniquely their own that they can protect themselves from having an accident or falling by tying a knot in their braces – the ancient symbol of the knot epitomizing safety and security.

STOCKINGS

It is generally held to be a good omen when dressing, to put your left stocking or sock on first; and also a sign of good luck to put either item on inside out or find that they are not a matching pair. Mind you, the luck is only certain if you keep the odd socks on! This is an interesting variation on the general idea that the left side of anything is unlucky because of its association with the Devil. If your stockings or socks should come down for no reason, then someone you love is thinking of you. And if when you are putting on one, your toes accidently go into the heel, then an important letter is on its way to you. There is an old Jewish superstition that, regardless of which stocking you put on first, always put your left shoe on before the right so that by finishing with the right-hand article you assure yourself of good luck for the day. There is a similar superstition that it is unlucky to finish off dressing one leg completely before beginning the other. And you might care to note the following verse from America, which indicates the omens to be drawn from holes in your stockings:

'Wear at the toe,
Spend as you go;
Wear at the heel,
Spend a good deal;
Wear at the side,
You'll be a rich bride;
Wear at the ball,
You'll live to spend all.'

STONES
There is a very ancient superstition that stones actually 'grow' while lying on the earth, receiving nourishment through a 'vein' which links them to the ground, and this no doubt has inspired most of the traditions about them. Any stone with a hole in the centre is said to bring good luck to its finder, if worn on a chain around the neck or attached to a key ring. Seamen particularly value these stones if they find them on the shore, and fishermen believe that to have one on board their boat will aid their catches. In America, there is a tradition that if a stone with a hole through the middle is hung over the bed of a woman in labour, this will make the birth less painful. The stone dolmens of France and Ireland are also claimed to have the power to make delivery easier for pregnant women who slide down them, and in addition to help young girls who sit on them to find husbands! And there are , of course, famous large

stone edifices all over the world which are said to bestow health and good fortune on those who stand under them or touch them.

STORK

Tradition once allocated to the stork the task of bringing babies to waiting mothers, and the bird still remains a powerful symbol of birth. Perhaps not surprisingly, therefore, the sight of a stork flying over a house is said to be an omen that there will be a birth there before long, and it is very lucky to have a pair nest on your land. Superstition also credits the bird with having flown around the cross of Christ offering sympathy. This association, together with that with new born children, has made it a very unlucky bird to kill. The bird is also renowned for its dedication to its young, and in a European superstition if two lovers see a pair of storks together then they can expect to conceive a child before very long.

STORMS

Storms were once said by superstition to be caused by enraged gods, but over the years the culprits have also been thought to be sorcerers, giants, demons and anyone who whistles! Many country folk and quite a number of seafaring folk also believe it to be unlucky for women to comb their hair and cut their nails when their men are out at work – particularly if they are at sea – as this will cause a gale to rise and put the lives of the men at risk. In several countries around the world it is said that hair and nails should only be cut at night, and that the clippings must be burnt afterwards, or they would be stolen by witches and used to stir up storms. A grim tradition from Scotland says that if a storm breaks out as a coffin is being lowered into a grave, then the deceased has obviously led a very wicked life and more than likely sold his soul to the Devil. In many parts of Europe, very heavy thunder storms are said to be omens of the death of an important person in the district. And in country districts of Germany and Austria there is a superstition that a raging storm can be stilled by opening a window and hurling a handful of meal out with the command, 'There, that's for you – now cease!'

STRAW
Straw was once believed to be a powerful means of bewitching people, and to get possession of a man's straw was said to provide witches and demons with all they needed to work their evil spells. Some ancient races such as the Persians and Syrians attached such importance to it that they even named the galaxy after it – Straw Road. In many cultures, too, straw has been used as a fertility charm by young girls – often bound as a garter around their legs – and in parts of England children still look for the first man wearing a straw hat each summer and wish for good luck when they see him. To find a piece of straw while sweeping a room is a sign of a visitor, according to German superstition, but to come across two pieces of straw crossed is an evil omen.

STRING
People in several English counties still believe that it is unlucky to burn string.

STUMBLE
For many centuries the act of stumbling was widely held to be an omen of misfortune to follow. Country people in some places, still believe that anyone who stumbles beside a grave is not long for this world, while a person who nearly takes a fall when setting out for work or starting any new enterprise is not going to enjoy much good fortune. The logic of these situations seems to be that a fall of any kind is, if not a catastrophe in itself, at least the outward sign of one to come.

SUICIDE
There is a belief still amazingly widespread that the spirit of anyone who has committed suicide must haunt the place where he took his life. Almost completely discredited, though, are the European superstitions that the body of a suicide cannot

sink, and that if a pregnant woman walks over a suicide's grave she will have a miscarriage.

SUN

Because of the worship that has been accorded to the sun since man's earliest days, it is believed to be unlucky to make any insulting gesture towards it, such as to point at it. And of course everyone is aware of the sayings that the sun only shines on the righteous, and 'happy is the bride the sun shines on'. In many countries of the world the superstition existed that if the sun 'hid his face' then misfortune and disaster was on the way – today we know that such occurrences were, and are, eclipses of the sun, and ill-luck does not necessarily follow them. In British tradition it is said that anyone born at sunrise will be intelligent and quick-witted, while those born at sunset will be slow and idle.

SUNDAY

Naturally, because of its significance in the Christian religion, Sunday has for long been held to be a lucky day particularly for those born then. Such children are believed to be especially gifted and secure from the attentions of witches and evil spirits – some may even be psychic and have the power to divine the future. Sunday is said to be the ideal day for a mother and new born child to first arise from bed, and indeed all cures for illness begun on this day are believed to be more likely to succeed than those commenced on any other day of the week. There is a quite unfounded superstition still repeated in parts of Britain that any agreement made on a Sunday is not legal because somehow it offends God. And in America a popular phrase warns against defying the Lord's command that this day should be a day of rest, 'Never make plans on a Sunday'. It is unlucky to put new sheets on a bed on Sunday, and to cut your hair or nails; and any member of a church choir who sings a false note on this day will, according to an English superstition, find their Sunday dinner scorched!

SWALLOW

This beautiful and graceful bird has long been regarded as especially favoured – heralding as it does the arrival of summer – and only misfortune will befall those who interfere with it in any way. According to a delightful Scandinavian legend, the bird hovered over Christ's cross crying, 'Svalê! Svalê!' (Cheer Up! Cheer Up!) and hence got its name, svalê or swallow. Throughout much of Europe it is said fortune favours the household where one of the birds builds its nest, although it is an ill-omen if it deserts the nest for any reason. Many farming folk believe that to kill a swallow will ruin the milk yield of their cows, while if one of the birds is disturbed the harvest will be a poor one. Although the swallow's timid nature makes it an unlikely thing to happen, a French superstition maintains that if one of the birds alights on your shoulder then your death is not far away. The Germans also believe that a swallow's nest built on a house will preserve it from fire and storm, and if a woman is unlucky enough to tread on the bird's eggs then she will become barren. The swallow is also a weather omen, for if it flies high the weather will be good, while if it is never far from the ground then rain is on the way. To see swallows fighting among themselves is also a signal of misfortune.

SWANS

Swans are, of course, protected birds, but it is also very unlucky to kill one and will result in the death of the person concerned within the year. It is also said that if swans stretch their heads and necks back over their folded wings during the daytime (in the style in which they sleep) this is a sign that a thunderstorm is brewing. Two superstitions about the bird which are rarely heard, but are worth mentioning, are that a swan cannot hatch its eggs except in a thunderstorm, and that because of its association with the Greek god of music, Apollo, it sings when it is dying, hence the term 'swansong'. Actually, there is no truth in either of them. Finally, there is a tradition in Scotland that if three swans are seen flying together then this is an omen of a national disaster.

SWEARING

There is a superstition still repeated in many German villages that swearing will increase the number of mice in the area – though why these rodents should be stimulated by bad language is anybody's guess! Jack-o-Lanterns, on the other hand, can only be driven away by swearing at them. By and large country people feel swearing is unlucky, and an invocation of the powers of evil.

SWEEPING

Throughout much of the world it is said to be unlucky to sweep any waste *out* of a house, for you may well sweep your good luck out with it. It is, though, quite in order to sweep the dust into the centre of the room and then to dispose of it without running any risk of misfortune. It is also believed to be unlucky to do any sweeping on New Year's Day or Good Friday; while a broom made of birch twigs (known as 'green broom') should not be used during the month of May because:

'If you sweep the house with broom in May,
You'll sweep the head of the house away.'

TABLE

There is a widely noted superstition that if you upset your chair when rising from the table after a meal, this is a sign that you have been telling lies in your conversation. According to American superstition it is very unlucky to change your place at the table once it has been allocated, and it is not a good sign for a young girl to sit at the corner of any table for she will never have a husband. Any engaged girl should also beware sitting on a table while talking to her fiancé for this will prevent her from marrying him! The Americans also believe that anyone who lies down on a table will die within a year. And when laying the table, according to a British superstition, if you should open the tablecloth and find a diamond or 'coffin' shaped crease in the middle then this is an omen of a death in the family.

TAXIS

Taxi drivers believe it is lucky to have the letter U on their number plates, and if any man's own number contains a seven, or any multiple of seven, he will enjoy a successful and prosperous career. Perhaps it is the lucky horse-shoe shape of the letter U which prompts this belief?

TEA

Reading the future from tea leaves is a pastime that has entertained people for many years, and one of the most widely accepted omens is that a tea-leaf floating on the surface of the drink indicates a visitor on the way. Less well known is the superstition that bubbles floating on the surface indicate kisses for the drinker. If you stir the pot before pouring the tea, this is said to stir up trouble (particularly anti-clockwise), while accidentally to leave the top off the pot is a sign of bad luck. Ladies perhaps ought to be careful about allowing a man to pour out a cup of tea with them, as a British superstition (doubtless rooted in sexual symbolism) says this will lead to their having a baby: in the North of England the story runs that if a girl allows a man to pour her out more than one cup of tea she will be unable to resist any attentions he may pay her. This is a curious variation on the idea that it was alcohol that always led to a girl's ruin! People also have differing ways of making cups of tea, but an English superstition which is still much repeated says that if young girls pour milk into the tea *before* putting in the sugar then they will die as spinsters! After taking that kind of risk one probably needs the advice of someone who can divine the future from tea leaves as quickly as possible!

TEETH

Children in many places still delight in the old 'superstition' that when they lose a tooth they should leave it on a plate beside their bed with some salt, and a fairy will come during the night and take it, leaving a coin in its place. The parents, of course, must play their part. There are a great many adults who believe that unless the tooth is removed before midnight the child will be subject to the attentions of evil spirits and almost certainly have bad luck thereafter. In many countries it is an ill-omen for a child to be born with any teeth; and there is still a tradition that if the first tooth appears in an infant's upper jaw it will die young, while a child that teethes very early is a sure sign that the mother is going to have another baby shortly. Superstition also says that the number of teeth a baby has by its first birthday indicates the number of brothers and sisters to come. The Scots and quite a number of other people believe that anyone with a wide gap between their two main front teeth will be lucky in life. On the other hand, teeth set wide apart in the jaws are a warning to young people that they would be well advised to seek their livelihood away from their birthplace if they wish to be successful. In America there is a continuing tradition that if a person dreams of teeth falling out, this is very unlucky and presages the death of a near relative. The Americans also claim that you will get toothache if you eat anything while a funeral bell is tolling. Although the surest way to cure a toothache is to visit the dentist, folk lore has many suggested cures. One of the most popular is to take a few strands of hair and some nail clippings belonging to the sufferer, and nail these to an oak tree to 'drive away' the pain. To protect yourself from getting toothache you might care to wear a little bag around your neck containing either a tooth from a corpse or the forelegs and one hind leg from a mole. If neither idea appeals, a walnut is said to do just as well!

TELEPHONE

The strange sensation you get when you 'know' that the telephone is going to ring before it actually does so, is perhaps what has prompted the superstition now quite widespread that it is an ill-omen if the phone rings intermittently, and no one is there when it is answered.

TENNIS

No tennis player likes to play again immediately with a ball for which a fault was called. The player will insist on a fresh one so that the bad luck is not repeated. And if you hold three tennis balls in your hand while serving a game, it will bring you bad luck.

THEATRES

It is perhaps not surprising, as actors are such a superstitious breed, that theatre people in general are influenced by various omens and beliefs. They naturally hold many in common with other people, perhaps the most widespread being those related to black cats, although they also believe it is very bad luck to kick a cat of any colour. It is also unlucky to whistle or open an umbrella anywhere in a theatre. No one should ever look out at the audience from the 'wrong' side of the drop curtain when it is down. Unfortunately, there is some confusion as to which is the 'wrong' side, for some people say it is the 'prompt' side which is ill-omened, while others say the opposite. Consequently, most managements place the peep-hole directly in the middle. It is also an omen of failure for the play if the drop curtain gets 'looped' at any time. At the box office it is said that if the first person who comes in to buy tickets for a new production is an old man or woman, then the play will have a long run: if it is a young person the reverse is true. Ushers, too, have their superstitions. For instance, the usher who seats the first person of the evening will be in for good tips – unless the seat number in question is number 13. However, it is unlucky for an usher to accept a tip from a woman (even in these liberated days!), and it is an ill-omen for the success of the play if a patron faints or dies in the audience. Most ushers like to hear the first line of a new play, as they believe this will bring them luck. If an usher seats the first person in their section in the wrong seat, he or she is likely to repeat this error at least twice more during the evening. Finally, most ushers always rub the first tip received on the first night of a new production on their uniform, and then keep it on their person for the rest of the season as a 'coaxer' for more.

THIEF

There is a curious superstition noted in a few middle European countries that if you steal something on Christmas Day and escape undetected, you can steal for the rest of the year without the risk of getting caught. Mind you, in Hungary there is said to be one sure way of tackling a thief the authorities are unable to catch – obtain one of his items of clothing and beat it soundly. This should cause him to fall seriously ill and curtail his activities.

THIRTEEN

The number 13 has a special place in superstition, and fear of its effect is known to have existed from the earliest times, although the main reason given for its ill-omen is its association with the Last Supper which was attended by 13 – Christ and his twelve apostles. Only the bravest soul would try to hold a gathering to which thirteen people were invited, and no host worth his salt would want a dinner party for the same number. According to the tradition, one member of such a group – the first to rise from the table – will die before the year is out. The number is rarely found on offices or shops, and even more infrequently on the rooms of a hotel or guest house. Airlines avoid the number for their flights and for the seats on board their aeroplanes, and there are whole cities, such as Paris, where there is scarcely a single house which bears the ill-fated number. (With typical aplomb, the French get round using the number by calling the designated property 'twelve *bis*' – twelve twice.) Friday the Thirteenth is, of course, a day when you are very careful about chancing your luck in any way. Indeed, there seems little doubt that *anything* associated with the number should be avoided, according to superstition!

THORN

In Hanover, Germany the superstition still persists that if a young girl accidentally gets a thorn attached to her dress or clothes it is an omen that she will marry a widower.

THREE

The number three features largely in superstition, though there is more good luck attached to it than bad. For many centuries it has been held that luck is to be found in odd numbers, particularly three and three times three, and the reader needs no reminding of the number of events in everyday life that have to be performed three times. Most folk remedies require part of the ritual to be performed three times, and when giving acclaim to anyone we always call for 'Three

Cheers'. In contrast, of course, the tax man will always ask us for our dues three times before taking action! The bad luck superstition attached to this number has best been summed up by the phrase 'one disappointment is followed by two others' used in Britain, and 'bad things happen in threes' in America. The number earned its bad luck element, it is said, because Peter denied Christ three times, while another explanation for its *good* luck is the fact that it is a mystical, powerful number and that as birth needed three people – mother, father and child – the number came to symbolize life itself.

THUNDER

The suggestion that the best thing to do when a thunderstorm strikes is to climb into bed and pull the sheets over your head is actually based on a superstition that if you did just that – having first moved your bed to the centre of the room – and then recited a pasternoster, you would come to no harm even if the house was struck. Thunder is believed to be an omen of death when heard at certain times of the year. If there is thunder on the first Sunday in a New Year, says one of the oldest British superstitions, then a member of the Royal Family will die, while if it thunders at any time between November and the end of the year (which seems likely) then some important person in the local community will die (which also seems a probability). In many countries it is believed that if church bells are rung during a thunderstorm this will disperse the bad weather, while if you open all doors and windows while the storm is blowing no thunderbolt will strike the house – though you may get very wet! There is also a superstition among some landlords who keep beer in barrels that a bar of iron should be put over them during a thunderstorm, to prevent the beer from turning sour – although it is the heat engendered by the storm which causes the spoiling rather than the thunder. The same superstition – and explanation – also applies to milk. In European tradition, thunder on each day of the week has some special significance, viz: on Sunday it is an omen of the death of a learned man, judge or author; on

Monday, of the deaths of women; Tuesday, of plenty of grain; on Wednesday, of the deaths of harlots, or of bloodshed; on Thursday, of plenty of sheep, cattle and corn; on Friday, of the death of some great man or a battle; and on Saturday it forebodes pestilence or sickness. Perhaps, though, this popular British rhyme seems more likely:

> 'Thunder in the morning,
> All the day storming;
> Thunder at night,
> Is the sailor's delight.'

THURSDAY

In German tradition, Thursday is the unluckiest day of the week and no marriages should be performed, important business undertaken, or children sent to school for the first time. Why this should be the case when the day is dedicated to such a powerful God as Thor is difficult to say.

TICKLING

Much as babies everywhere love tickling, superstitious folk in Georgia, USA maintain that this will cause them to stutter when they learn to talk.

TOAD

Throughout much of the world the toad is regarded as a good omen, for its presence is said to indicate plenty of water, although to kill one will bring on rain! In England it has been associated with witchcraft, and consequently some rural people believe it is a harbinger of misfortune. For centuries there was also a superstition among burglars that if you carried a toad's heart in your clothes you would never be caught while breaking in. Perhaps, though, the superstition about the creature that still flourishes most widely is that that concerns weddings, and the claim that if a toad crosses the path of the bride on the way to church both she and her husband will enjoy prosperity and happiness.

TOAST

Although it may be slightly embarrassing at the time, it is actually lucky to spill some drink while making a toast, for this will ensure the person's health and happiness. Should the glass break in the hand at this moment, though, this is an omen of death.

TOES

In America it is said that if a woman's second toe is longer than her big one, she will 'wear the trousers' in any marriage she makes.

TONGUE

If you bite your tongue while eating, says a superstition very widespread in Europe and America, the reason is that you have recently told a lie. The Indians, however, put a different interpretation on tongue biting – it is an omen that you will receive a gift of sweets or pleasant news of some kind.

TORTOISE

In a number of countries the tortoise is regarded as a symbol of immortality and strength, so to kill one is extremely unlucky. The Chinese have always especially revered the animal, and the North American Indians believe that earthquakes are caused by movements of the tortoise who is said to support the world.

'TOUCH WOOD'

The expression 'touch wood' is so familiar to most people that it is scarcely recognized as a superstition – yet such it is, and has been for a very long time. It is often said during a discussion touching on good health or prosperity, when we wish to seek the protection of fate for the future. The request must be accompanied by touching some item of wood with the *right* hand. The origin of the superstition is believed to date from the time when man regarded trees as the home of powerful 'wood spirits', and thought that by touching them reverently one gained their protection. With the passage of time, the belief has been broadened to include wood of any tree in any form, natural or crafted, although those woods considered sacred are still said to be best. (Some authorities claim that Christ's crucifixion on a cross of timber gave all wood an aura of holiness.) The act is also associated in many respects with man's superstitious dread of boasting, or of appearing too sure about something. From the earliest time he has been afraid that to assume too much will lead to dire consequences and the fates must be pacified – in many places, for instance, it is considered unlucky to compliment children, or to praise the beauty of women, lest you draw the attentions of the evil eye to them. As well as wood, iron can serve the same purpose, but it is doubtful whether children who touch their own heads achieve anything but a laugh! The Dutch, for their part, believe you should always touch the *underside* of a table when using the expression.

TOWEL

If two people dry their hands on a towel at the same time, says an old superstition recorded in many parts of England, they will almost certainly quarrel and probably encounter some kind of misfortune. Lovers should also not share the same towel to dry themselves after a bath or swim, or they will part. If you drop a towel or dishcloth then you can expect a visitor – although this old Scottish supersititon adds that you can prevent this if you wish by smartly stepping over the cloth backwards!

TREES

Trees have played an important part in man's life from the earliest times when they were believed to be the homes of wood spirits, and naturally superstitions about them abound. It was once a crime punishable by death to cut down a tree (and law still exists today against the felling of certain trees), while in some primitive societies it was held that a man who cut off the branch of a tree might well lose one of his own limbs, or cause it to wither. Below are some of the widely held superstitions about the more famous trees:

The *apple* tree has several omens associated with it, including one that if an apple remains on it through the winter until the following spring, a member of the family owning it will die. And if an apple tree bears blossom and ripening fruit at the same time, this is another sign there will be a death in the family. If the sun shines through the tree on Christmas day this is an omen that there will be a good crop to follow – although to ensure this you should place a piece of toast in the fork of the biggest tree in the orchard! This superstition is associated with the 'Wassail Parties' held in cider making counties of England, where local men would chant old verses to ensure a good crop and satisfy the spirits that look after apple trees. The men would often take along barrels of cider to drink while they sang, and then at the conclusion throw the dregs over the trees. Of the *crab apple* tree it is claimed that if it overhangs a well and blossoms out of season, there will be more births and marriages than deaths among those who live nearby.

The mythologies of several nations claim that the first man on earth was created from the *ash* tree, and consequently many cures are attributed to it. If the winged seeds of the ash do not appear then this is an omen that a reigning monarch is to die. The seeds can also be used in love divination, as explained in a rather saucy verse still repeated in England:

'Even-ash, even-ash, I pluck thee,
This night my own true love to see,
Neither in his bed nor in the bare,
But in the clothes he does every day wear.'

To find an ash leaf that has an equal number of division on each side is considered particularly lucky, for these are very rare indeed. If you should find one, pick it carefully and either wear it or carry it in your clothes, and you will be both happy and safe from misfortune. It helps the charm, too, if you recite these words as you pluck the leaf:

'Even ash, I do thee pluck,
Hoping thus to meet good luck.
If no good luck I get from thee,
I shall wish thee on the tree.'

In parts of Northern England, a girl could learn who her future husband might be by placing one of these leaves in her left shoe, after which the first man she met would be her intended. The ash is also associated in a rhyme which foretells future weather thus:

'If the ash leaf appears before the Oak,
Then there'll be a very great soak.
But if the oak comes before the ash,
Then expect a very small splash.'

The *aspen* tree is famous for the superstition which surrounds the trembling of its leaves. It is said that the cross on which Christ was crucified was made from aspen, and the tree was so stricken with horror that its boughs have trembled unceasingly ever since – earning it the nick-name 'shiver tree'. The tree does, though, have the power to cure a fever – cut a hole in the trunk, insert the nail clippings of the sufferer, and then cover up the hole. All this, mind you, must be done at the dead of night to prevent the fever getting out again!

The *bay* tree, it is said, is never struck by lightning, and people have been known to carry branches of it over their heads in a storm. It is believed that if its leaves wither on the branch it is an omen of a death to follow. The leaves are also a test of good fortune if thrown on the fire – if they crackle violently good luck is in store, if there is no sound, beware. It has also been claimed that bay leaves hung in the house ward off disease, while a sprig placed under your pillow at night will give you pleasant dreams. The widespread admiration for the tree is probably because it was held by the Ancient Greeks to be sacred to Apollo and his son, Aesculapius, the god of medicine.

A cross cut from a *birch* tree placed above the front door will protect the house and its occupants from evil and bad luck.

In Europe the *cherry* tree is said to bear plenty of fruit if the

235

first cherry to ripen is eaten by a woman who has recently given birth to her first child. The stones of the cherry will also tell you when, or if, you are to marry – you count one by one all those you have eaten at a meal and repeat, 'This year, next year, sometime, never.'

The *elder* is another plant with religious associations, for it is said to be the tree on which Judas hung himself in penance. Because of this, country people have always been especially cautious about it – believing, though, that it too can never be struck by lightning. It should not be taken into the house, and only bad luck will result from using it as fuel for the fire.

If a *fir* tree is touched, withered or burned by lightning, superstition says this is an omen that the master or mistress of the land on which it stands is about to die.

While the *hawthorn* is generally regarded as a harbinger of good luck, legend does say that the crown of thorns which Christ wore on the cross was made from it, and a widespread superstition states most emphatically that none of its flowers should ever be brought into the house or a death will result. This apart, a branch of the tree hung over the doorway will ward off evil spirits, though to cut down the entire tree will lead to misfortune. It performs perhaps its greatest service to mankind as a weather omen – for not until the last winter frost has passed and spring is about to appear will the hawthorn flower.

Twigs of *hazel* worn in the hair are known in the superstitions of many countries as 'wishing caps', and if you should make a wish while so attired your wish will be granted. A forked shoot from the tree is also used by diviners in their search for water hidden underground.

The Welsh believe it is extremely unlucky to cut down a *juniper* tree and to do so will result in your death within a year. The tree is credited with having saved the infant Jesus during his parents' flight from King Herod into Egypt, and consequently is attributed with special powers to ward off evil and illness.

The white flowers of the *lilac* should never be used for

decoration, and especially never given in a spray to anyone who is ill, for it will surely cause a relapse. There is little good, in fact, attached to the tree, except that it is lucky to find a five-petalled blossom, especially in purple.

The *maple* tree is said to possess the power to ensure long life for children, if they are passed through its branches while they are still very small.

Myrtle is believed to be a particularly lucky tree, and when one or more flourish in a garden it is an omen that the household is particularly happy. In some parts of England such a show can also indicate that there will be a wedding before long for a member of the family.

When the *mulberry* tree begins putting out small shoots on its branches, says a widespread superstition, then you can be sure there will be no more frosts that year.

The *oak* has been regarded as a sacred tree from the earliest times, and ill-luck is supposed to beset those who chop one down. If the leaves on the tree are seen to be particularly curled, this is an omen of hot weather. The galls or 'oak apples' often found on the trees are actually made by insects, and many people claim that if a worm is discovered in one then the finder will be rich, if a fly then he can expect misfortune, while a spider presages illness. The acorn from the tree can also be used to test love, says another belief: two of these should be dropped into a bowl of water and if they float together then the couple who placed them will marry, while if they drift apart so will the young people.

If a *plum* tree blossoms in December, it is an omen that a member of the household will die during the winter months.

The Scots believe that the *rowan* tree offers a special protection against witches and evil spirits when a branch is hung over the house door or animal quarters.

The *walnut* acts as a good omen for farmers, for if it bears a heavy crop then they know they are in for a hard winter, but can look forward to a fine corn harvest the following year. Nut trees in general indicate a hard winter by producing a heavy crop, and vice-versa.

The *willow* is the traditional emblem of grief and much associated with those who have been jilted in love. It used to be believed that if a person who had been foresaken wore a sprig of willow, the 'heart' of the tree, which was so used to grieving, would take on the pain.

And finally the *yew* tree has for centuries been regarded as the guardian of the dead, and is still commonly found in churchyards all over Europe. As a consequence it is said to be unlucky to cut one down or remove any of its branches. It is maintained that some churches were actually built near yew trees because they have been known to live for over nine hundred years, and were therefore seen as symbols of immortality.

TURPENTINE

To smell turpentine when there is none about is an omen of death, according to a strange old English superstition which appears also to be known in Europe and America.

TWINS

Since time immemorial there appears to have been a belief that any woman who eats two fruits that have grown into one will bear twins. In South America, though, there is a nice variation, that any man who eats two bananas which have grown together will cause his wife to give birth to twins! The more commonplace superstitions about twins are that they are somehow in tune with each other and share each other's joy and sorrow. In life they can sense danger to each other even when apart, and if one dies before the other, the survivor takes on the strength and vitality of his twin. Naturally, these superstitions apply especially to identical twins.

'TYING THE KNOT'

The popular expression about a couple 'tying the knot' when they get married, originated with the Ancient Babylonians who believed that it ensured good luck for newly weds if a thread of cotton was taken from the clothes of each of them, and tied together – thereby symbolizing their union.

U

ULCER
  A cure for ulcers still recorded in certain areas of Britain is to eat the tongue of a dog!

UMBRELLA
  The superstition that it is unlucky to open an umbrella indoors – either for the person concerned or for those who live in the house – appears to have developed in the East where the umbrella, or sun shade, was used only by Royalty. It was naturally associated with the sun because of its shape, and with the passage of time it became regarded as ill-omened to open it anywhere but in the presence of the sun – hence it is particularly unlucky to open one indoors during fine weather. In parts of Europe to open an ordinary umbrella, as distinct from a parasol, during fine weather, is said to run the risk of bringing on rain. The Americans curiously reverse this belief by maintaining that by *not* carrying an umbrella one ensures fine weather! Finally, if you drop an umbrella, let someone else pick it up for you or the omens are not good, particularly if you are a woman, since an American superstition says that any lady who does so will be a spinster all her life.

UNDERWEAR

It is widely believed that to mend underwear while still wearing it will bring bad luck (this applies to all clothing, in fact), just as to button or hook anything up in the wrong hole or catch when dressing in the morning bodes ill for the day. Conversely, if you first put something on inside out, then you can look forward to a successful day. When petticoats were much the fashion, it was said that if they were longer than a girl's dress and showed, it indicated that her father loved her more than her mother! And there was also a saucy suggestion that if any item of a girl's underwear should slip down for no apparent reason (this included stockings) then it was a sign she was thinking of her lover! Should the same thing happen to a married woman, she has a problem in store for her – which one might imagine the falling undergarment alone would provide! Although the appearance of a ladder or hole in stockings or tights can be very annoying, superstition says that if two of these appear simultaneously then it is an omen of a gift coming to you in the next week. Also if stockings or tights should curl up while they are hanging on the line to dry, this is a sign of happiness or a new love. And for girls who wear suspenders, if the catch slips three times while you are trying to fasten it, this is a sure sign you are in for a good day. An old European superstition claims that any young girl who obtains a piece of underwear which has belonged to a woman recently married – a garter is said to be most effective – will herself soon be on the way to the altar. The Welsh believe that if a girl wears valerian in her bra or pants she will become attractive to men – which seems a much cheaper kind of perfume than any of those currently on the market! In the Midlands of England it is believed that a girl who gets married wearing no underwear will be lucky in later life. This superstition appears to stem from the custom, observed until the middle of the last century, that husbands became responsible for any debts their wives had incurred before their marriage. It was believed that a man could evade this liability if his bride went to the altar wearing nothing more than her wedding dress, because no creditor would have the heart to seek payment from such an obviously impoverished woman! These marriages were known as 'smock' weddings. In Britain, too, a bride who loses a garter during her honeymoon should see it as a sign that her marriage will not last. And people here also say that a nylon stocking, taken warm from the leg of a new bride and wrapped round the throat before going to bed, is a fine cure for hoarseness! A rather unhygienic superstition persisted among rural German folk until quite recently that a woman should not change her underclothing for a period of six weeks after giving birth to a child, or she would give birth to a baby every year thereafter. This idea would seem to be a prescription at once for fertility and contraception! By contrast, there is a charming superstition in the Mediterranean countries that if a girdle unexpectedly slips down the legs of a woman who is pregnant, this is an omen that she will have an easy delivery! Perhaps just as delightful is this verse from Maryland in America, about using a petticoat in love divination:

'This Friday night while going to bed,
I put my petticoat under my head,
To dream of the living and not of the dead,
To dream of the man I am to wed,
The colour of his eyes, the colour of his hair,
The colour of the clothes he is to wear,
And the night the wedding is to be.'

And here is one final tip, in case your day is going badly and you could use a little good luck – turn all your underwear inside out and things should change dramatically!

UNLUCKY DAYS

Often for no apparent reason, people have come to believe that certain days of the year are unlucky for them, so they are ill advised to begin anything of importance then. These days, of course, vary from person to person, but it is interesting to note that there is a specific superstition found in various parts of England that three particular Mondays of the year are very unlucky: the first Monday in April, the day on which Cain was born and his brother, Abel, slain; the second Monday in August, the day on which Sodom and Gomorrah was destroyed; and the last Monday in December, the day on which Judas Iscariot, the betrayer of Christ was born. Because of this belief, there are still country folk who steadfastly refuse to carry out any activity of significance on these days. Friday is, of course, considered an unlucky day and is dealt with in detail elsewhere. Here, though, for what it is worth – and however accurate it may or may not be – is the full list of ill-omened days as collected 'according to the opinion of astronomers' and published by the English printer and historian, Richard Grafton, in his *Manual* (1565): 'January 1, 2, 4, 5, 10, 15, 17, 29, very unlucky. February 26, 27, 28, unlucky; 8, 10, 17, very unlucky. March 16, 17, 20, very unlucky. April 7, 8, 10, 20, unlucky. 16, 21, very unlucky. May 3, 6, unlucky; 7, 15, 20, very unlucky. June 10, 22, unlucky; 4, 8, very unlucky. July 15, 21, very unlucky. August 1, 29, 30, unlucky; 19, 20, very unlucky. September 3, 4, 21, 23, unlucky; 6, 7, very unlucky. October 4, 16, 24, unlucky; 6, very unlucky. November 5, 6, 29, 30, unlucky; 15, 20, very unlucky. December 15, 22, unlucky; 6, 7, 9, 28, very unlucky'. In Britain and parts of Europe, December 28, Holy Innocents' Day, is said to be the unluckiest day of all, and any personal venture begun on this day is doomed to failure. The explanation given is that it was on this day that King Herod ordered the slaughter of the innocents, and indeed history is dotted with stories of important state and public functions which were first planned for this date and subsequently changed when the implications were realized. It is also not a good idea to wear new clothes for the first time on this day (they will quickly wear out), nor should any housework be done for it will immediately be spoiled. What better excuse could be needed!

URINE

Human urine has been regarded as an excellent protection against ghosts and evil spirits in many superstitions. It has healing properties as well. But probably the most unusual belief concerning it is that if a girl urinates in a man's shoe he will fall madly in love with her! The superstition is said to be of German origin.

V

'V' SIGN

The 'V' sign, familiar today both as a signal of triumph and of abuse, has its origins in superstition. A salute using the first and second fingers of the right hand signifies triumph when the palm of the hand faces the person to whom the sign is being made, and derision when the back of the hand is seen. The great British statesman and war-time leader, Sir Winston Churchill, of course made the former signal world famous, but it is doubtful if even he knew that originally it signified the Devil's horns. It was said that if the sign was made – normally with the fingers pointed downwards rather than upwards this would force the Evil One back into hell. Perhaps unconsciously Sir Winston was signifying his desire to drive the 'evil one' Adolf Hitler back to defeat.

VALENTINE'S DAY

February 14, St Valentine's Day, the most popular day for lovers in the entire calendar, has now become thoroughly commercialized, so the old idea that men and women should send each other cards which they had designed and drawn themselves has virtually disappeared, giving way to ready made cards. The day is named after the patron saint of lovers, a young priest who was killed for defying an edict forbidding young men from marrying, on the ground that marriage turned them into poor soldiers. The same date also honours, however, two Greek gods who symbolized woman and marriage. The yellow crocus is the special symbol for the day, and the chance of a girl meeting a future partner is all the better if she wears one in her buttonhole. In both Britain and America it is believed that a girl can tell what kind of man her future husband is going to be by the kind of bird she first sees on St Valentine's Day. Here is the most reliable list:

> Blackbird – clergyman or priest
> Robin Redbreast – sailor
> Goldfinch (or any yellow bird) – a rich man
> Sparrow – farmer
> Bluebird – a happy man
> Crossbill – an argumentative man
> Dove – a good man.

But if the girl should see a woodpecker, she will never marry. It should perhaps be just added here that it is very unlucky to sign a Valentine Card – for doing so defeats the object of sending it!

VEINS

There are two superstitions still extant in America concerning veins visible on the face of a child. In Maine and Massachusetts it is believed that a blue vein on a child's forehead extending down to the nose is a sign that he or she will meet an early death. And throughout the whole country a blue-coloured vein running across the nose is also a death omen. In Europe, however, such a vein on the bridge of the nose is a sign the person will never marry.

VENETIAN GLASS

Venetian glassware is said to be an infallible guide to whether the food or drink it holds contains any poison, for if it does the glass will crack and fall to pieces when handled. This belief was once widespread throughout Europe and is still held in parts of Italy.

VIOLETS

It comes as a surprise to hear English country folk say that such a pretty flower as the violet is ill-omened, but they insist that if anything less than a full handful of them is taken indoors then they bring in bad luck. Farmers particularly believe that one or two of the flowers carried into their homes will cause their young chickens and ducks to fall ill or die. If violets bloom in the autumn it is said to be a death omen for the people on whose land they are growing.

VIRGINITY

Tests of virginity have been many and varied over the ages, most of them firmly rooted in superstition, and a few have survived into the present century. In Britain, for example, it was said that if a girl could look into the sun it was a sure sign she still possessed her virginity – though such an action would be terribly dangerous for her eyes! In Germany and Austria, only a virgin could blow back into life a still glowing candle, while in Hungary the one sure proof that a girl still had her maidenhead was that she could walk through a swarm of bees without being stung. The bees, apparently, would not touch a pure woman. Old Russians also remember that it used to be said in the Caucasus region that it was a sign that a girl had lost her virginity if her breasts had developed to any size. A girl in Britain who forgot to put a salt-sellar on the table while she was laying it was also believed to be giving away the fact she was no longer a virgin. In the depths of Poland an extraordinary claim was once advanced that a virgin had the power to roll water up in balls, while it would perhaps be hard to find a nastier belief than that which claimed that sexual intercourse with a virgin would cure venereal disease. And, finally, surely the most bizarre of all was the notion originating from Central Europe that a woman who gave birth to seven illegitimate children thereby regained her virginity!

VISITORS

Although most of us wave off departing visitors until they have gone from sight, a superstition still observed by some country people says that this is unlucky if both parties do it, as it means that they may never see each other again. And in Germany there is a belief that if you visit a house where there are children you should always sit down, albeit briefly, otherwise you will take the children's 'peace of mind' with you when you leave.

W

WAITERS

Waiters, as a rule, have a belief that it is an ill-omen if a customer sits in a seat other than the one they have indicated. Strangely, too, they believe that it is unlucky to get a good tip early in the day, as this bodes badly for the rest of their shift. They also have a particular apprehension of one-armed customers.

WALKING

There is a superstition still widely observed in America, but which probably originated in England, that if you are out walking with a friend and you part company temporarily to walk on the opposite sides of an obstruction, then you will later quarrel or have bad luck unless one or other of you accompanies the act with the words 'Bread and butter'. You will also fall in for some bad luck if you stumble over a street curb and do not go back and step over the stone again properly.

WALKING STICKS

In Germany and several other European countries, walking sticks are said to be particularly effective, especially when filled if hung over the front and back doors of a house. Glass walking

248

sticks are said to be particularly effective, especially when filled with coloured sand, hair or white beans, for these items are good luck charms. Should an evil spirit come across one of these when about to work mischief in the house, he will be so fascinated by it that he will quite forget what his mission was and eventually go away.

WAR OMENS

Sudden and unexpected displays of electricity in the skies have long been cited as omens of war, and two of the best and most quoted instances of this are the flashes reported over Northumberland before the Stuart rebellion in 1715, and the remarkable display of nature's electricity over Michigan and Ohio just before the Japanese attack on Pearl Harbor which brought America into the Second World War. Strong red streaks seen in the lights of the Aurora Borealis are also said to be war omens according to a European tradition which connects the streaks with the blood to be shed in the conflict. In Sweden some country people believe that the appearance of the hoopoe bird is an omen of war – which is perhaps strange, since the bird has turned up in the country quite frequently and, of course, Sweden has been free of wars for a great many years! For centuries the people of Britain prayed that St Paul's Day, January 25, would be bright and sunny – for if the sun did not shine at all on that day it was believed to be an omen that war and other disasters were shortly in store for the nation. It has always been considered unlucky to kill a martin, and in parts of Britain it is believed that if the birds are seen fighting amongst themselves then this is an omen of war and human misery. When more boys are born than girls in any particular period it is said to be an omen that nature is preparing to replace with new stock the young men doomed to die in the forthcoming conflict. For the same reason, superstition says that more boys than girls are born during wartime. In Britain it is claimed that a drum belonging to the great sea captain Francis Drake will begin beating when the nation is in peril, while in the United States the ghost of Abraham Lincoln will appear in the White

House should war be on the horizon. There is, of course, no more widespread superstition among fighting men than the one that says that no one will die unless there is a specific bullet 'with his number on it'. And, finally, there is an English superstition of some antiquity – which surely can no longer be held to be true, or we should be permanently in battle – that if children begin without prompting to play at soldiers in the street, this is a sign of a real war approaching.

WARTS

Although there is no evidence whatsoever to support the belief, there is a widespread superstition still repeated today that if you place your hands in water that has been used to boil eggs, you will get warts! Readers with some knowledge of superstition will probably have heard many different remedies for curing warts, and indeed there are innumerable cures to be found around the world, the more interesting and unusual ones of which have been included under other general headings. String, fresh meat, bacon, butter, lard, toads and snails are among the most popular ingredients! Perhaps, though, the remedy still most widely repeated in country districts, and the least unpleasant to carry out, is tie up some pebbles in a small bag and include with them a silver coin. Leave this in the road, and whoever picks up the bag and keeps the money (this is important) will inherit the warts. It is a bit selfish, though!

WASHING

Monday has always been considered the housewives' ideal day for washing clothes, and the later in the week the washing is done, the unluckier it is likely to prove, as this North of England verse indicates:

'They that wash on Monday, have the whole week to dry.
They that wash on Tuesday, are not so much arye.
They that wash on Wednesday, will get their clothes so clean.
They that wash on Thursday, are not so much to mean.
They that wash on Friday, wash for their need.
But they that wash on Saturdays, are dirty folks indeed!'

Superstition advises against washing on New Year's Day for this 'washes one of the family away', while Good Friday is probably the most ill-omened of all because it was on this day that the washerwoman insulted Christ on his way to Calvary.

WASHING UP

Even the chore of washing up has a superstition attached to it, which is still fairly universal. If a plate or cup is dropped, then you can expect two more items of crockery to be smashed before the end of the day. The chances are in fact that after a break you will be taking extra care for the rest of the day – but should that second fall happen and you wish to avoid the third, there is a way to do so. Take an old broken piece of crockery and smash it deliberately – this will fulfil the superstition without losing you a valuable piece of glassware or china. There is also a superstition repeated in northern Ohio, which readers may suspect was invented by a woman:

> 'Wash and wipe together,
> Live in peace together.'

WASPS

Most of us devote much time and energy to getting rid of these pests, and perhaps for this reason it is interesting to find that there is a superstition that if you kill the first wasp you see in any season, this will ensure you good luck and a lack of problems in the months to come. Unfortunately, it says nothing about keeping the number of wasps in your vicinity down!

WATER

Water features in many superstitions recorded in this book, but nowhere is there one quite so delightful as that noted in the South of France, where it is said that between eleven and twelve o'clock on Christmas Eve water in stone jugs turns to wine. Oh, to be there and find it true! Water has, of course, always been looked upon as a deterrent for evil spirits, and for this reason it is unlucky to throw any of it out of the house

251

after nightfall. There is an English country superstition that water placed in a bedroom for washing or drinking should never be boiled, as this will bring misfortune to those using the room. Apparently the Devil has a particular dislike for boiled water, and coming across some will make life most unpleasant for those he finds nearby. The waters of a number of wells and rivers in the world are said to have healing qualities, while in Wales spring water drawn at midnight on any Saints' Day is claimed to have special health-giving properties – which, in the light of the special mineral contents of many natural springs may well be true. Beware, though, spilling a bucket of water drawn from a well or pool, for this presages misfortune ahead. There are a number of superstitions concerned with ordinary tap water, including one that it is bad luck for two people to wash in the same water. If you sprinkle around you the water you use for the first wash of the day, though, you will enjoy good luck – and no doubt upset the person who has to clear up the mess! There is also an omen to be read by any young girl who seems unable to avoid splashing herself or her clothes when washing – for this is a sign she is going to get a drunken husband. Finally, in India it is said that to spill some water before setting off on a journey is a good omen for the trip, while to dream of water – rough water in particular – is an omen of misfortune.

WAVES

Seamen of many lands – and now surfers – believe that the ninth wave of any sequence is always the greatest: though there is no scientific reason why this should be thought so.

WEASEL

The weasel is a creature of ill-omen wherever it is found, and should one appear near a house and make its squeaking sound then a death is imminent. You are in for a bad day if one crosses your path – particularly if it runs away to the left – and it is all the more unfortunate if the creature should be white in colour. It seems the weasel has earned its unhappy reputation

252

because it was once believed that witches could turn into them, to carry out their missions of evil. In parts of Europe it is said that it is impossible for a human to catch a weasel asleep.

WEATHER

Weather omens and superstitions are almost limitless, and it would be dangerous to claim that anything like the full range have been included in this book. Nonetheless the portents for most conditions are included under one or other of the appropriate headings, and this entry is devoted to perhaps the most unusual and striking of them all – the belief, said to be of German origin, that if it rains while a couple are having sexual intercourse (not necessarily out in the open!) then a girl child will result. Sex during fine weather will produce a boy.

WEDDING

Many of the omens and superstitions related to weddings are dealt with under the headings 'Marriage' and 'Brides', but it should perhaps be added here that there are certain ill-omened times for weddings to take place. May has been thought unlucky since Roman times, when the month was reserved for making offerings to the dead – and there is a Scottish saying still widely heard, 'Marry in May, rue for aye.' Lent is also said to be an unlucky period, just as is Advent – though both seem to be objected to purely on religious grounds. The following is a list of the good days of the year – at least according to a much reprinted list compiled by the seventeenth-century almanac writer, Andrew Waterman, who 'assembled it from many sources'. These were supposed to be days when 'women will be fond and loving': January 2, 4, 11, 19 and 21. February 1, 3, 10, 19, and 21. March 3, 5, 13, 20 and 23. April 2, 4, 12, 20 and 22. May 2, 4, 12, 20 and 23. June 1, 3, 11, 19 and 21. July 1, 3, 12, 19, 21 and 31. August 2, 11, 18, 20 and 30. September 1, 9, 16, 18 and 28. October 1, 8, 15, 17, 27 and 29. November 5, 11, 13, 22 and 25. December 1, 8, 10, 19, 23 and 29. A wedding conducted after sunset is believed to be irretrievably doomed, according to superstition, for not only will the couple's life together be miserable, but they will lose their children and both go to an early grave. And here is a wedding night tip. It should always be the husband who locks the front door before going to bed, not the wife, or there will be a quarrel during the night; and superstition adds that whoever falls asleep first on this night will be the first to die.

WEDDING CAKE

The wedding cake has been a feature of the marriage ceremony since the very earliest times, and it symbolizes fertility and good luck. The Romans sometimes used to crumble a slice of the cake over the newly-weds to ensure them prosperity, and the ancient Chinese may well have started the custom of giving a slice of cake both to those friends who were present at the rites and to those who could not attend – thereby ensuring good luck for everyone. In England for some centuries there was a custom that guests at a wedding should each bring a small bun with them. These would be piled up in a mound in the room where the festivities were to be held. If the bride and groom could lean over the pile from opposite sides and kiss each other without disturbing the mound then they would enjoy a long and happy life together. Interestingly, in some Pacific Islands the actual eating of the wedding cake constitutes a marriage ceremony! It is said to be very bad luck if the bride takes any part in the making of this cake, and indeed she should not even taste it before the wedding day or she will very quickly lose her husband's love. The custom of the bride and groom cutting the first slice of the wedding cake together is to show that they intend to share everything between them, and superstition warns that if the bridegroom attempts to do it on his own then the marriage will be childless. It is unlucky for anyone to refuse a slice of cake – both for the person concerned and for the newly-weds. The bride would be well advised to keep a slice for herself, for this will ensure that her husband remains faithful. And, finally, if young, single girls sleep with a piece of wedding cake under their pillows, they will dream of their future husbands.

WEDDING RING

Since the very earliest times the wedding ring has signified the uniting of man and woman, the circle shape representing eternity. The reason for wearing the ring on the fourth finger of the left hand is also a very ancient one – and not unassociated with superstition. Apparently for many centuries it was believed that a special vein ran from this finger direct to the heart, and it was therefore the most suitable finger to bear a symbol of love. It is said to be an unlucky omen if the ring is dropped during the wedding ceremony, and only the person conducting the service – the clergyman, priest or Registrar – should pick it up, or the life of the couple may turn out unhappily. Bad luck may also attend a couple if the wife loses her ring later in life, and to avoid trouble the husband should immediately buy another one, replace it on his wife's finger and at the same time repeat the lines of the marriage vow.

WEDNESDAY

Wednesday is felt to be an unlucky day in most European superstitions, but the Americans feel quite differently, as this rhyme from New England indicates:

> 'Monday for health,
> Tuesday for wealth,
> Wednesday the best of all,
> Thursday for losses,
> Friday for crosses,
> And Saturday no luck at all.'

WEEDS

Superstition claims that weeds were the curse God placed upon the ground when Adam disobeyed His command, and consequently no amount of human labour will ever completely clear them from the soil. In some parts of England it is also believed that anywhere where weeds grow in profusion despite all a gardener's efforts is somehow ill-omened for all crops.

WHALE

Superstition has always believed the whale to be a lucky creature, with misfortune attaching to those who kill them, but the appearance of these creatures in places where they are not usually seen is an omen of trouble to come. For many years the wives of whale fishermen in several countries believed that they must take to their beds and fast while their husbands were at sea, or they would not have a good catch.

WHIPPOORWILL

That strange bird, the whippoorwill, is the most ominous of all the birds in America, and its cry heard late at night near a house is said to be a sure sign of a death to come. Only the owl is held in anything like the same superstitious awe.

WHISTLE

Whistling in certain specified places is said to be unlucky – no miner would whistle below ground for fear of an explosion, while sailors believe that to whistle at sea will raise a storm. Theatre folk also say that anyone who whistles in the theatre, particularly in the dressing rooms, dooms the current production. 'A whistling woman and a crowing hen' are said to be two of the most unlucky creatures for anyone to come across, although just why has never been satisfactorily explained. Some scholars believe that the idea may have originated from the story that a woman stood by whistling while the nails were being made which were used to crucify Jesus Christ.

WHITE HEATHER

White heather, as distinct from the purple variety, is said to be a good luck bringer, and many people who visit moorland districts return with a sprig in their buttonholes, or tied to the front of their cars. The plant is also attributed with the power to stop a drunkard from drinking! In Scotland, however, white heather is looked upon as ill-omened, for a sprig of it was given to the ill-fated Bonnie Prince Charlie when he landed in August 1745.

WILL

The belief still persists that it is unlucky to make a will, in case this somehow hastens your death. In this context it is interesting to note that wills once used to be read over the dead person's coffin before they were buried, presumably giving them the opportunity to protest in some way if things were not done as they had instructed!

WILL-'O-THE-WISPS

Will-'o-the-wisps, Jack-o'-Lanterns, or Corpse Candles as they are sometimes known, are the strange, flame-like lights which are occasionally seen over marshy ground, and which are now known to be caused by the spontaneous combustion of gases rising from decaying vegetable matter. Long before the explanation of these lights was discovered, they were regarded with superstitious awe as omens of death or disaster. They were often seen in remote, damp churchyards, and in Wales particularly it was believed that they were the spirits of someone who had arisen to fetch a relative who was on the point of death. The path which the candle took was said to indicate the route the funeral party would later follow. If only one small light was seen, the death of a child was indicated, while the bigger the glow the older the person concerned. Sometimes whole groups of the candles were to be seen, and in Wales a number of such instances are said to have presaged mining disasters.

WIND

Wind crops up in many superstitions mentioned elsewhere under other headings, but there should be space here for the delightful nautical superstition related in a verse still much repeated around Cape Cod in Massachusetts:

> 'Comes the rain before the wind,
> Then your topsails you must wind;
> Comes the wind before the rain,
> Haul your topsails up again.'

WINDOW BLINDS

In Europe and America, a window blind that suddenly falls down for no apparent reason is said to signify a death in the family. The bobbins at the end of the sash are often acorn-shaped, in tribute to the superstition that the oak tree, and by implication the acorn, could never be struck by lightning. It is unlucky to watch a burial from behind window blinds – or through any window for that matter – for if you do, says an English superstition, you may soon be buried yourself.

WINE

A superstition attached to the serving of wine, which is still observed in several of the European wine growing countries such as France, Germany and Spain, says that the bottle must always be passed round in the direction of the sun. To ignore this, it is said, will seriously affect the quality of the wine. In many countries it is the tradition to serve Port in the same manner and for the same reason. Many Mediterranean fisher-men still believe that stormy waters can be stilled by pouring a glass of wine into the sea – as a symbolic sacrifice to the spirits of the waves. And you may take your choice about the omen involved in spilling wine, for according to the Greeks it is lucky, while in Britain it is said:

> 'Drink up your cup,
> But do not spill wine.
> For if you do
> 'Tis an ill sign.'

WINKING

There is a superstition practised by many American girls that the way to ensure your boyfriend loves you – and will continue to do so – is to wink at the largest star you can find just before going to bed. (There have also been reports that the girls of Texas think they can attract love by carrying a toad around with them – though how they could bear to do so and quite how the toad would work its love magic is not known!)

WISH

Among the many omens on which you may have a wish granted are: saying the same thing at the same time as someone else, breaking off the larger part of a wish-bone, sneezing, and seeing the first star of the evening. To this list may be added an itching palm, which calls for you to repeat the following verse as you wish:

> 'Rub it on brass,
> It's sure to come to pass.'

WISHBONE

The wishbone's association with good luck derives from its resemblance to the horseshoe, and one of the most popular superstitions connected with it is that if two people hold the ends and then snap the bone, whoever holds the bigger portion should then make a wish and it will come true. In the North of England it is said that any young girl who secures the wishbone during the Christmas festivities should hang it over the door of her home on New Year's Day, and the first man who walks underneath it is destined to be her future husband.

WISHING WELLS

Wishing wells are to be found all over the world, each said to have some special quality which will endow luck on the person who leans over them and makes a wish. This idea of wells as harbingers of good fortune derives from the ancient belief that spirits lived in them, and so they were sacred places. It was said that a stone dropped in the water would reveal what the future held – if the water bubbled it was a good sign, but if it clouded over the person concerned had better watch out. In these commercial times, of course, a coin has taken the place of the stone.

WITCHCRAFT

The fear of the Devil, evil spirits and witches can be seen at the back of many omens and superstitions. The subject is, of course, an enormous one which has been dealt with in innumerable books. The fear of those said to be in league with the 'Evil One' reached a climax in Europe during the Dark Ages, when people tended to assume a supernatural explanation for anything they could not immediately explain. Many folk were accused of being witches who were no more than practitioners of simple country medicine, and others were tortured and put to death during the witch hunts which lasted through the Middle Ages for no better reasons than hatred, suspicion and jealousy. The fear of witchcraft is a world-wide phenomenon – it still persists in many countries today – and it is remarkable how many of the protective charms against it, though developed separately, are similar throughout the world. Many of these charms will be found under other headings, as will the other omens associated with witchcraft. For a fuller discussion of this subject the reader is directed to the shelves of any well stocked library.

WOLF

The wolf is an ill-omened creature, and it used to be said in Britain that if a wolf sees a man before the man sees him, then the unfortunate man will be struck dumb. In many European countries it is believed to be unlucky to say the word 'wolf' in the month of December, for you run the risk of being attacked by one. In Canada, however, the wolf is rather more highly regarded and its representation on a crest grants power to the wearer. There also used to be a belief in France that the tooth of a wolf hung around a child's neck would protect it from evil spirits.

WOODEN LEG

There has been a belief in Britain for many years that it is a sign of good luck to see a man with a wooden leg coming towards you – but if you see only his back, or have to turn around to get a look at him, then the omens are bad.

WORK

People in many professions such as shopkeepers, carpenters and dressmakers will often refuse to brush away the waste material from their premises at times when work is hard to come by, in the belief that by doing so they will 'brush away' any future jobs. 'Dust the table with a piece of paper,' says an expression used by people in the garment industry, 'and you dust away the work.' The window cleaner, whose life is so bound up with the ill-omened ladder, is much beset by superstition, the strongest belief being that to change the manner in which he erects his ladder to do his work will bring bad luck. Another man who deals in heights, the steeplejack, will often twist his braces, holding to the old idea that a twist, or knot, symbolizes security. Many professions cling to the idea that some days are better than others for certain tasks, and that it is unlucky to talk about particular projects before they are completed. Other notions are that green coloured products rarely succeed, and – in a nutshell – that it never pays to take chances with the gods of fortune!

WORM

The worm is said to be an omen in determining the health of a sick person, and an old English belief claims that if on the way to visit someone who is ill you pick up a stone and find there is no living thing underneath, then this is a sign that the person will die. If you find a worm there, however, the person is going to recover.

WREN

Today the wren is cherished in much the same way as the robin, although for generations it was unmercifully hunted for financial gain. It was believed that the bird's feathers would protect anyone from drowning, so naturally there was a lively and profitable trade to be conducted with sailors and fishermen. Fortunately this cruel superstition has now been replaced by the belief that it is very unlucky to kill the bird – particularly by sailors and farmers. In England, anyone who harms the bird or destroys its nest will suffer a broken bone shortly afterwards. The French also tell their children not to touch the wren's nest – for if they do, it is said they will break out in pimples!

Y

YACHTING

Amateur yachtsman believe it is unlucky to take first place in any practice race for a major competition, and would rather finish second so as not to anger the gods of the sea by presuming to be able to win the same event twice. Superstition also says a yachtsman can raise wind when he is becalmed by scratching the mainmast with his fingernails.

YAWNING

Although it is quite easy to make oneself yawn – and how catching it can be if someone else does it in your presence! – the yawn has a place in superstition. The habit of covering the mouth when yawning – apart from being good manners – appears to have originated from the belief that while a person yawned, evil spirits took the opportunity to slip into the mouth and thereby into the body. In Turkey, though, a yawn is said to be dangerous because it will allow your soul to escape unless you close your mouth quickly. The North American Indians say that a yawn means Death is calling you, and you should quickly snap your middle finger and thumb or he will carry you off.

YEAST

To dream of yeast is a mixed blessing, according to superstition, for it is a sign that your next undertaking will be successful, and that the most important woman in your life is pregnant, whether you want her to be or not!

YELLOW

Yellow is a generally ill-omened colour, though in most superstitions it is said that evil spirits are afraid of it. In Britain a yellow leaf on a pea or bean plant is said to foretell a death in the household.

YELLOWHAMMER

The yellowhammer is an ill-omened bird in superstition, because the strange markings on its eggs are said to have been made by the Devil who is its master. For this reason it was once much persecuted and its eggs and nest destroyed to avoid bad luck.

XYZ

It is said to be unlucky for any author to have the letters X, Y and Z in the last sentence of any book, for this is an omen that he will never write another. This author is prepared to take the chance, and for once actually defy superstition for the sake of the record! (Although you will notice they are not actually *all* in this last sentence!)

Also available in Magnum Books

DR LAURENCE PETER

Quotations for our Time

Here is a stimulating and witty collection of quotations from the man who discovered the Peter Principle. The focus is on ideas rather than words and the book includes gems of wit and originality from minds ancient and modern: from Plato to Freud, from Shakespeare to Woody Allen.

Art

'A painter who has the feel of breasts and buttocks is saved.' – *Auguste Renoir*

Computers

'The computer is a moron.' – *Peter Drucker*

Marriage

'Marriage has many pains but celibacy has no pleasures.' – *Samuel Johnson*

Life

'Let us endeavor so to live that when we come to die even the undertaker will be sorry.' – *Mark Twain*

Sincerity

'A little sincerity is a dangerous thing, and a great deal of it is absolutely fatal.' – *Oscar Wilde*

'A compendium, full to overflowing, of the remarks that illuminate the world, usually by their wit and truth, and sometimes by their stupidity. Open it anywhere and you will laugh – or wince.'

– *Isaac Asimov*

ROBERT HELLER

Superman

The complete guide to realizing your full potential in body and mind.

The human body is the most remarkable machine in existence, controlled by the most remarkable computer, the human brain. Seldom do these two operate at full potential, but anybody can use the powers of the mind to gain the freedom of the body.

Now Robert Heller, one of the world's most brilliant analysts of business management, turns his attention to the management of the human body and mind. He shows, first of all, how you can make yourself 50 per cent fitter and improve your memory and reading speeds by one-third. Beyond these basic improvements, he demonstrates how you can get more out of your life by minimising stress, maintaining good health, planning your life, successfully earning money and learning how to spend it.

He writes with authority and is easy to read ... If you are ambitious and want to be a superior person, read this – *Daily Telegraph*

Ed by ANTHONY HOWARD

The Crossman Diaries

'As a literary record, as a *book*, the *Diaries* are a triumphant success, and will be read with horrified attention when other, more portentous, recollections have been submitted to compulsory pulping.'
– *The Times*

Bestsellers in hardback, the three volumes of Richard Crossman's *The Diaries of a Cabinet Minister* are now available in this condensed paperback version. *The Crossman Diaries* cover the years 1964 to 1970 and together form one of the most significant and revealing political documents of the century.

The most hilarious, the most dispiriting, the most trivial and the most penetrating political memoirs ever composed by a senior Cabinet Minister at the centre of affairs during a key period of Britain's history' – *The Guardian*

ROSEMARY STURGESS

The Baby Book

A reliable and readable guide for every mother-to-be and new mother. *The Baby Book* is a mine of down-to-earth practical advice which will dispel many of the fears which arise during pregnancy, and during your baby's first years.

Dr Rosemary Sturgess has been a hospital paediatrician and is the mother of three children. She has written an authoritative yet sympathetic book for the expectant mother, and discusses all aspects of motherhood, from the first suspicions of pregnancy, through labour, until your child is toddling.

The Baby Book is a valuable source of advice which all parents and would-be parents can turn to with confidence.

DR ARTHUR C. WASSMER

Making Contact

Do you feel tense and anxious when you meet someone for the first time? Are you shy at parties or in crowds? Are you nervous at interviews? Dr Arthur C. Wassmer's warm and perceptive book will show you how to feel more positive about yourself and get full enjoyment from life.

No matter how often or how severely you experience shyness, you can change. Dr Wassmer's practical advice explains how to gain confidence in family and personal relationships, and in social and business situations. You too can enjoy the advantages of better contact with other people.

'Refreshingly non-preachy book ... Wassmer's techniques – simple, easy to master and apply – should be a boon to many' – *Publishers Weekly*

DAVID BEATY

The Complete Skytraveller

The complete new guide to air travel, which reveals:
    How to choose the best seats on the plane.
    What are your chances of getting hi-jacked.
    How a pilot negotiates his way through dense fog.
    Where to go, at what time of year and what to take
with you on your trip abroad.
    How to 'read' a weather map -- and much more
fascinating information.

H. MONTGOMERY HYDE

Oscar Wilde

Oscar Wilde's wit continues to delight readers and audiences all over the globe, and the drama of his life remains one of the really astonishing and moving true stories in the world of letters. This is the most complete biography to date, with new information which has come to light in recent years; and it is the most outspoken about his homosexual affairs.

'a biography that is thorough, fair, immensely readable' – Anthony Powell, *Daily Telegraph*

'It is as near "definitive" as we are likely to have' – C. P. Snow, *Financial Times*

'judiciously accurate ... superlatively accomplished' – Kay Dick, *The Times*

'thoroughly prepared, well informed and well written' – Keith Robertson, *Oxford Mail*

Other non-fiction available from Magnum Books

Biography

417 0191	Montgomery of Alamein	Alun Chalfont	£1.25
417 0201	Elizabeth of Glamis	David Duff	£1.75
417 0263	Corps Commander	Sir Brian Horrocks	£1.25
417 0267	The Crossman Diaries: Condensed Version	ed Anthony Howard	£2.95
417 0193	Oscar Wilde	H. Montgomery Hyde	£1.50
417 0270	Christopher and his Kind	Christopher Isherwood	95p
417 0278	Kevin Keegan	Kevin Keegan	95p
417 0334	Charlie Chaplin	John McCabe	£1.25
417 0300	Charles -- the Clown Prince	Simon Regan	90p
413 3680	Henry VIII	J. J. Scarisbrick	£1.50

General

417 0364	The Complete Skytraveller	David Beaty	£1.25
417 0293	Back Door Britain	Anthony Burton	£1.25
417 0457	Superman	Robert Heller	£1.25
413 3186	The Electric Muse	Dave Laing	75p
417 0162	Capital City	McRae/Cairncross	85p
417 0316	The Baby Book	Rosemary Sturgess	£1.25
417 0273	Almost Human	Barbara Woodhouse	90p

These and other Magnum Books are available at your bookshop or newsagent. In case of difficulties orders may be sent to:

Magnum Books
Cash Sales Department
P.O. Box 11
Falmouth
Cornwall TR10 109EN

Please send cheque or postal order, no currency, for purchase price quoted and allow the following for postage and packing:

U.K.   30p for the first book plus 15p for the second book and 12p for each additional book ordered to a maximum charge of £1.29.

B.F.P.O. & Eire   30p for the first book plus 15p for the second book plus 12p per copy for the next 7 books, thereafter 6p per book.

Overseas customers   50p for the first book plus 15p per copy for each additional book.

While every effort is made to keep prices low, it is sometimes necessary to increase prices at short notice. Magnum Books reserves the right to show new retail prices on covers which may differ from those previously advertised in the text or elsewhere.